COOLMORE STUD

COOLMORE STUD

IRELAND'S GREATEST SPORTING SUCCESS STORY

ALAN CONWAY

MERCIER PRESS
IRISH PUBLISHER – IRISH STORY

MERCIER PRESS

Cork

www.mercierpress.ie

ISBN: 978 1 78117 455 5

10 9 8 7 6 5 4 3 2 1

A CIP record for this title is available from the British Library

Printed and bound in the EU.

CONTENTS

For Eddie and Noah

Acknowledgements

Writing a book of any size cannot be done alone and there are a number of people I would like to thank for enabling me to write a book that has been a lifetime in the making.

To my parents, Michael and Mary, I want to thank you for always believing in me and standing by me as I have pursued my love of sport and of writing. Without your love and support, this book would not have been possible. My sister, Michelle, and brother-in-law, Dermot, have also played a huge role, not just in the development of this book but in the course of my life, be it ferrying me to and from the Curragh, or simply having a chat when it seemed that meeting a deadline was impossible.

Having a loving and caring partner beside you is one of life's joys and I am blessed to have my partner, Eileen, in my life. She has been my rock for so many years and has listened to me ramble on about my love for Coolmore/Ballydoyle for so long that she could easily have written the book instead of me! Thank you so much, Eileen, for being in my life and for never shushing me when I would go off on one of my horse-racing tangents and for believing that I could write this book. You have believed in me when I found it difficult to believe in myself and for that I am eternally grateful. This book is as much yours as it is mine.

To my friends: Ross, Kirstin, David, Derek, Stephen, Phillip, Patrick, Eoin, Tarah, Daniel, Jennifer and Nathan, I hope you think my endless chatter about horse racing has been worth it.

An author is only as good as the publisher they deal with and I was blessed to deal with a wonderful publishing house in the form of Mercier Press. They have worked tirelessly to produce this book. To Mary and everyone at Mercier Press, thank you.

Thanks to everyone at Coolmore Stud, who were all very gracious with their time, information and advice. I would also like to thank Paul Rhodes, David Betts for his wonderful images, which are used throughout the book, and Daragh Ó Conchúir for his tremendously passionate foreword.

Finally, I would like to thank the people and horses that have made Coolmore into the entity it is today. From *The Minstrel* through *Sadler's Wells*, *Danehill*, *Montjeu* and *Galileo*, right through to *Australia*, *Gleneagles* and *Air Force Blue*, it is the horses that have made Coolmore, and indeed this book, possible. They have given me so many wonderful moments that I do not know where my life would be without them. So thank you from the bottom of my heart.

Alan Conway

FOREWORD

Reading Alan Conway's book is a reminder of how so many of us not reared around horses have grown to love them. Or to be more specific, have grown to love racing. Certainly, the story related here is close to a carbon copy of my own experience, with only the generation changing.

I had a father with a passion for racing that ramped up another few levels when Vincent O'Brien was involved. Ballydoyle, and all who sailed in her, held absolute primacy when it came to the flat. Lester Piggott. Pat Eddery. Robert Sangster. And so on.

At that time, Sangster was the colourful public face of 'The Syndicate', whose number included O'Brien – much more than a trainer – and a little-known figure named John Magnier. I say little-known, but that was to me. He didn't ride, he didn't train and he didn't do interviews. I wasn't aware of the former stud manager at that time and that is just how he would have liked it. But I knew all about the horses. *Golden Fleece. El Gran Senor. Assert. Alleged* and *The Minstrel*, who had come before. *Sadler's Wells.*

Coolmore Stud initially operated like all other bloodstock entities, within narrow, domestic confines. In fact, it started life as a farm in the truest sense of the word. But when this trio of visionaries-cum-gamblers came together, beauty was born. They were ambitious and yearned for something bigger, something global, something innovative. And most of all, they yearned for dominance.

The result was an enterprise that has been described as one of Ireland's best business ideas ever, along with Guinness and Ryanair. The concept was so simple but the implementation required military precision, huge financial input and, initially at least, massive risk.

Prospective stallions had to have value, so they had to perform on the track in the races that counted. But the process began at the sales, sourcing the best-bred animals that might – *might* – do the business on the track and then *might* produce similarly successful progeny. They took the view that they would be best served delving into the *Northern Dancer* bloodline, a process O'Brien began early in the 1970s, to considerable effect. It was a decision that paid huge dividends, though, ironically, probably not from the expected source.

Sure, the Classic winners came, but that was only a thread of the business model. At its core was the creation of world-renowned stallions, whose services would be in demand among prime-time players who would cough up eye-watering amounts for a premium service. A racing record only got you on the map. Producing racing champions and then breeding champions ensured longevity. That was where the real money lay.

Sadler's Wells was a brilliant racehorse, winning the Irish 2000 Guineas, the Eclipse Stakes and the Irish Champion Stakes in 1984. But even that year he was by no means the stable star at Ballydoyle. Pride of place went to *El Gran Senor*, the brilliant dual Classic victor and, like *Sadler's Wells*, a *Northern Dancer* colt.

Once the racing career is over, though, for this business entity it is what you do in the barn that counts when you're a stallion, more than anything. Or, being specific, it is what results from those activities in the shed.

El Gran Senor had low fertility and sired less than 400 foals throughout his career. He produced fifty-five stakes winners and twelve horses that won at Group or Grade 1 level, which is by no means poor, given the relatively few sons and daughters he produced. But his offspring did not go on to be successful stallions.

Compare that to *Sadler's Wells*, who changed the face of the thoroughbred breeding industry and shot Coolmore to the top of the tree, putting it in the type of position where it could purchase the breeding rights to Triple Crown champion *American Pharoah* for its Ashford Stud operation in Kentucky in 2015. *Sadler's Wells* was champion sire fourteen times in Britain and Ireland, and sired eighty horses that were successful in at least one Group or Grade 1 contest. Crucially, he is a sire of sires. *Montjeu* remains an influential stallion, but it is *Galileo* who now stands astride the entire industry, the keystone to a colossus.

After an inauspicious start, *Galileo* was 'discovered' as a stallion by Jim Bolger, who, ironically, would have closer links with Coolmore competitors, Godolphin. It was Bolger who advertised *Galileo*'s talents and the Derby double hero of 2001 has become the new king.

Indeed it was an emphatic nod to Coolmore's position when Godolphin bought into *Teofilo*, the Bolger-bred and trained champion two-year-old. Ignoring the bloodline had become a self-defeating exercise that Sheikh Mohammed could no longer sustain.

At present, *Galileo* is halfway towards the number of champion-sire crowns garnered by his own sire, but at six-in-a-row, has some distance to travel to match the thirteen-in-a-row achieved by *Sadler's Wells*. Yet, the pace with which he is ratcheting up top-level winners is greater than the old horse managed. *Sadler's Wells* needed sixteen crops to reach the century. *Galileo* managed it in eleven. It is fitting, and the complete authentication of the original plan, that the son succeeded the father as world leader.

John Magnier is now 'The Boss' at Coolmore and it is a massively profitable business enterprise, maintained by its own profits rather than being propped up by wealthy benefactors. Ballydoyle is still a vital cog, albeit now under the stewardship of another O'Brien. Aidan may be unrelated to his Cork-born predecessor but in shrewdness, eye, remarkable ability and national hunt roots, he could be a clone of the late, great Vincent.

There is no end in sight and Coolmore is at the forefront of placing little Ireland in the vanguard of a multi-billion euro/pound/dollar/guinea industry. The dream has come true and now the story will be told.

It is a corker.

Daragh Ó Conchúir
Editor of the *Irish Racing Yearbook*

INTRODUCTION

Royal Ascot 2015: the Group 1 St James's Palace Stakes has just taken place. The race is the day one centrepiece of a five-day extravaganza and traditionally crowns the winner as the leading three-year-old mile racehorse in the world. The winner this year is *Gleneagles*, trained in Ballydoyle, County Tipperary, by Aidan O'Brien, and owned by the Coolmore triumvirate of John Magnier, Derrick Smith and Michael Tabor. The three men gather around their latest champion and exude a sense of quiet satisfaction. Unlike many owners who pose and preen for the cameras after a big race win, the Coolmore operation keeps its celebrations muted because, in a sense, this is just another day at the office.

Gleneagles is the latest champion who will take up residence at his owners' base at the end of his racing career, where he will, it is hoped, breed a horse of similar ability. For horse-racing fans, the sight of a Coolmore-owned Group 1 winner is something very familiar, and for the Coolmore operation, *Gleneagles* will be another tantalising stallion prospect when he retires to its headquarters.

Gleneagles' father is the world's leading sire, *Galileo*, who also raced for the Coolmore operation, winning the 2001 Epsom and Irish Derbies as well as the King George VI and Queen Elizabeth Diamond Stakes, before retiring to stud, where he has become the breed-shaping stallion of his generation. His dam, *You'resothrilling*, was also raced by Coolmore, as was her brother the 'Iron Horse' *Giant's Causeway*, himself a hugely successful stallion in North America. So it could be said that when *Gleneagles* was born, he was stamped with the mark 'Made in Coolmore'.

One could wait for decades and not find a horse as blue-blooded as *Gleneagles*, yet for the last five decades Coolmore Stud has produced a steady stream of similarly well-bred horses, as it has become not just a hugely successful stud farm, but also the supreme leader in its field and a name that commands instant respect wherever it is spoken. Nestled in a secluded part of County Tipperary, Ireland, the stud has, over the last fifty years, grown to become the world leader in production of top-class racehorses. When Coolmore Stud is mentioned, the mind opens up and memories of all the top-class horses that have come from the farm come flooding back. The likes of *Sadler's Wells*, his sons *Galileo*, *High Chaparral* and *Montjeu*, the incredible *Danehill* and his offspring, including *Rock Of Gibraltar*, who won seven consecutive Group 1 races, all stood at Coolmore Stud when their racing careers came to an end.

Gleneagles, ridden by Ryan Moore, wins the 2015 St James's Palace Stakes at Royal Ascot. He now resides at Coolmore with his sire, *Galileo*. *Courtesy of Getty Images*

Originally founded by Tim Vigors, Coolmore began life as a farm dedicated to general agriculture. It wasn't until the group of men who became known as 'The Syndicate' purchased the land on which Coolmore is situated that the stud blossomed and began to stand stallions who would shape the breeding of thoroughbred horses for generations to come.

In 1975 John Magnier, a successful stud manager from County Cork, joined forces with the leading racehorse owner at the time, Robert Sangster, and approached the world's leading trainer of thoroughbred horses, Dr Vincent

O'Brien, with a plan. The three gentlemen would source the world's best potential racehorses from sales around the globe, train them to win the most prestigious races throughout their careers, retire them to stud and breed the next generation of champions. Sounds easy, right?

The Syndicate struck gold almost immediately. In their first foray to the world's leading yearling sale in Kentucky, America, the group purchased the winner of the 1977 Epsom Derby, *The Minstrel*. They then sold a half share of the horse back to his breeder, the famous E. P. Taylor, who would oversee the horse's stallion career. *The Minstrel* was valued at an eye-watering $9 million.

Around that time, The Syndicate also purchased a yearling colt by the world's leading sire, *Northern Dancer*, for a European record (at the time) of 127,000 guineas (gns). The colt, which went into training at O'Brien's base at Ballydoyle, was named *Be My Guest* and became Coolmore's first champion sire of Great Britain and Ireland when he took the sires' championship in 1982. The first acorn had been planted.

Coolmore's business plan of purchasing potential winners and turning them into champions was beginning to take shape, but it wasn't until a triple Group 1 winner retired to stud that Coolmore took off into the stratosphere. *Sadler's Wells* may not have been the horse with the best racing record to have passed through the hallowed gates of Ballydoyle, but at Coolmore there has never been a horse that has had such an influence on the breed. During his phenomenal stud career, *Sadler's Wells* won a record fourteen sires' championships in Great Britain and Ireland, surpassing a record that had stood since 1798. He sired *Galileo*, *High Chaparral* and *Montjeu*, all top-class sires in their own right, and provided the foundations for Coolmore to develop into the global entity it has become today.

Under the watchful eye of John Magnier and the Coolmore team, *Sadler's Wells* sired the likes of *In The Wings* (Breeders' Cup Turf), *Salsabil* (1000 Guineas, Oaks, Irish Derby), *Barathea* (Breeders' Cup Mile), *Entrepreneur* (2000 Guineas), *Kayf Tara* (Gold Cup twice), *Dream Well* (Prix du Jockey Club, Irish

Derby), *Imagine* (Irish 1000 Guineas, Oaks), *Islington* (Breeders' Cup Filly and Mare Turf) and *Yeats* (Gold Cup four times). He also sired *Istabraq*, who became a national hero in Ireland by landing three consecutive Champion Hurdles at the Cheltenham Festival at the start of this millennium. At the time of his retirement in 2007, *Sadler's Wells* had sired the winners of 106 Group 1 races, along with every one of the Classic races in both Ireland and England. His legacy will endure for generations to come.

When Vincent O'Brien retired in 1994, John Magnier quickly set about finding a replacement to fill the sizeable void in Ballydoyle, Coolmore's private training establishment (owned by Magnier), and to continue the production line of potential champion sires in Coolmore. Magnier found his man in Aidan O'Brien (no relation to Vincent, but blessed with similar genius). Magnier and O'Brien gelled instantly and Coolmore began to reach new heights. With Magnier supplying the raw material, O'Brien turned potential into excellence. Under his watch the likes of *Galileo*, his Derby-winning son *Australia*, *High Chaparral* and his son *So You Think*, as well as the likes of *Giant's Causeway*, *Holy Roman Emperor*, *Duke Of Marmalade*, *Dylan Thomas*, *George Washington* and *Mastercraftsman* have flourished and then retired to Coolmore, where the next generation of champions will be conceived and raised.

It seemed only fitting to tell the story of Coolmore through the lives of its personalities, both human and equine, and the great successes that they have achieved. Thus, in the pages following you will read about the men who have made it what it is and some of the brightest lights of the horse-racing and breeding world, including *Northern Dancer*, *Sadler's Wells* and *Montjeu*.

Back in the winner's enclosure at Royal Ascot, *Gleneagles* is led away by his handler, and his owners move forward to collect their prize. It will sit proudly in the Coolmore office, a place that expects and demands only one thing – perfection. Something that Coolmore Stud has become over the last fifty years.

COOLMORE'S PLACE
IN WORLD SPORT

As *Galileo* is brushed by his devoted groom, a small but select group of people is waiting. Waiting is not something the head of this particular party is used to, but sometimes even royalty must do it. It's 2011 and HRH Queen Elizabeth II is at the 'Home of Champions' waiting for the king of the stallion world, *Galileo*. Here, it is *Galileo* who is treated like royalty. It is a measure of the esteem in which Coolmore Stud is held that when Queen Elizabeth arrived in Ireland for her historic visit in 2011, one of the places on her wish list was the stud farm owned by John Magnier, which has been developed into the finest example of equine entrepreneurship and excellence Ireland has ever seen.

The queen's trip healed many wounds from the past, both from an Irish and English perspective, but it was her trip to County Tipperary to see the likes of *Galileo* at stud that showed the standing of Coolmore outside the sporting world. The fact that the queen wanted her trip to be a private affair emphasises the point further.

Throughout the world, the name Coolmore is synonymous with excellence. It is an Irish success story, one of the greatest to come out of Ireland since the foundation of the State. Its impact has been immense. From the farm to the winner's enclosure, excellence is not just a word but a lifestyle that runs through Coolmore, from the people mucking out the stalls to the men and women purchasing multi-million-euro foals and yearlings with the dream that they will retire to Coolmore and become the next generation of super stallions or blue-hen broodmares.[1]

Excellence is evident from the moment you pass the statue of *Be My Guest*

---

1   Blue hen refers to mares that are among the best-bred in the world.

Be My Guest, immortalised in bronze at Coolmore Stud.
Courtesy of Coolmore Stud

at Coolmore's head office in County Tipperary. When you walk past the bridles of champion sires such as *Danehill*, *Sadler's Wells* and *Galileo*, and step into the reception area, where you are greeted by a friendly face behind the horseshoe desk, you immediately feel surrounded by greatness. The old cliché that it's something that money cannot buy certainly rings true here.

Before 1975, in the period of Irish horse racing known as BC (before Coolmore), Irish racing and Ireland as a nation were searching for an identity, searching for who we were both as a people and as a country. The fuel crisis of 1973, along with conflict in Northern Ireland, left Ireland wandering around in the dark looking for a door that would let in some light and allow us to believe that there could be a brighter future.

In horse racing, people were also looking for that ray of light. As Ireland stumbled from one crisis to the next, the best horses of the 1950s and 1960s were all exported to England and further afield, so the chances of finding another *Arkle*, widely considered the greatest National Hunt horse in racing history, were slim.

Irish racing itself had been plodding along for many years at the same pace until 1962, when the Irish Derby was turned into a sweepstake by Joe McGrath. A stroke of a pen turned the 1 mile 4 furlong Group 1 into the richest race in Europe. It was a masterstroke and led to the Irish Derby becoming one of the most hotly contested races anywhere in the world, with a prize fund of £60,000. In the 1962 race, twenty-four horses and riders went to post, led by Epsom hero *Larkspur*, who was looking to become the first horse since 1907 to complete the English/Irish Derby double. The crowd, which some say was between 40,000 and 70,000 strong, witnessed a thrilling race that was won by *Tambourine* and Etienne Pollet, trainer of the immortal *Sea-Bird*.

This new-look Irish Derby was a big step in the right direction for Irish racing, but it wasn't until Vincent O'Brien began to source *Northern Dancer*-bred horses from the big sales in America that the tide really began to turn. Not only did Vincent and his partners bring back to Ireland some world-class talent, including the great *Nijinsky*, they also brought their wealthy owners and encouraged them to spend time and money in Ireland while their horses were winning on the racetrack.

After the success of *Nijinsky*, who in 1970 won the Epsom and Irish Derbies, the 2000 Guineas at Newmarket and the St Leger, the trickle soon turned into a flood, and suddenly the best horses in the world and some of the most powerful owners in the world were setting up operations in Ireland. The Syndicate of Vincent O'Brien, John Magnier and Robert Sangster turned Irish racing from a cottage industry into the number-one source of equine and human talent in the racing world.

With the likes of *The Minstrel* winning the Epsom and Irish Derbies, along with the King George at Ascot, Irish racing's reputation began to grow, and suddenly people were looking to Ireland, rather than America or England, as a place where they could develop their racing interests. Although *The Minstrel* was sold to America as a stallion, every champion that Coolmore subsequently had was retired to stud at its base in Tipperary, and soon the farm grew into the powerhouse it is today.

The decisions made by a small group of people had a profound and lasting effect on Irish racing and on Ireland as a country. The success that Coolmore enjoyed not only brought financial rewards but also boosted Ireland's confidence that it could not only compete on the world stage but also win. The names Vincent O'Brien and Coolmore were suddenly in bright lights. The sight of the Irish flag being hoisted high at Epsom, Longchamp, Washington or Melbourne became familiar, as Irish horses and trainers targeted foreign prizes that were previously a distant dream.

As Coolmore grew and developed, so too did the class of horse bred there. Thanks to leading sires *Sadler's Wells* and *Danehill*, some of the most renowned horses in racing were gifted to the world. Think *In The Wings*, *High Chaparral*, *Montjeu* and *Galileo*, who were all sired by *Sadler's Wells*, and *Rock Of Gibraltar*, *Danehill Dancer*, *Duke Of Marmalade* and *Dylan Thomas*, who all had *Danehill* as their sire. All these horses touched the lives not just of the people at Coolmore,

Look at the affection: Vincent O'Brien with his dual Derby winner *The Minstrel*.
Courtesy of Jacqueline O'Brien

but also of the wider racing public, many of whom developed a love of horses thanks to the stud.

Many people would argue with the assertion that Coolmore is the dominant force in the bloodstock industry when it is compared it to the juggernaut that is the Godolphin/Darley operation, spearheaded by Sheikh Mohammed, the ruler of Dubai. Since the 1980s the distinctive red and white colours of Sheikh Mohammed and, in more recent times, the royal-blue silks of his Godolphin operation have been immensely successful, winning many Group/Grade 1s throughout the world. It raised the standard of horses in Europe to such an extent that there was a time when people worried what the horse-racing industry would do if the Arab money dried up, such was the impact it had on British racing.

However, while Godolphin/Darley has enjoyed tremendous success and is, quite rightly, lauded as a wonderful ambassador for its region, Coolmore has built its success over the last fifty years without the enormous financial muscle that Sheikh Mohammed and his associates have had at their disposal. If the Dubai operation wanted a particular horse, it could simply wave its chequebook and that horse would soon be running in its livery. While there is nothing wrong with that, Coolmore simply didn't have the financial clout to operate that way in the 1980s. Instead it had to develop its own stars through the likes of *Sadler's Wells* and *Danehill*. An indication of Coolmore's success in its approach is that in the last few years Godolphin/Darley has changed its modus operandi to echo that of Coolmore and has started to successfully develop its own stallions, headed by the hugely successful *Dubawi*. He finished runner-up to *Galileo* in the 2015 sires' championship.

An example of the stranglehold that Coolmore has enjoyed over the breeding industry came in 2005, when Darley Stud boycotted the purchase of any Coolmore-sired stock auctioned at public sales. It was an extraordinary move and one that many racing insiders couldn't fathom. With *Sadler's Wells* still siring Group 1 horses, and with his three sons *Galileo*, *High Chaparral* and *Montjeu* in the early stages of their stallion careers, it appeared to make little sense for

Sheikh Mohammed and his team to pass up the opportunity to own the next great potential champion racehorse. One could almost understand where the Dubai operation was coming from, as Coolmore tended to purchase stock sired by their own stallions and, in the main, didn't purchase non-Coolmore-sired stock. However, when the best young stock is sired by Coolmore stallions, could anyone really blame John Magnier and his associates for continuing to purchase stock by *Sadler's Wells*, *Galileo* and others at the bloodstock sales?

Coolmore also played its part in the fall-out with Darley, as for six years it didn't send any Ballydoyle horses to Dubai's signature event, the Dubai World Cup, now held in March at the futuristic Meydan Racecourse. This was a big blow, because without any Coolmore horses there was a certain lustre missing from a meeting that prides itself on its international flavour, as was witnessed when the Irish-trained *Sole Power* landed the Group 1 Dubai Golden Shaheen at the 2015 meeting.

Whatever the reasons, the boycott was damaging for the entire bloodstock industry. Sheikh Mohammed's Godolphin suffered two years of poor racetrack performances, as its crop of horses at the time was simply not up to standard, while breeders who were taking a Coolmore-sired yearling to the sales knew that their customer base would be cut dramatically while the Sheikh and his supporters boycotted Coolmore progeny.

Eventually, in a nod to the influence Coolmore has in the industry, Sheikh Mohammed bought into the Coolmore bloodlines by purchasing a controlling stake in the 2006 European champion two-year-old colt *Teofilo*, who was trained by Jim Bolger. This son of *Galileo* enjoyed an undefeated five-race juvenile campaign before an injury brought an end to his racing career. *Teofilo* was subsequently retired to Sheikh Mohammed's Kildangan Stud in County Kildare, where he became a noted stallion, siring the likes of *Pleascach*, who won the Irish 1000 Guineas and the Yorkshire Oaks for Godolphin and Jim Bolger in 2015.

While nobody would admit it, having access to Coolmore's bloodlines was

Dr Jim Hay (centre), who has a number of horses in partnership
with the Coolmore operation. *Courtesy of Tattersalls*

just the kick that Godolphin/Darley needed as it looked to re-establish itself
among the elite players in flat racing. It is also fair to say that Godolphin came
off worse in its 'feud' with Coolmore. Because it chose not to purchase young
stock sired by Coolmore stallions, it deprived itself of horses able to compete
at the highest levels of flat racing for a number of years. It wasn't the wisest
decision the Godolphin/Darley operation ever made.

Coolmore also signalled its intention to develop a more harmonious working
relationship with Sheikh Mohammed when in 2011 it sent its Irish Derby and
Irish Champion Stakes winner *Cape Blanco* to contest the $10 million Dubai
World Cup, a Grade 1 race run on Meydan's track. It was a move initiated by

Dr Jim Hay, who bought a stake in *Cape Blanco* along with fellow Irish Derby winner and future Ascot Gold Cup winner *Fame And Glory*, becoming one of the few people to own a horse in Ballydoyle aside from the Magnier, Tabor and Smith axis.

Speaking at the time to *The Guardian*, Hay said of the decision to bring *Cape Blanco* to Dubai:

> You could maybe see this as a move that could bring the two sides together. These squabbles are just part of life, they come, they go. I think, hopefully in the years to come, we'll see a lot more of the [Irish] folks with top-class horses here, which must be good for Dubai. It should be win, win, win.

Since 2011 both Coolmore and Godolphin have enjoyed many battles on the racetrack, most memorably when the Godolphin-owned *Encke* denied the Coolmore-owned *Camelot* the English Triple Crown when running out a narrow winner of the 2012 St Leger at Doncaster.[2] The following year, in May 2013, *Encke* was one of twenty-two Godolphin-owned horses to test positive for anabolic steroids in an out-of-competition test conducted by the British Horseracing Authority (BHA) and was banned from racing for six months.

While Godolphin/Darley continues its quest to once again become the greatest force in world racing, Coolmore seamlessly continues its domination of global racing, both on the racetrack and in the breeding sheds. In 2012, one year after *Sadler's Wells* passed away, Coolmore achieved something unique in the world of breeding when its stallions became the champion sires in Europe, America and Australia. *Galileo* secured the European crown, while *Giant's Causeway* and *Fastnet Rock* became champion sires in America and Australia respectively. It was a tremendous achievement and one that may not be equalled for quite some time.

---

2   The Triple Crown is awarded to the horse that wins the St Leger Stakes, the Epsom Derby and the 2000 Guineas in the same year.

Coolmore's importance to Irish sport continues to grow. One wouldn't need many fingers to calculate the number of Irish entities that command the worldwide respect that Coolmore has enjoyed for the last fifty years. During the breeding season, which begins in early February, Coolmore hosts mares from America, Australia and even Japan, as breeders from all over the world want access to stallions such as *Galileo*. It is this international reputation that places Coolmore among the most successful and important sporting entities to emerge from Ireland.

When thinking of Irish sporting successes in a worldwide context, many would automatically mention the tremendous success that the Irish rugby team has enjoyed in recent times, or the outstanding achievements by our boxers or athletes over the decades, but few people outside the small world of horse racing would mention Coolmore/Ballydoyle. Yet both Vincent O'Brien and Aidan O'Brien should be held in similarly high regard for their achievements. To have achieved so much, on both a domestic and international stage, in National Hunt and flat racing, and to be so consistent, are the true marks of greatness.

With Aidan O'Brien at the helm, the Coolmore/Ballydoyle operation looks well placed to continue the success it has enjoyed over the last twenty years. One can't help but feel that its next big goal is to own a Triple Crown winner. Having come so close with *Camelot* in 2012, when the colt was narrowly beaten in the final leg of the English St Leger, there must be a tremendous desire within the organisation to have the next horse to win the Triple Crown and follow in the hoofprints of the last colt to win it – *Nijinsky*, in 1970.

I was at the Curragh Racecourse on the day *Camelot* was defeated in the St Leger. When Aidan O'Brien and his son Joseph, who rode *Camelot* that day, arrived to contest the Group 1 National Stakes, the crowd clapped them all the way from their helicopter in the middle of the track to the weight room. It was an extraordinary gesture that showed the high regard in which both Coolmore and Ballydoyle are held by many of the Irish racing public.

For the last five decades, Ireland has consistently produced trainers and horses who have shone on the world stage. It is an extraordinary achievement to have that much success over that length of time and one that should be shouted from the rooftops. Think of the likes of Dermot Weld, who became the first non-Australian to win the Melbourne Cup with *Vintage Crop* in 1993 and the first Irish trainer to win an American Classic race with *Go and Go* in the 1990 Belmont Stakes; Jim Bolger, who has won big Group 1 and Grade 1 races throughout the world; and John Oxx, who masterminded the wonderful career of *Sea The Stars*. However, the successes of Coolmore and Ballydoyle are at the top of this list.

When *Australia* landed the 2014 Epsom Derby, he gave Aidan O'Brien an unprecedented third triumph in the race following on from *Camelot* (2012) and *Ruler Of The World* (2013). It was the first time in the history of that great race that any trainer had saddled the winner for three consecutive years. Even more remarkably, the Coolmore owners were winning the race for the fourth year, as *Pour Moi* had taken victory for France in 2011.[3] To have horses good enough to run in four editions of the Derby is an achievement in itself, but to own the winner and for the winners to come from your own stallions, well that is an achievement beyond comparison.

Horse racing is big business in Ireland and Coolmore is at the forefront, driving the industry to ever greater heights. One example of the money gene-rated by the bloodstock industry came in November 2013 when a regally bred daughter of *Montjeu* came up for auction at a horses-in-training sale at Goffs in County Kildare. *Chicquita*, who was trained to win the 2013 Darley Irish Oaks by Alain de Royer-Dupré, was part of Paul Makin's dispersal of his bloodstock interests. Not only was she a beautiful-looking filly, she had gold-plated Group 1 form on her résumé. As well as winning the Irish Oaks in dramatic style (she veered across the racetrack with her jockey Johnny Murtagh and looked to have thrown the race away on several occasions), the mare had previously

---

3   The Coolmore owners have a select number of horses in training outside Ballydoyle.

finished second to subsequent dual Prix de l'Arc de Triomphe winner *Treve* in the French Oaks that same summer.

Given her race record and her looks, there was a buzz around the auditorium when she came up for auction. Henry Beeby, CEO of Goffs, led the sale and started the bidding at an eye-watering €3 million. The sale was off and running in spectacular fashion and the bids kept on coming. €3.1 million, €3.2 million, €3.3 million. Eventually there were only two bidders left: a bloodstock agent bidding for Sheikh Fahad Al Thani, one of the biggest and most recent players to come into the elite end of flat racing, and the father-and-son team of Peter and Ross Doyle, who were bidding on behalf of Coolmore.

These two superpowers went toe to toe. €4 million, €4.5 million, €5 million. Both sides refused to give an inch in the battle for this filly. With the tension in the room reaching near breaking point, the bids continued. €5.5 million, €5.6 million, €5.7 million. Then it came – the moment when the Doyle operation and Coolmore finally outbid Sheikh Fahad. A bid of €6 million was made on behalf of Coolmore, and the Sheikh's bloodstock agent walked away. Coolmore had won the battle and got its filly for a record-breaking price. In that instant *Chicquita* became the most expensive horse ever sold in Ireland and Coolmore showed, once again, that it was the biggest dog in the bloodstock yard.

It was an amazing purchase and one that illustrated the pulling power that Ireland has as a horse-producing country. This point was expanded upon when Henry Beeby, speaking in the excellent documentary *Power in the Blood*, said of the sale, 'It demonstrated that

Sheikh Fahad, a major new player in the bloodstock world, who will be a challenger to Coolmore in the coming years. *Courtesy of Tattersalls*

Ireland is top of the tree and is the spiritual home of the thoroughbred. We had two of the biggest superpowers in world racing here at Goffs bidding in an Irish sales ring for an Irish-bred filly. That's very important.'

Since she had sold for a colossal amount of money, expectations were high that *Chicquita* would continue her excellent racecourse performances for her new trainer, Aidan O'Brien. Sadly she could never regain the winning thread and she failed to win in four attempts for her new connections, finishing down the field in the 2014 Prix de l'Arc de Triomphe, before ending her racing career with a disappointing fifth place in the Breeders' Cup Turf at Santa Anita. It will be interesting to see if she will be able to produce a top-class son or daughter during her time as a broodmare.

The strength of the Irish bloodstock industry was again illustrated in September 2015, when history was made. For the first time four yearlings were sold for more than €1 million at Goffs. Prices of €2 million, €1.7 million, €1.2 million and €1.05 million, paid by four separate buyers, set a new record for Goffs as the highest number of million-plus lots in the history of the sale. Henry Beeby said of the record-breaking sale:

> Never before have we sold four seven-figure lots at a Goffs [Orby] yearling sale nor three in a single day, so we are naturally elated to have catalogued this quartet of truly illustrious yearlings. The fact is that a deeper analysis of Orby shows a sale that has grown by 41 per cent in just two years, so we have essentially consolidated those gains, and the sale remains a firm favourite with vendors and purchasers alike whilst, very significantly, we are attracting an increasing number of the very best, as demonstrated by the million-euro lots. This year we have welcomed increased numbers of overseas buyers following a number of international trips and with the assistance of Irish Thoroughbred Marketing.[4]

---

4   http://goffs.com/news/record-number-millionaire-yearlings-orby-sale/

The continued success of Coolmore is one of the reasons it deserves to be ranked alongside the famous boxers, athletes, rugby and soccer players who have represented Ireland with such distinction. However, the private nature of the operation means that people outside horse racing may never fully appreciate what a world-class entity Coolmore Stud really is. Simply put, its people are the very best in the world at what they do.

Coolmore is one of the brightest diamonds that Ireland has, and in the age of the bankers and jokers who brought Ireland to its knees, it's comforting to see people like John Magnier thrive, and know that as a nation Ireland can still shine on the world stage. From little acorns, as the old saying goes, mighty oaks grow, and Coolmore will continue to grow and grow for generations to come.

VINCENT O'BRIEN

He strode into the barn. All around him horses and their jockeys went about their business. Expressions remained neutral. This was no time for joking. As each horse passed the man who was known as 'The Boss', opinions were formed in the greatest mind that has ever held a training licence. Instructions were passed along and carried out with military precision. That's how in a small part of County Tipperary things were expected to be done. Nothing less than perfection was accepted. It was a way of life, but one that brought untold riches to this part of Ireland.

As the string of horses made their way past The Boss and back into their immaculate stables, they were groomed and another work morning passed without incident. For Vincent O'Brien, it was another morning when he learned that little bit extra about his string, something he may not have known before and would store away to use when the time was right. Later his horses would travel to races in Ireland, England, France or America. It didn't matter. Wherever a horse trained by M. V. O'Brien turned up, it would usually win. It's what all those early mornings were for.

He was the man who started it all. Along with John Magnier and Robert Sangster, he was one of the founders of Coolmore Stud, which grew from a small breeding operation into the premier source of world-class stallions. Whenever Irish horse racing and bloodstock are discussed throughout the world, one of the first names people will mention is Michael Vincent O'Brien. Born in Churchtown, County Cork, in 1917, he rose to heights that were never scaled before and haven't been equalled since he retired in 1994. Along with Patrick 'Darkie' Prendergast, O'Brien took Ireland, which at the time was a bit-part player on the world racing stage, and positioned it as the place where the best horses in the world were trained and where the best stallions resided. He also took Ballydoyle, which was a working farm at the time, and converted it into a disciplined, state-of-the-art training facility light years ahead of its time. His impact on the world of horse racing was immense.

To understand O'Brien's genius one must go all the way back to the very start. His father, Dan, was a well-respected horse trader in Cork, and this is where the young Vincent learned his trade. In 1943, after Dan went racing at the Curragh, he contracted pneumonia and passed away. Vincent, who was the first son of Dan's second marriage, held no rights to the family farm, so was essentially homeless and without work. Out of that family tragedy came the seeds of a remarkable training career.

O'Brien travelled to England to purchase some horses to kick-start his training career. While he was there he was asked to train a horse named *Good Days* for a man called Sydney McGregor. During that same trip, O'Brien bought a horse called *Drybob*. Those two horses played a pivotal role in his story. Because he didn't have much money to play with, the only way he could make training racehorses pay was to gamble on the horses he had trained and hope that they would win.

O'Brien initially targeted two big handicap races at the Curragh in 1944 – the Irish Cambridgeshire and the Irish Cesarewitch. He put a £2 each-way double on both his horses at 20/1. *Drybob* dead-heated for the Cambridgeshire and *Good Days* won the Cesarewitch. The gamble had paid off and O'Brien took £1,000 from the bookmakers. It was just the start that he needed to his training career, and from that moment on he never looked back.

Remarkably, for a trainer who became synonymous with training flat horses, it was in the jumping sphere that O'Brien carved out his reputation, and his trips to the Cheltenham Festival became the stuff of folklore. His first really good horse was the fleet-of-foot chaser *Cottage Rake*, who in 1948 won the first of his three consecutive Cheltenham Gold Cups, something that had never before been achieved. The esteem in which O'Brien and *Cottage Rake* were held by the racing public was such that each time *Cottage Rake* and his jockey, Aubrey Brabazon, powered up that famous finishing hill at Cheltenham, punters would cry:

Aubrey's up, the money's down.

The frightened bookies quake.

Come on, my lads, and give a cheer.

Begod, 'tis *Cottage Rake*!

For many trainers having a horse the calibre of *Cottage Rake* would have been the pinnacle of their career, but for O'Brien *Cottage Rake* served as the launch pad for his raids across the Irish Sea. As well as landing three Gold Cups with *Cottage Rake* (*Knock Hard* made it four Gold Cups for O'Brien in 1953), the trainer landed the most prestigious hurdle race at the Cheltenham Festival with the boot-tough *Hatton's Grace* for three consecutive years from 1949 to 1951. (It was after his success in 1951 that he moved to Ballydoyle.)

While these successes brought O'Brien into the spotlight, he was not content with what he had achieved. He was famous for never looking back at past glories and was always striving for better ways to prepare his horses. That approach saw him fly three horses in a converted RAF fighter plane to the Cheltenham Festival in 1949. O'Brien was the first person to use air transport for his horses and the rest of the racing world scoffed, but his tactics paid off. All three horses won their races and the derision soon stopped.

O'Brien's exploits at the Cheltenham Festival may have put him on the road to success as a trainer, but it is what he did at Aintree's Grand National Festival between 1953 and 1955 that truly made people take notice of his training ability. Nowadays the Grand National is a watered-down version of a once great race, but back in the 1950s the 4 mile 4 furlong test around Aintree truly was the ultimate challenge for both man and horse. The fences were more unforgiving. The famous Becher's Brook fence was so steep that jockeys reported it was like falling off the edge of the earth. To win the Aintree Grand National one needed not just a man and a horse, but a great deal of bravery to even attempt to take home the great prize. Vincent O'Brien had all three.

O'Brien purchased his first Grand National winner, *Early Mist*, for owner

Vincent O'Brien transported horses to Cheltenham by air in 1949, the first trainer to do so.
Courtesy of Jacqueline O'Brien

Joe Griffin. It was the start of a remarkable period in his training career. *Early Mist* was not the easiest horse to train, and O'Brien and his staff had a job on their hands to get the horse ready for the 1953 Grand National. Carrying 11st 2lbs and sent off at 20/1 by the punters, *Early Mist*, ridden by Bryan Marshall, survived a number of heart-stopping jumping errors to win the world's most famous race by twenty lengths.

This Grand National success was greeted by unprecedented scenes of joy in Ireland. The horse was paraded down O'Connell Street in Dublin and a reception was held at the Mansion House in the city centre. While the celebrations were in full flow, O'Brien was already looking ahead to the following year's race and had identified the horse that would represent him.

Royal Tan didn't have much luck around Aintree before taking his place in the 1954 Grand National. The horse, then owned by Harry Keogh, had run twice previously at the track, in the 1951 and 1952 Grand Nationals, and was placed second on both occasions, both times having made dreadful mistakes at the final fence when in contention for victory. An injury kept the horse off the track for the 1952–53 season, and when he returned to training, he continually tested the mettle of his young trainer. Now in the ownership of Joe Griffin, who was looking for his second consecutive Grand National winner, *Royal Tan* defied training problems and less-than-perfect preparation to give Vincent O'Brien his second Grand National win by beating *Tudor Line* by the narrowest of margins. The pair was separated by only a neck at the end of 4½ miles in a race that was widely regarded as one of the finest Grand Nationals of its era.

With back-to-back Grand Nationals secured, O'Brien launched a four-strong assault on the great race in 1955. *Quare Times* had progressed rapidly

The beginning of an era. Vincent O'Brien watches his string, led by
Royal Tan, at Ballydoyle. *Courtesy of Jacqueline O'Brien*

from making his debut as an unfurnished six-year-old to being a Cheltenham Festival-winning gelding with the size and scope over a fence that made him an ideal candidate for the 1955 Grand National.[1] Like *Royal Tan*, *Quare Times* had his own training problems in the lead up to his Grand National.

On the day of the race the rain poured down, drenching the course and, it seemed, making the going unsuitable for *Quare Times* and apparently washing out any chance of the horse giving O'Brien his Grand National hat-trick. However, with Pat Taaffe (who later rode the incomparable *Arkle*) in the saddle, *Quare Times* showed that he had the courage to complement his unquestionable class. They powered through the Liverpool mud to come home twelve lengths ahead of their rivals and secure their place in history, along with Vincent O'Brien, who became the first trainer ever to saddle the winner of the Grand National for three consecutive years.

Of all the achievements that came to O'Brien later on in his career, it is his success in the Grand National that will forever remain his finest. Think of how hard it is to prepare one horse for a race and to win that race, then imagine trying it with three different horses in three different years and with two different jockeys. It was simply remarkable.

Having conquered the National Hunt world, O'Brien turned his attention to the world of flat racing. It is a testament to his self-belief that he decided to change tack and move away from the jumpers who had brought him so much success and notoriety.

Ballymoss may not be high up in the overall list of talented horses that O'Brien handled, but he was the first high-class colt who got the trainer up and running on the flat. Owned by American businessman John McShane, *Ballymoss* gave O'Brien his first win in an English Classic when he landed the St Leger in 1958 under a terrific ride from Scobie Breasley. The following month, in unsuitably heavy going at Longchamp, Breasley and *Ballymoss* dug as deep

---

1   Unfurnished in this context means a horse that will take a number of years to fully grow into their frame.

as they could and captured the Prix de l'Arc de Triomphe to give Vincent his biggest win in flat racing.

While it seemed that nothing could derail Vincent O'Brien and his team at Ballydoyle, a race at the Curragh in 1960 would provide the trainer with perhaps the toughest challenge that he would ever encounter.

Chamour is not one of the more recognisable names in Vincent O'Brien's training career, but it is one of the most important. After *Chamour* won a £200 maiden race at the Curragh in 1960, the Irish Turf Club sent a letter to O'Brien to inform him that samples taken from the horse after the race contained a drug or stimulant. The drug in question was a substance that resembled methyl-amphetamine. Even more remarkably, the amount that was allegedly found in the horse's system was one ten-thousandth of a grain.

Given how little evidence there was against O'Brien and his horse, The Turf Club was damning in its sentence. They warned off the trainer until November 1961 and made Vincent a disqualified person, which meant that he could not set foot on a racecourse or in his training yard at Ballydoyle, even though there was absolutely no evidence that he had given the horse the drug. So, with a young family, O'Brien had to vacate his home at Ballydoyle, and the training of the horses was handed over to his two brothers, Phonsie and Dermot.

The ban hit O'Brien hard. In the excellent 2011 documentary, *The Master*, Phonsie O'Brien explained just how much having his licence taken away from him hurt O'Brien: 'He was so upset about the ban, it was unbelievable. The horses became irrelevant and he wouldn't talk to me about them. At one point he considered leaving and going to train in France, but thankfully he calmed down after a period of time and decided to stay.'

The ban hurt not only O'Brien and his operation at Ballydoyle, but also the wider racing public in Ireland, who felt a huge degree of anger towards The Turf Club. When *Chamour* came to contest the Irish Derby, the huge crowd didn't hold back and they vented their feelings towards the organisation that had taken their hero from them. Having won the Irish Derby, *Chamour* was led into the winner's enclosure, which was jammed up with spectators shouting, 'We want Vincent! We want Vincent!' It was a remarkable display of support from a public who could see that banning the trainer was completely illogical.

The anger of the racing public in Ireland did not break The Turf Club. It stuck to its guns and refused to overturn the decision, which O'Brien fought. It took a full year before his training licence was restored and he had his name cleared by The Turf Club, which issued a full apology. In a twist of fate, the day that O'Brien was reissued with his trainer's license (27 May 1961) a foal was born that changed O'Brien's life for ever. That colt was *Northern Dancer*.

It wasn't long before O'Brien focused his attention on the world's most famous race, the Epsom Derby. Run over 1 mile 4 furlongs, the Derby is considered *the* race for future stallion prospects. In 1962 Vincent ran a colt called *Larkspur*, who was owned by the American Raymond Guest. In a hugely eventful race, which saw seven horses fall as they descended from the top of Tattenham Corner, *Larkspur* and his jockey, Neville Sellwood, managed to evade the carnage and land the prize at the generous odds of 20/1.

While there may have been a degree of luck with *Larkspur*'s Derby win in 1962, Vincent's second Derby winner needed no luck whatsoever. Named *Sir Ivor* and owned, again, by Raymond Guest (who was by this time ambassador to Ireland), the big bay colt arrived at Epsom in 1968 as an undefeated champion juvenile as well as a Classic winner, thanks to his success in the 2000 Guineas the previous month. Ridden by Lester Piggott, who had cemented his reputation as the 'big-race king' at that point, *Sir Ivor* produced a turn of foot rarely seen at the highest level to cheekily defeat *Connaught* and his jockey, Sandy Barclay, and win by a comfortable length.

His victory not only gave his owner a second Derby win, but also won Raymond Guest a large amount of money. The enthusiastic owner backed *Sir Ivor* before he had even run and struck a bet with William Hill of £500 each way at 100/1. When Piggott and *Sir Ivor* crossed the finish line at Epsom, Guest collected £62,500 along with his share of the prize money. Not a bad day's work!

Sir Ivor's Derby victory in 1968 established O'Brien as a Classic-winning trainer, but it was that drive inside him to always try to be better and never to settle for what he had already accomplished that led the trainer to Canada. Sometimes in life you make your own luck, but there are also times when a person is simply in the right place at the right time. In 1968 O'Brien was in the right place and began a journey that would fundamentally alter his life and the world of horse racing.

Lester Piggott and Vincent O'Brien on the gallops at Ballydoyle. *Courtesy of Jacqueline O'Brien*

Charles Engelhard, a hugely wealthy American owner, had asked Vincent to travel to Canada to inspect a yearling by the high-class horse *Ribot*, who landed back-to-back Prix de l'Arc de Triomphe in 1955 and 1956. O'Brien wasn't too enthused about travelling such a long way to inspect a single horse, but still took up the offer. After inspecting the yearling, O'Brien dissuaded Engelhard from purchasing the colt. 'He had a slight malformation that I didn't like,' O'Brien said in *The Master*. But having travelled such a long distance, O'Brien decided to see what other horses were on the property. He approached a paddock and spied a beautiful, imposing colt that fitted the criteria of a prospective champion. O'Brien relayed what he saw to Engelhard and advised that he should purchase the colt when he went under the hammer that summer.

A price of CAD$84,000 was handed over for the colt by *Northern Dancer*, who was just starting out in his stallion career. The colt's mother, *Flaming Page*, had also performed with distinction on the racetrack. The colt was called *Nijinsky*. He was flown back to Ireland, trained by O'Brien at Ballydoyle and proved to be a revelation. Despite having some temperament issues when he first arrived at Ballydoyle, *Nijinsky* quickly settled into a routine and took to his work with tremendous ease. His debut win in the Erne Stakes at the Curragh in the June of his juvenile season was so impressive that all of Ireland was talking about him. *Nijinsky* finished his two-year-old campaign with a performance in the Dewhurst Stakes of such authority that he was crowned the leading juvenile of his generation by some distance.

A win in the 2000 Guineas at Newmarket the following May kick-started *Nijinsky's* three-year-old season before he landed a pair of Derbies with easy wins at Epsom and the Curragh. He then travelled to Ascot for the King George VI and Queen Elizabeth Stakes, which he won without breaking a sweat. It was a performance that had to be seen to be believed, and one that would not be replicated until *Montjeu*, who ran in the Coolmore colours, produced similar results in 2000. In a nod to the horse's performance, O'Brien led *Nijinsky* into the winner's enclosure himself, something that he did not do again until his final winner at Royal Ascot, *College Chapel*, in 1993.

Nijinsky went on to win the English St Leger at Doncaster two months later, thus capturing the English Triple Crown, something which had not been achieved for thirty-five years. It is a record that stands to this day, although another Coolmore-owned horse, *Camelot*, came close in 2012, only to be denied by three-quarters of a length by the Godolphin-trained *Encke* in the St Leger.

O'Brien's success with *Nijinsky* confirmed his belief that the *Northern Dancer* bloodline was one worth exploiting. It was from this thought that the foundation was laid for the Coolmore business plan that is still in effect to this day. In 1975 O'Brien, John Magnier and Robert Sangster came together with a plan to source the finest bloodstock from the world's leading yearling sales, train them at Ballydoyle and then stand them at stud for huge sums of money as an ongoing business venture.

The majority of the pressure would fall on O'Brien's shoulders. He would be supplied with the raw material, but it was up to him and his team at Ballydoyle to turn potential into championship material. The Syndicate, as they became known, struck gold from the outset. *The Minstrel*, who was very closely related to *Nijinsky*, was one of their first purchases. Having bought the colt for $200,000 at the Keeneland Yearling Sales, O'Brien trained him to win the Epsom Derby under a ferocious drive from Lester Piggott in 1977. The colt was later sold to America, where he would remain for the duration of his stallion career.

In the same year that O'Brien trained *The Minstrel* to Derby glory, he was also masterminding the career of Coolmore's founding stallion, *Be My Guest*, as well as the dual Arc winner *Alleged*. A son of *Northern Dancer*, *Be My Guest* became Coolmore's first champion sire in 1982 and laid the foundations for Coolmore's success today. A life-size bronze statue of the horse stands outside the offices of Coolmore Stud.

O'Brien's talent for training racehorses was something to behold. Each season he would take the finest horseflesh that was sent his way and, in his own

Vincent O'Brien relaxing at Ballydoyle with the brilliant two-time Arc winner *Alleged*.
Courtesy of Jacqueline O'Brien

quiet and meticulous way, carefully hone and develop each horse and squeeze out every inch of potential. O'Brien's hunger to win was insatiable. The likes of *El Gran Senor, Golden Fleece, Gladness, Valoris, Pieces of Eight, Long Look, Boucher, Thatch, Lisadell, Abergwaun, Home Guard, Apalachee, Artaius, Try My Best, Cloonlara, Godswalk, Be My Guest, Mariinsky, Lady Capulet, Solinus, Jaazeiro, Thatching, Monteverdi, Solford, Bluebird, Lomond, Godetia, Storm Bird, Kings Lake, Caerleon, El Prado, Woodstream, Capricciossa, Prince of Birds, Dark Lomond* and *College Chapel* all enjoyed successful racing careers under his guidance.

Of all the horses O'Brien trained, none had a bigger impact on Coolmore and world racing than *Sadler's Wells*. The son of *Northern Dancer* captured three Group 1s while at Ballydoyle, but it is his deeds at stud for which he will be for ever remembered. During his time at Coolmore Stud, *Sadler's Wells* captured fourteen sires' championships in Great Britain and Ireland and became a noted sire of sires as well as a phenomenal broodmare sire.

Vincent's love of the *Northern Dancer* line provided him with his last and probably most romantic win on the world stage. The Breeders' Cup was still a relatively new event in 1990. In fact since its inception in 1984, no Irish horse had even been placed in a Breeders' Cup race, let alone walked into the winner's enclosure.

In 1990 Vincent sent a colt called *Royal Academy* to contest the Breeders' Cup Mile. Owned by Classic Thoroughbreds, a consortium established by Vincent and his business partners, *Royal Academy* was expected to put up a bold show against his American counterparts. Ridden by Lester Piggott, who had guided so many of Vincent's past champions to glory and who had come out of retirement just a few weeks previously, *Royal Academy* put in a withering late run to catch the American-trained (and wonderfully named) *Itsallgreektome* in the shadows of the post, filling a notable gap on O'Brien's glittering CV. Vincent, who hadn't travelled to America due to an illness, watched the race from Ballydoyle, while his devoted wife, Jacqueline, and their son Charles collected the trophy that registered high on the emotional Richter scale.

The final winner of O'Brien's career came when Christy Roche guided *Mysterious Ways* to victory at the Curragh in September 1994. In a beautiful tie-in, this final winner came exactly fifty years after the famous *Good Days/Drybob* double that started the ball rolling for Vincent. The end of his career as a trainer came in October 1994 with a short statement:

> Racing has been good to me and has enabled me to pursue a career which combined work with pleasure. When I started training, the bloodstock industry in Ireland was still developing. Now we are one of the major thoroughbred racing and breeding countries in the world. I have had the wonderful fortune to have had many wonderful horses and owners and have been ably assisted by friends and by a dedicated staff down the years. To these and all my friends, I am most grateful.[2]

---

2   Ivor Herbert and Jacqueline O'Brien, *Vincent O'Brien: The Official Biography* (London, 2005).

Vincent O'Brien leads in his last Royal Ascot winner *College Chapel*, ridden by Lester Piggott in 1993. *Courtesy of Trevor Jones, Thoroughbred Photography Ltd*

When O'Brien exited stage left in 1994, he left behind a legacy of galactic proportions. Ballydoyle, the stable he purchased for £17,000, was globally recognised as the world's premier racing stable. O'Brien pioneered transporting horses by air, something that is taken for granted nowadays. He was also the first trainer to install an all-weather gallop in his yard. His career was a litany of firsts.

Vincent and his wife enjoyed a wonderful retirement, splitting their time between Perth in Australia and Ireland. They visited racecourses to watch their horses, trained by their son Charles, run. Even after his retirement, the impact that O'Brien had had was not quickly forgotten. Speaking some years later, John Magnier said:

> He understood all aspects of racing. A vital element of Coolmore's success was Vincent's early recognition of the *Northern Dancer* bloodline back in 1968. At Coolmore, as well as being a part-owner, he was our most valued adviser. Three of our champion sires, Be My Guest, Caerleon and Sadler's Wells, were all trained by Vincent. Many of the horses which were trained so brilliantly by Vincent played their part in making today's racing industry a thoroughly international affair.[3]

Vincent O'Brien passed away on 1 June 2009, in Straffan, County Kildare. He was ninety-two. His passing marked the final chapter in a glittering life that brought Ireland to the forefront of Irish horse racing. Many people have contributed to the success that Ireland has enjoyed over the last fifty years, but no person has had such an influence on his sport as Vincent O'Brien had.

At the time of Vincent's passing, Pat Eddery, who guided *Golden Fleece* to victory for O'Brien and Sangster in the 1982 Derby, said:

> Vincent O'Brien was an amazing trainer, a genius with a gift that can't be taught. I was there for five years, and they were the best five years of my life.

---

3   *Ibid.*

Every year, they went to the sales with his eye for horses, and they would buy good ones, but not only that, he could train them and improve them too.[4]

His brother Phonsie, speaking in the *Irish Racing Yearbook 2010* said of Vincent, 'He was a brilliant man. He was so single-minded. He didn't care what other people thought of him. And I do believe that if he had started life selling shoes, he would have been the most successful shoe-seller in the world.'

Michael Vincent O'Brien stands alone as the greatest Irish racehorse trainer ever. There could be no finer epitaph.

M. V. O'BRIEN'S RECORD

Cheltenham Gold Cup: *Cottage Rake* (1948, 1949, 1950), *Knock Hard* (1953)

Grand National: *Early Mist* (1953), *Royal Tan* (1954), *Quare Times* (1955)

Champion Hurdle: *Hatton's Grace* (1949, 1950, 1951)

Irish 2000 Guineas: *El Toro* (1959), *Kings Lake* (1981), *Sadler's Wells* (1984)

Irish Derby: *Chamour* (1953), *Ballymoss* (1957), *Nijinsky* (1970), *The Minstrel* (1977) *El Gran Senor* (1984)

Irish National Stakes: *Sir Ivor* (1967), *Roberto* (1971), *Storm Bird* (1980), *El Prado* (1991)

English 2000 Guineas: *Sir Ivor* (1968), *Nijinsky* (1970), *El Gran Senor* (1984)

Epsom Derby: *Larkspur* (1962), *Sir Ivor* (1968), *Nijinsky* (1970), *Roberto* (1972), *The Minstrel* (1977), *Golden Fleece* (1982)

St Leger: *Ballymoss* (1957), *Nijinsky* (1970), *Boucher* (1972)

King George VI and Queen Elizabeth Stakes: *Ballymoss* (1958), *Nijinsky* (1970), *The Minstrel* (1977)

Prix de l'Arc de Triomphe: *Ballymoss* (1958), *Alleged* (1977, 1978)

Breeders' Cup Mile: *Royal Academy* (1990)

---

4   http://www.theguardian.com/sport/2009/jun/06/derby-epsom-vincent-obrien-aidan-obrien

Northern Dancer

He was the one, the horse that changed everything. Like Michael Jordan in basketball, Jack Nicklaus or Tiger Woods in golf, or Lionel Messi in soccer, *Northern Dancer* redefined what we could expect from a stallion. He changed the thoroughbred industry with his deeds in the covering shed, in the process making many people very rich, but also producing some of the best animals the world of horse racing has ever seen.

At 15.2 hands, *Northern Dancer* wasn't very big – think more *El Gran Senor* than *Nijinsky* – but by God could he run. There was an element of the street fighter in him. It was as if he knew he was smaller than his competition and that, if he was going to win, he would have to out-muscle every single one of them. With a crooked blaze running down his face, he wasn't the *beau idéal* thoroughbred that owners and breeders crave. In fact he didn't even make the $25,000 reserve that was placed on him by his owner and breeder E. P. Taylor when he was being auctioned for sale in 1962. If horses truly have feelings, one can imagine how cheesed off *Northern Dancer* would have been when nobody wanted to give him a home as a young horse.

Thankfully for *Northern Dancer*, and the breeding industry as a whole, his owner brought him back to his Windfields Farm in Ontario, Canada, the same farm where he would begin his outstanding stallion career. While it seemed no one wanted to purchase the young *Northern Dancer*, E. P. Taylor, a huge supporter of horse racing in Canada, was more than happy to retain his home-bred colt. A businessman by trade, Taylor's love and affection for horses grew almost as quickly as his fortune. Born in Ottawa, Ontario, on 29 January 1901, Taylor started his first business, breeding and selling rabbits, when he was just twelve years of age. That love of building a business from the ground up followed Taylor throughout his life. Famously, he grew tired of the local bus service in his hometown, so he and a friend successfully started up their own bus service before selling it to the leading bus company of the time, Capital Bus Line.

Having made his fortune, Taylor began to dabble in the horse-racing industry and soon he was making a major impact. In the 1940s and 1950s Taylor reorganised Canadian racing, which had been managed in a haphazard way before his intervention. He developed Woodbine into the top-class racing facility it is today and established Windfields Farm, where he cultivated his own breeding operation.

One of his first good horses was *Nearctic*, who won twenty-one of forty-seven starts and was crowned Canadian Horse of the Year in 1958, a season in which he won nine races. *Nearctic* retired to Taylor's farm where his most successful

son was *Northern Dancer*. Having developed into something of an oligarch of Canadian racing, Taylor was more than happy to keep *Northern Dancer* and elected to put him into training with Horatio Luro, who was in charge of the Windfields racing stable at that time. Luro liked what he saw from *Northern Dancer* in his early days. Although the horse didn't have the long, flowing stride that one would normally associate with a potential champion, Luro was impressed with the colt's attitude. Whatever was asked of *Northern Dancer*, he carried out his task with relish and determination.

Northern Dancer preparing to work.
Courtesy of sportshorse.data.com

Many people will not remember 2 August 1963 with any great clarity, but for the horse-racing fraternity it is a date that is steeped in importance, for it is the date that *Northern Dancer* made his racecourse debut. Fort Erie Race Track in Ontario was the chosen location for *Northern Dancer* to have his first public outing. Ron Turcotte, the jockey who went on to ride the Triple Crown winner *Secretariat*, was the chosen pilot for *Dancer's* first race. Acutely aware that a horse's first experience at a racetrack is their most crucial, Luro impressed upon Turcotte the importance of *Northern Dancer* enjoying his first race and dissuaded him from using the whip on the immature colt.

Despite a sluggish start, *Northern Dancer* travelled sweetly for Turcotte and was in a challenging position running into the final 2 furlongs of the 5½ furlong contest. Coming to the final furlong, Turcotte and *Northern Dancer* were battling for the lead when Turcotte switched his whip from his right hand to his left and gave *Northern Dancer* a crack, completely disregarding the trainer's instructions. *Northern Dancer's* response was electric. The colt positively took off, sprinting towards the finish line and finishing eight lengths clear of his nearest rival. It was a performance that revealed immense potential and hinted that he could be the next champion to emerge from Taylor's Windfields Farm.

After that first victory, Horatio Luro kept *Northern Dancer* working as a two-year-old. The colt ran a further eight times in 1963, winning six times, including the Summer Stakes and the Coronation Futurity Stakes in Canada and the Remsen Stakes in America. Those performances earned *Northern Dancer* recognition as the leading juvenile in Canada that season.

Northern Dancer developed well over the winter months and the 1964 Kentucky Derby, run on the first Saturday in May at Churchill Downs, became the long-term goal. Prep began for the 'Run for the Roses' with a warm-up race ahead of his first big target of the season, the Grade 1 Flamingo Stakes in Florida.[1] With first-choice jockey Bill Shoemaker unavailable, E. P. Taylor

1   The 'Run for the Roses' is the Kentucky Derby's nickname, which comes from the blanket of roses draped over the winning horse.

and Horatio Luro chose Bobby Ussery to become the fifth jockey to partner *Northern Dancer* in just ten career starts.

As it was the colt's first race after a long break, Ussery was instructed to give *Northern Dancer* an easy time of things and, again, not to touch the colt with the whip. Having endured a troubled passage throughout the race, Ussery used the whip on *Northern Dancer* in the final strides and the pair finished third. Luro was incensed and publicly criticised Ussery for the ride he gave *Northern Dancer*. The experience was not lost on the horse, and in his next workout ahead of the Flamingo Stakes, *Northern Dancer* refused to go onto the track and do his work. The more he was encouraged the more he refused to cooperate. It now appeared that the colt associated the track with the whip. If this continued, the colt's racing career would be thrown into serious doubt.

With careful handling from Luro and his staff, *Northern Dancer* was encouraged to forget about his experience. An exhibition race was put on and, ridden by Bill Shoemaker, the colt ran away from his two rivals, *Chieftain* and *Trader*. It seemed that the Kentucky Derby was back on the agenda.

Wins in his next two races, the Flamingo Stakes and the Florida Derby, put *Northern Dancer* in prime contention for the Kentucky Derby, but on the eve of his final prep race, the Grade 1 Blue Grass Stakes, Bill Shoemaker, who had been asked to commit to riding the colt at the Kentucky Derby, jumped ship and elected to ride another Grade 1 winner, *Hill Rise*.

Without a jockey for their star colt, Taylor and Luro sought the services of Bill Hartack, who guided the colt to victory in the Blue Grass. On Kentucky Derby day, *Northern Dancer* and Hartack were ready to run the race of their lives. Having seen off nine horses in the first three-quarters of the race, *Northern Dancer* had to fend off one last challenge in the final furlong of the 1 mile 2 furlong Grade 1. *Hill Rise* and Bill Shoemaker were the last to challenge and they pushed Hartack and *Northern Dancer* all the way to the line. But the gutsy Canadian colt would not be denied and he flashed by the line the winner, becoming the first Canadian-owned-and-bred horse to win the most famous American horse race. Not only that, but *Northern Dancer* also became the first horse to run the 1 mile 2 furlong test of the Kentucky Derby in two minutes. *Dancer* stopped the clock at an unbelievable 2.00.00 flat and became the first horse in the Derby's eighty-nine-year history to achieve such a fast time. He showed that although he didn't have the height or stature expected of champions, he had the heart of a champion and guts and determination to boot.

Winning the Kentucky Derby was a tremendous achievement for all concerned and thoughts soon turned to the Triple Crown. As *Northern Dancer* had recovered from his efforts at Churchill Downs better than expected, Horatio Luro aimed him at the Preakness Stakes, which is considered an easier run than the Derby. Despite *Northern Dancer* coming into the race as the Kentucky Derby winner, the punting public were with *Hill Rise*, who they sent off at 4/5 favourite.

Again ridden by Bill Hartack, *Northern Dancer* displayed his customary enthusiasm for racing, galloping along sweetly in third place for much of the race. As the field swung out of the backstretch and the race heated up, Hartack moved *Northern Dancer* up to the lead. As was the case in the Derby, Shoemaker and *Hill Rise* tracked *Northern Dancer* into the final furlong. However, when Shoemaker pushed *Hill Rise*, the horse's response was disappointing and *Northern Dancer* quickly drew away. *Hill Rise* was nudged out of second place by *The Scoundrel*.

It was another top-class performance from *Northern Dancer* and, with only one leg of the Triple Crown to go, hopes were high that he could secure his place in racing history by winning the Belmont Stakes to become the latest Triple Crown winner. However, on a grey afternoon in New York, the Triple Crown dream would die as *Northern Dancer's* stamina ran out over the punishing 1 mile 4 furlongs of the Belmont Stakes and he faded into third place behind the eventual winner *Quadrangle* and runner-up *Roman Brother*.

It was a bitterly disappointing end to *Northern Dancer's* Triple Crown dream, but his owner pressed on and sent his boot-tough champion back into battle in Canada's Queen's Plate, a race in which he treated the rest of the field with contempt, winning by seven and a half lengths. That victory in the Queen's Plate proved to be the last of *Northern Dancer's* career. He developed tenderness in one of his front tendons, no doubt brought on by his aggressive running style. E. P. Taylor made the decision to retire his star colt to Windfields Farm, where he would begin his stallion career.

Northern Dancer was showered with honours at the end of his racing career. He was named both the American and Canadian Horse of the Year for 1964, along with becoming the first horse to be inducted into the Canadian Sports Hall of Fame in 1965. He won fourteen of his eighteen starts and never finished out of the first three places in any of his races. Class, determination and courage were just some of the qualities he displayed during his racing career and it was hoped that he would be able to pass on these traits to his offspring. When the colt arrived back at Windfields Farm at the end of his three-year-old season, expectations were high for his future career as a stallion.

A Grade 1 winner as a juvenile and the winner of six Grade 1s in his classic year, *Northern Dancer* certainly had the race record to make a fine addition to E. P. Taylor's stallion ranks, and while he may not have had the poster-boy good looks of a top-class stallion, breeders flocked to him when he retired to stud. A fee of $10,000 was set for his first season at stud. Little did anyone know that it would prove to be the bargain of a lifetime.

Unlike nowadays, when stallions cover huge books of mares in both hemispheres, *Northern Dancer* was restricted to a select book of mares while he was at stud. When he started his stallion career, there were thirty-two shares available in what became known as the *Northern Dancer* Syndicate. A further four shares were retained for breeding purposes, so in essence the stallion would cover a book of thirty-six mares. This goes some way to explaining why his offspring cost so much when they went under the hammer at public auction.

As with his performances on the racetrack, *Northern Dancer* hit the ground running as a sire. One of the first top-class horses he sired was *Fanfreluche*, a beautiful-looking filly who had buckets of talent to match her looks. *Fanfreluche* was an exceptional race mare. During her career, she won eleven of her twenty-one starts, including five Grade 1 races. However, she is best remembered for an incident that occurred after she retired. In June 1977 *Fanfreluche* was kidnapped from her stable at Claiborne Farm in Kentucky while she was in foal to Triple Crown winner *Secretariat*. In scenes that would be repeated a few years later in Ireland, when wonder horse *Shergar* went missing, *Fanfreluche* went on the missing list for five months until the FBI found her safe and well some 158 miles away from Claiborne in the small town of Tompkinsville, where she was staying with a family who found her wandering down a country road. Having returned safely to her stable, *Fanfreluche* gave birth to her foal, a colt who was given the French name *Sain et Sauf*, which translates as safe and sound.

Fanfreluche was doing her bit to advertise *Northern Dancer* as a potential top-class sire in North America, but it was one of his sons who did more than most to show *Northern Dancer*'s potential as a stallion, particularly in Europe. Named after the Russian dancer Vaslav Nijinsky, the equine *Nijinsky* was the first of *Northern Dancer*'s offspring to race in Europe and became the trailblazer of a sire line that completely dominates European racing.

Trained by Vincent O'Brien in Ballydoyle, *Nijinsky* backed up a champion two-year-old campaign by becoming the first horse in thirty-five years to win the English Triple Crown in his three-year-old season. It is a feat that has not been equalled at the time of writing in 2016. The success that O'Brien had with *Nijinsky* persuaded the trainer to continue purchasing *Northern Dancer* stock. All the hallmarks that shone through his racing career – toughness, soundness, grit, determination and class – were being passed on by *Northern Dancer* to his offspring.

O'Brien became the greatest supporter of *Northern Dancer*. Along with Robert Sangster and John Magnier, he travelled to America, purchased the best *Northern Dancer* stock available, brought them back to Europe and trained them to become champions. They were either sold for a huge profit or retired to Coolmore Stud where they could breed their own champions without Coolmore having to dip into their sizeable pockets at the sales.

It proved to be a phenomenally successful plan and was the seed that saw Coolmore develop into the world's pre-eminent stud farm. *Be My Guest*, Coolmore's first champion sire, was by *Northern Dancer*, as was the incomparable *Sadler's Wells*, who was champion sire in Britain and Ireland a record fourteen times. *El Gran Senor*, *The Minstrel*, *Storm Bird*, *Lomond*, *Try My Best* and *Monteverdi* were all colts by *Northern Dancer* that Vincent O'Brien trained to great success on the gallops at Ballydoyle. The offspring of *Northern Dancer* were beginning to transform the very fabric of European racing, and during the 1980s the competition for his sons and daughters became so fierce that it threatened to tip the bloodstock industry over the edge, as the prices for yearlings were becoming unsustainable.

Each July the big hitters from Ireland (O'Brien, Sangster and Magnier), Dubai (led by Sheikh Mohammed) and America all locked horns and spent tens of millions of dollars on *Northern Dancer* progeny, hoping that they would have the next *Nijinsky* in their stable. The bidding for *Northern Dancer* stock came to a head when Sheikh Mohammed paid a world-record (at the time) $10 million for a colt by the great sire out of a mare called *My Bupers*. *Snaafi Dancer* was the name given to the expensive colt, who was sent to the highly respected stable of John Dunlop. But he was reportedly so slow that he never saw the racetrack. Even worse was to come when he was sent to stud. *Snaafi Dancer* suffered from fertility problems and could sire only four foals, three of which didn't show much at the racetrack. He was retired from stud duty and faded into oblivion.

Snaafi Dancer aside, *Northern Dancer* continued to be the most in-demand stallion of the twentieth century. Having started his stud career as a $10,000 sire, his price quickly shot up to such an extent that in the mid-1980s his covering fee was $1 million without a guarantee of a live foal. It was an extraordinary figure, but not one that deterred breeders, who still queued up for his services.

Famously, at the height of his powers, *People Magazine* said of *Northern Dancer* that 'he was the only celebrity that could earn a million dollars before breakfast'.

In 1984 twelve yearlings by *Northern Dancer* sold for an unrivalled price of $3,446,666. The Keeneland sales in July turned into the *Northern Dancer* show. Staggeringly, over a twenty-two-year period, *Northern Dancer*'s progeny made $160 million at Keeneland.

Such was the clamour to have a stake in *Northern Dancer* that in 1981 a bid of $40 million to purchase him was made by a group of French breeders. E. P. Taylor flatly rejected it. 'Over my dead body,' was the response from Windfields Farm. The stallion remained in North America and continued to regularly sire both champion fillies and colts. His offspring began to produce their own collection of champion horses, and *Northern Dancer* morphed from a champion sire into a sire of sires. *Be My Guest, Danzig, Fairy King, Lyphard, Nijinsky, Northern Taste, Nureyev, Sadler's Wells*, and *Storm Bird* all became top-class sires in their own right, ensuring that the *Northern Dancer* line would live on.

Aside from *Be My Guest* and *Sadler's Wells*, the other *Northern Dancer* line that has flourished at Coolmore over the last forty years is the *Danzig* line, mainly thanks to his son *Danehill*. Injury cruelly cut *Danzig*'s racing career short, but he made amends at stud, siring a host of top-class horses and becoming one of the most influential sires of the twentieth century alongside his own sire. *Danehill*'s impact on the breed, both in the northern and southern hemisphere, is considerable. Many horses from the *Danehill* sire line, including *Holy Roman Emperor, Mastercraftsman, Fastnet Rock* and up-and-coming stallion *Zoffany*, stand at Coolmore's three worldwide bases. Coolmore, perhaps more than any other stallion station, has benefited from *Northern Dancer*'s success as a stallion. Thanks in the main to Vincent O'Brien for spotting his potential, *Northern Dancer* transformed Coolmore into what it has become today.

The legacy of *Northern Dancer* carried on with *Sadler's Wells*, who took Coolmore into a different league. He, in turn, sired the most dominant stallion of the twentieth-first century in *Galileo*. *Galileo* has kept up the tradition of his paternal side by siring the likes of *Australia*, *Gleneagles* and *Ruler Of The World*, all horses that now stand at Coolmore's Irish base in County Tipperary. It is a sire line that looks likely to remain dominant for generations to come.

Northern Dancer is the great-grandsire of *California Chrome*, winner of the 2014 Kentucky Derby and 2014 Preakness Stakes, and the great-great-grandsire of *Sea The Stars*. Undefeated racehorse *Frankel* is inbred 3×4 to *Northern Dancer*, meaning *Northern Dancer* appears once in the third generation and once in the fourth generation of his pedigree. *American Pharoah*, winner of the 2015 US Triple Crown, is 5×5 inbred to *Northern Dancer*, through *Storm Bird* and *El Gran Senor*. *Northern Dancer* is the great-great-grandsire (all paternal) to undefeated Australian mare *Black Caviar*.

One only has to look at the sire's championship table in Great Britain and Ireland to see the influence that *Northern Dancer* has had on the breed over the last fifty years. Since 1970 *Northern Dancer* and his descendants have won thirty-two sire championships. Apart from the four titles he won himself, one title each was won by his sons *Be My Guest* and *Nijinsky*, fourteen were won by his son *Sadler's Wells*, two by his grandson *Caerleon*, three by his grandson *Danehill* and seven by his grandson *Galileo*.

Despite having such unadulterated success in Europe, *Northern Dancer* didn't have quite the same impact in North America, where he was champion sire in 1971 and in 1977 when international earnings are taken into account. Amazingly, despite having won the Kentucky Derby himself, *Northern Dancer* had only a single runner in the race during his stallion career, when *Giboulee* ran down the field in the 'Run for the Roses' in 1977. Other North American horses of note he sired were the likes of *Dance Number*, *Northernette* and *Lauries Dancer*, all fillies and all Grade 1 winners. His stock had the ability to travel off a strong pace and unleash a tremendous turn of speed in the latter part of their races. The very best of them also possessed a will to win that is very hard to find in horses. You could count on the *Northern Dancer* stock to put their head down and battle all the way to the line. It's what their father did and would have expected from his progeny.

As with all life, be it animal or human, there comes a point in time when one has to step aside, exit stage left and give way to a new generation. For *Northern Dancer* that moment happened when he was retired from active stud duties in 1987 at the age of twenty-six. His retirement marked the end of an era, but with sons like *Nijinsky*, *Be My Guest* and *Sadler's Wells* at stud, his legacy was in safe hands. *Northern Dancer* lived out his days at the Windfields Farm property in Maryland, spending them in his paddock and enjoying his retirement. Just three years after the decision was made to retire the stallion from the breeding world, he was gone. He was put down at the age of twenty-nine and laid to rest on 16 November 1990.

Alan McCarthy, the vet who looked after *Northern Dancer* for the last ten years of his life, was with the sire on his last day and spoke in an interview with *The Baltimore Sun* about the final few hours when *Northern Dancer* fought the horrific bout of colic that brought the stallion to the end of his life:

> 'It got to the point where he was going to inflict damage to the people around him,' McCarthy said about the horse, who was in such tortuous abdominal pain that he was almost uncontrollable, even in the face of death. 'He was a difficult horse to work with anyway … When he was down and I was trying to ease his pain, he'd turn around and try to bite me. It was very, very sad. But I'm confident we made the right decision. I talked to veterinarians at the New Bolton Center [the University of Pennsylvania Veterinary Clinic in Kennett Square] and they said that in many old horses there is some strangulation of the small intestine caused by fatty tissue. But we don't know for sure what caused *Northern Dancer*'s problem, and we wouldn't know unless we opened him up.
>
> I called Windfields' manager, Ric Waldman, in Kentucky, and he is the one who OK'd putting him down. He died at 6.15 a.m. His body was loaded and shipped out by 7.30 a.m. and he was in Canada by 9 p.m. They dug his grave while he was in transit.

It was a sad end for the horse who transformed racing across the globe. *Northern Dancer* was laid to rest at Windfields Farm, Ontario, in between the barn where he was born and the barn where he bred his first runners. Sadly, from a horse-racing fan's perspective, access to his burial site is restricted as the land was purchased by the University of Ontario and is not accessible to the public.

Northern Dancer preparing for track work. He would later play a crucial role in the early success of Coolmore Stud. *Courtesy of sportshorse.data.com*

Northern Dancer's legacy continues to this day with the deeds of his great-grandsons and great-granddaughters. One only has to look at the pedigree of the majority of horses in Europe to see the impact *Northern Dancer* has had on the world of horse racing. While he may now be at the great racecourse in the sky, alongside his sons and daughters who did so much to cement his legacy as the world's most influential stallion of his generation, his name will be uttered in revered tones for many, many years to come. *Northern Dancer* was the stallion who defined an era and it was Vincent O'Brien who recognised his potential and used it to build one of the strongest lines of stud mares and stallions in the world.

MAJOR WINS

Coronation Futurity Stakes (1963)

Summer Stakes (1963)

Remsen Stakes (1963)

Flamingo Stakes (1964)

Florida Derby (1964)

Blue Grass Stakes (1964)

Queen's Plate (1964)

AMERICAN CLASSICS WINS

Kentucky Derby (1964)

Preakness Stakes (1964)

AWARDS

US Champion Three-Year-Old Colt (1964)

Canadian Horse of the Year (1964)

Leading Sire in North America (1971)

Leading Broodmare Sire in North America (1991)

Leading Sire in Great Britain and Ireland (1970, 1977, 1983, 1984)

HONOURS

Canada's Sports Hall of Fame (1965)

Canadian Horse Racing Hall of Fame (1976)

United States Racing Hall of Fame (1976)

Canadian postage stamp (1999)

Northern Dancer Boulevard in Toronto, Ontario

Northern Dancer Drive in Warwick, Maryland

Northern Dancer Turf Stakes at Woodbine

Northern Dancer Stakes at Churchill

Northern Dancer Plate at Hyderabad Race Club (India)

Life-size statue at Woodbine Racetrack

THE OLD SYNDICATE

They sat as a group saying nothing. In the warm Kentucky summer, the men were as cool as the breeze that punctuated another sweltering July day. There were no smiles. They were there for business and, with so much money on the line, serious faces and attitudes were the order of the day. The laughing could wait until the bar later that night.

Each man walked in front of, to the side of and to the back of the horses. The yearlings (one-year-old colts and fillies) were being inspected by some of the most respected names in the business. It wouldn't be long before buyers would begin to pay huge prices for yearlings. One can understand why nobody was making jokes.

In the middle of the group was Vincent O'Brien, the main man. A trainer like no other. *Sir Ivor, Nijinsky, Roberto, The Minstrel, Alleged, Ballymoss, Gladness* – all were champions trained by O'Brien at his stables in Ballydoyle, County Tipperary. He was in Kentucky to find his next champion.

O'Brien took his time choosing which horses would make his select list. The young men holding the horses occasionally let out groans of exasperation, but O'Brien would not be rushed. He gazed at each animal's body, legs and finally its head. He looked deeply into the horse's eyes and asked the question he had asked a thousand times before: 'What will you do for me?' It would be the feeling that O'Brien got from the horse, a gut instinct, that would either see the horse earn a flight back to Ballydoyle or be passed over.

Standing next to O'Brien was Robert Sangster, a millionaire from Liverpool, England, who had become one of the major driving forces in world racing. His reach spread right across the globe, but it was there with O'Brien that he felt most at home. His colours were as familiar as the sun. Why wouldn't they be? Robert Sangster's silks had been carried to victory by some bona fide legends of the turf, horses that ignited a passion for horse racing in so many. Horses that started a love affair with this most wonderful of sports: *The Minstrel, El Gran Senor, Golden Fleece, Sadler's Wells, Assert, Rodrigo de Triano* and *Caerleon*, all top-class horses that won at the highest level of flat racing and shaped the breed for generations.

Sangster's horses won twenty-seven European Classics and more than a hundred Group 1 races, including two Epsom Derbies, four Irish Derbies, two French Derbies, three Prix de l'Arc de Triomphe, as well as the Breeders' Cup Mile and the Melbourne Cup. He was also the leading owner in England five times, yet it is his association with Vincent O'Brien and John Magnier that he is best known for.

Born in Liverpool on 23 May 1936, Sangster was brought up in comfort. In 1926 his father, Vernon, established the Vernons Pools. These pools were a betting system based on predicting the outcome of top-level association football matches taking place in the coming week. The pools were typically cheap to enter and the prize was a considerable sum of money.

While he was growing up it wasn't horse racing that interested the young Sangster, but rather cricket and boxing. He excelled at boxing and, during his time in the army, won a heavyweight boxing championship in Berlin. The gritty determination he showed in the boxing ring was something he carried with him throughout his life. Having completed his time in the service, Sangster joined his father's organisation, rising to become the company's managing director, before serving as chairman from 1980 to 1988. Following this he sold the Vernons Pools business to Ladbrokes for £90 million.

Before Sangster joined forces with O'Brien and Magnier, and proceeded to turn the world of international breeding on its head, he had enjoyed his own share of luck on the racetrack. His first win in a major flat race came when his horse *Brief Star* won the 1969 Ayr Gold Cup. It was the race that hooked Sangster.

The final man in that Kentucky group was John Magnier, a quiet and reserved gentleman whose mind ran more efficiently than those of the majority of his peers in the bloodstock industry. Magnier, like Sangster and O'Brien, would have looked at a yearling, but he would have been thinking ahead three, four and even five years down the line to where this horse might end up.

Born on 10 February 1948 and educated privately at Glenstal Abbey in County Limerick, Magnier had to leave school at the age of fifteen following the untimely death of his father, Tom. He helped his mother, Evie, run Grange Stud, and visitors to the farm recall seeing a young John Magnier milking the family's dairy herd. His business philosophy was a simple one: breed or purchase the best raw talent in the world, have them trained to Group 1 success, retire them to stud and hopefully breed the next generation of superstar racehorses.

Ideally for Magnier, a colt (such as his 2015 champion *Gleneagles*) would retire to Coolmore Stud. If the colt had enjoyed a successful racing career and become a multiple Group 1 winner, he would start his stallion career commanding a six-figure sum per covering, and when a stallion can have up to 150 covers per year, the math is simple.

The pivotal moment in their relationship, for both Robert Sangster and John Magnier, came in 1971, when Sangster was at Haydock sponsoring the Vernons Sprint Cup (now known as the Haydock Sprint Cup). The pair met and were impressed with each other. A friendship developed that would change the course of horse racing and horse breeding. Sangster and Magnier approached the world's greatest trainer, Vincent O'Brien, who was fresh from guiding the great *Nijinsky* through his Triple Crown season in 1970, with a proposal. The plan was that the three men would target the major bloodstock sales throughout the world, purchase stock by *Northern Dancer*, sire of *Nijinsky* and a stallion Vincent O'Brien had the utmost confidence in, win the biggest races on offer and then stand the stallions in Ireland.

At the time, Coolmore Stud was not the behemoth it later became. Having started out as a relatively small farm, the property came into the Vigors family in 1945, when a training operation was established there. Tim Vigors, a famous fighter pilot in the Battle of Britain and in the Far East, inherited it. On leaving the Royal Air Force, Vigors had joined the world-renowned Goffs bloodstock auctioneers before setting up his own bloodstock agency in 1951. He moved to Coolmore in 1968, went into partnership with Vincent O'Brien, and started to establish Coolmore as a stud. He later sold his interest to O'Brien and John Magnier owing to a messy divorce through which he was going.

All the pieces for the project seemed to be in place. They had the best trainer in the world, who could train the horses to win the races that mattered most year after year. In John Magnier they had one of the sharpest minds in the business, a man who could map out the stallion careers of the horses who made it to Coolmore and could select which races were the most important in making a champion racehorse into a lucrative stallion prospect. In Sangster they had the most important element: cold, hard cash.

In a rare interview, given in 1975, the twenty-seven-year-old Magnier outlined his plans for Coolmore Stud:

> If we keep stallions here and stand them very cheaply … in a short time we would be buying tenth-rate stallions, and when we went to the yearling sales, nobody would want our produce. We have got to avail ourselves of the outside markets and stand stallions which will have international appeal as well.[1]

That international vision, the ability to see the bigger picture, was a trait Magnier always possessed.

Grange Stud, where Magnier grew up, was close to Fermoy in County Cork, in an area that had been synonymous with National Hunt breeding for years. When asked about Magnier, Vincent O'Brien said:

> He is a man of exceptional ability; he thinks big, deals shrewdly, and is most

---

1   http://www.the-racehorse.com/breeding/breeding_business/coolmore_part_one_the_early_years

knowledgeable about bloodlines and everything to do with the stud business. John is so able I feel he would have reached the top of whatever profession he chose, and our very close association has been the greatest pleasure to me – it is a joy to work with someone of his calibre.[2]

Magnier was equally enthusiastic about O'Brien:

Not only would I describe him as a great trainer – he is on a plane apart when it comes to breeding matters – Vincent can compete with anybody in buying on looks alone. He could, I am certain, pick a potential winner, even a future champion, without even looking at the pedigree. Nobody before Vincent, or likely to come after him, could ever match his knowledge of pedigrees and bloodlines. It's uncanny really.

Truthfully, however, without Sangster's deep pockets, the project would have been doomed to fail. It was he who paid for the initial purchases that allowed The Syndicate to start their rise to the top of the bloodstock world.

As well as the three members of The Syndicate, a key member of the partnership was the late Billy McDonald, who passed away in November 2009. McDonald was involved in the purchase of young horses. He spotted *Alleged* at a breeze-up sale in California and convinced Robert Sangster to purchase the colt, which he did, privately, for $120,000. McDonald also played a key role in securing *Fairy Bridge*, the dam of *Sadler's Wells*, as John Magnier described during the 2005 Cartier Racing Awards in London:

One year, during the July Sales at Keeneland, I was on the way to breakfast one morning through the bar at the old Hyatt and I spotted Billy McDonald's catalogue in the trash can. Inside the catalogue was a pass-out for a filly that he'd bought the day before. He'd paid $40,000 for her, and there wasn't a lot

---

2   *Ibid.*

of her there. As luck would have it again, she turned out to be champion two-year-old filly *Fairy Bridge*.

I learned afterwards that Billy had given a $100 bill at Claiborne to the yearling manager Gus Koch – obviously a turned-on guy – to find out his pick of the draft and he said a little *Bold Reason* filly was the fastest in the paddock; it was obviously money well spent. *Fairy Bridge*'s first visit to *Northern Dancer* at Windfields resulted, as luck would have it, in *Sadler's Wells*.[3]

With the likes of McDonald in their ranks, the 'triumvirate', as they became known throughout the breeding world, struck gold from the off. They travelled back from Kentucky in 1975 a shade under $1.8 million lighter in the pocket. The trio brought with them *The Minstrel*, who landed the Epsom and Irish Derbies in 1977. It was just the start the partnership needed. Buoyed by the success of *The Minstrel*, Sangster and The Syndicate reinvested and continued to strike gold. From 1975 onwards a steady stream of beautifully bred, expensive horses carrying Sangster's colours and trained by Vincent O'Brien won the biggest races in Europe before retiring to stud where they stood for enormous covering fees.

It was a golden time for the trio. Ably assisted by Lester Piggott, the world's greatest jockey at the time, The Syndicate could do no wrong. Sangster was instrumental in convincing Piggott to give up his freelance career in England to ride for the Coolmore/Ballydoyle operation. It looked on paper like a partnership that would last the test of time. Sangster said:

> Lester was a fantastic jockey and very tough. He could get the very best out of the horses when he needed to. When he won the Epsom Derby on *The Minstrel*, I think he would have been banned for six months for his use of the whip [Piggott didn't receive a ban for this ride] but nobody else would have got that horse home that day. He was simply the best.[4]

---

3   http://bloodstock.racingpost.com/news/bloodstock/alleged-sadlers-wells-fairy-bridge-racing-mourns-the-death-of-agent-billy-mcdonald/655301/
4   https://www.youtube.com/watch?v=6Se0kMospmc

Because Piggott was the best, The Syndicate had to pay sizeable amounts to retain the jockey's services. Sangster admitted:

> He was on half a million dollars. Ten times more than the Prime Minister. Any horse that won a Classic, Lester got a breeding right to, which was the equivalent to 2.5 per cent. In those days we were syndicating horses like *Storm Bird* for $28 million, *Assert* for $24 million. *The Minstrel* was $9 million and *Alleged* was $12 million, so it was big bucks.

It was indeed the era of big deals, and The Syndicate was right in the thick of things. Be it purchasing colts or fillies at auction, or breeding them from Sangster's Swettenham Stud, his own separate breeding operation, The Syndicate had a whole host of beautifully bred horses, year after year, who scored at the highest level. Think of *Sadler's Wells*, the supreme stallion of his generation, who won three Group 1 races for The Syndicate in 1984 and, remarkably, wasn't considered the best horse in Ballydoyle at the time. That title fell to *El Gran Senor*, a drop-dead gorgeous horse who had any amount of ability to go with his noble looks.

A champion at two, *El Gran Senor* motored away from one of the best 2000 Guineas fields that has ever been assembled. Champions like *Chief Singer, Lear Fan* and *Rainbow Quest* were all dismissed in effortless fashion by *El Gran Senor*, who then lost the Epsom Derby in sensational style on his next start, when he failed to get the better of *Secreto* in a tussle that is still talked about to this day – many felt that Pat Eddery mistimed his challenge and cost *El Gran Senor* the race.

Golden Fleece was another horse that carried The Syndicate's colours with distinction, despite having just a few fleeting moments of brilliance on the racetrack. A son of *Nijinsky*, *Golden Fleece* landed the 1982 Epsom Derby in breathtaking fashion under Pat Eddery, before being cruelly cut down, first by injury and then cancer. He passed away in 1984.

Sangster was the public face of The Syndicate and with good reason. While O'Brien and Magnier were reserved men, Sangster was more affable, a man

Vincent O'Brien and Robert Sangster watch *The Minstrel* run in the Irish Derby.
Courtesy of Jacqueline O'Brien

who embraced life and squeezed from it every ounce of enjoyment he could. His friend Julian Wilson, a hugely respected broadcaster who passed away in 2014, followed Sangster during the early days of The Syndicate and detailed his unrelenting passion for life:

> In the late 70s he allowed me to film a documentary on his racing life.
>
> BBC TV, ever generous towards and enthusiastic about horse racing, approved the project – providing we did not exceed two days' shooting.
>
> So began a typical 36 hours in Robert's life. We filmed at Barry Hills's stable on Monday morning; flew to the Nunnery, Isle of Man, for lunch;

flew on to Dublin; drove to Mick O'Toole's stable at the Curragh to film a Sangster-owned star galloping at, of all things, teatime; and downed a jar (or three) at O'Toole's early evening.

Our next port of call was Ballydoyle, home of the great Vincent O'Brien, for dinner.

'Hadn't we better go,' I nagged urgently, as time ticked by.

'Don't worry, Wiz. Everyone's late in Ireland.'

We arrived at Ballydoyle an hour and a quarter late. The O'Briens were coming towards the end of their main course.

'Sorry we're a bit late, Vincent,' said Robert. 'Julian insisted on having another drink at our last port of call …'

Vincent and Jacqueline gave me the evil eye throughout dinner – and only one glass of wine.

The following morning we filmed at Ballydoyle – it was the era of *The Minstrel* and *Alleged* – and at Coolmore Stud, where Vincent explained, memorably, what he looked for in a yearling.

Robert's eight-seat plane collected us from Ballydoyle and we flew into Heathrow. From there we relocated to Robert's penthouse suite at the Dorchester, to toast the project in Dom Pérignon.[5]

That was the life of Robert Sangster. He lived life in the fast lane and didn't care who noticed.

While many people assumed that The Syndicate was made up of three individuals, this isn't quite true. Fringe members of The Syndicate, who owned a portion of a number of horses that were trained at Ballydoyle, included Paris-based Jean-Pierre Binet, Bob Fluor of the American-based Fluor Corporation, whose best horse was dual Arc winner *Alleged*, Swiss billionaire Walter Haefner, London insurance broker Charles St George, Scottish aristocrat Simon Fraser, Irish property developer Patrick Gallagher and Yorkshire-based David Aykroyd.

---

5   http://www.theguardian.com/sport/2004/apr/09/horseracing1

Chief among the very rich people who looked to get a piece of The Syndicate's action was the Greek shipping tycoon Stavros Niarchos. Niarchos first became involved in horse racing in the early 1950s, with his first stakes race success coming when *Pipe of Peace* won the Group 1 Middle Park Stakes at Newmarket. Despite that initial success, Niarchos made the decision to leave the horse-racing industry for roughly two decades, until he made his return in the 1970s, when he took a share in a number of The Syndicate's horses. He acquired the Haras de Fresnay-le-Buffard horse-breeding farm in Neuvy-au-Houlme, France, and Oak Tree Farm in Lexington, Kentucky, which he made into his own equine paradise. It was from Kentucky that in 1984 he bred his most successful horse, *Miesque*.

Niarchos was a player in The Syndicate's most famous, or infamous, moment, depending on your perspective, which came on a balmy July day in 1985. Sangster and his group were at the height of their powers. They had over the previous decade transformed the bloodstock industry to a point where people were paying extraordinary amounts of money, running into the tens of millions of dollars, for horses that had never seen a racetrack. On this day, however, sanity was lost and replaced by hubris and ego. The colt at the centre of attention was a beautifully bred horse by *Nijinsky*. He was out of the hugely talented *My Charmer*, who had already become a broodmare of note having thrown two champions in *Seattle Slew*, who landed the American Triple Crown in 1977, and *Lomond*, who had won the English 2000 Guineas for The Syndicate just a few months previously. Certainly on paper the colt ticked all the boxes and as a physical specimen he had the looks to match his regal pedigree. There was a buzz of anticipation when he was led into the sales complex, although the youngster was not intimidated by the huge crowd in the jam-packed auditorium.

Incredibly, bidding for the horse opened at $1.25 million. It was a sensational opening, but it was only the beginning. After sixty seconds, the bidding passed $8 million, with Sangster, O'Brien and Magnier leading the charge. Another forty seconds elapsed, and bidding shot past $9.8 million with only The

Syndicate and an American consortium, led by Racing Hall of Fame trainer D. Wayne Lukas, left. The two groups settled in to duke it out. On they went. $10 million, $10.5 million, $11 million, $11.5 million, $12 million, $12.5 million, $13 million, $13.1 million. Then it happened. Lukas blinked, and in that instant The Syndicate knew they had won the day.

Lukas walked away and the hammer fell on the most expensive yearling to be sold in the world. The Syndicate had flexed their muscle and showed that, for all the new money that was coming into racing and breeding, Sangster, O'Brien and Magnier were still at the top of the tree. It was a startling show of financial strength that highlighted the culture of ego and excess that existed at the time.

The $13.1-million animal was totally unaffected by the hoopla that surrounded his purchase and remained unfazed as he was led out of the sales arena destined for his new home at Ballydoyle. Named *Seattle Dancer*, the colt would have to live up to huge expectations to justify his enormous price tag. However, problems beset *Seattle Dancer* from the outset. A virus swept through Ballydoyle during the 1986 season, which kept the young and still immature *Seattle Dancer* on the sidelines. It was a big blow for The Syndicate, as *Seattle Dancer* missed all the major two-year-old races, which are vital in showcasing a horse's talent and enhancing its stallion CV. Having sat out all of the 1986 season, *Seattle Dancer* made his belated debut in April 1987 at the Curragh. Wearing the colours of Stavros Niarchos, who took a share in the colt to help ease the financial burden on The Syndicate, *Seattle Dancer* finished third. It was a respectable first outing considering that it was his first time at a racetrack and the fact that he had to overcome a virus the previous season.

Despite their disappointment, The Syndicate pressed on and pitched *Seattle Dancer* higher for his next start. He took the Group 3 Gallinule Stakes at the Curragh before backing up that performance with another classy display in the Group 2 Derrinstown Stud Derby Trial Stakes at Leopardstown, as he began to demonstrate why his owners had forked out such a colossal amount of money for him. Sadly that proved to be the final success in *Seattle Dancer*'s racing career.

A disappointing sixth place effort in the Group 1 Prix du Jockey Club was followed by second place in the Grand Prix de Paris before an injury brought his career to an end after just five starts.

Having failed to cut the mustard on the racetrack, *Seattle Dancer* was retired to Ashford Stud, Coolmore's American branch, in Kentucky, where it was hoped he could pass on some of his talents to his offspring. Unfortunately his stud career proved to be a mirror image of his time as a racehorse. *Seattle Rhyme*, winner of the 1991 Group 1 Racing Post Trophy and *Que Belle*, a dual Classic winner in Germany, were the highlights of a stallion career that saw *Seattle Dancer* sire thirty-seven stakes winners. As well as his time at Ashford Stud, *Seattle Dancer* spent time at Coolmore's head office in County Tipperary, before being sold to Japan, then spending the last five years of his stud career in Germany. He died of a heart attack in 2007. His name will be for ever linked to the heady days of the 1980s when the bloodstock industry lost the run of itself. He is also a reminder that nothing in sport, or life for that matter, is a guaranteed success.

Seattle Dancer caused The Syndicate to change its approach. After they met with their greatest rival, Sheikh Mohammed of Dubai, a truce of sorts was called, and the dizzying prices that yearlings were being sold for soon became a thing of the past. It didn't help that the bloodstock industry was about to slip into a deep recession, which had repercussions throughout the breeding world.

The Syndicate was seen less and less at the major auction sales. A consortium called Classic Thoroughbreds, a public company which allowed people to purchase shares, was formed in 1987 by Sangster, O'Brien and Magnier, but quickly died a slow and painful death, with *Royal Academy*'s 1990 Breeders' Cup Mile win the major highlight of the venture. With the business evolving, the syndicate of Sangster, O'Brien and Magnier dissolved in 1991, as the three men turned their attentions elsewhere.

Sangster began to focus on his thoroughbred racing and breeding empire, including interests in England, Australia, Venezuela, the United States, Ireland, France and New Zealand. He had bought Swettenham, a 200-acre stud farm in

Cheshire, when he was twenty-eight, and in 1985 had paid £6 million for the famous Manton House stables near Marlborough in Wiltshire. This became the focus of his racing operations in England. He had installed Michael Dickinson, the brilliant National Hunt trainer who trained the first five home in the Cheltenham Gold Cup of 1983, as his first trainer, but when Dickinson moved to North America, Sangster replaced him with Barry Hills, then Peter Chapple-Hyam and John Gosden.

Sangster largely withdrew from buying at the yearling sales, instead selling horses bred at his own studs. He won his final Classic when *Rodrigo de Triano* won the 2000 Guineas at Newmarket in 1992 under Lester Piggott. He also saw horses he bred win major races for other owners, including *Dr Devious*, who won the Derby in 1992, *Balanchine*, who won the Oaks and the Irish Derby in 1994, and *Carnegie*, who won the Arc in the same year. In 1993 Sangster sold his interest in Coolmore to John Magnier, although he retained breeding rights to a number of stallions, notably *Sadler's Wells* and *Danehill*. His attention remained on his own breeding operations, which were by then focused mainly on Australia. Sadly Robert Sangster passed away in 2004, after a battle with pancreatic cancer.

John Magnier moved away from the racing side of things and set about quietly developing Coolmore as a breeding powerhouse. With the likes of *Sadler's Wells* and *Danehill* performing exceptionally at stud, Magnier and Coolmore were doing very well. However, the stallion master knew that he would need a new generation of super stallions if Coolmore was to continue to grow and develop. With Ballydoyle lying idle following the retirement of Vincent O'Brien in 1994, Magnier selected Aidan O'Brien to become the new trainer there and carry on what Vincent O'Brien had started. The pair has gone on to enjoy wonderful success. O'Brien trained the magnificent *Galileo*, who has established himself as the dominant stallion of his generation and has begun to eclipse the records set by his own sire, *Sadler's Wells*.

The impact The Syndicate had on the world of racing cannot be overestimated. Before them, owners bred horses to race, but The Syndicate flipped that notion on its head and instead raced to breed. While people had seen the business of breeding horses as a hobby, The Syndicate saw it as a business. In the process, they made vast fortunes but also changed the way people viewed horse breeding.

The Syndicate introduced large book sizes for their stallions (traditionally stallions would cover around forty mares per year; Coolmore increased that number to around 150) and began to send their horses to the southern hemisphere, where they would cover another set of mares. It was such a simple concept that it's staggering to think that nobody had thought of it before. They also gave us some of the best horses the world has ever seen. One can't help but think back to that hot day in Kentucky and wonder could Messrs Sangster, O'Brien and Magnier have known how great an impact they would have on the world of horse racing. Perhaps they would have allowed themselves a wry smile if they did. They were a unique trio of men.

SADLER'S WELLS

In horse racing, as in life, sometimes the most talented individual doesn't fulfil the grand expectations set out for them. Sometimes it is the one who goes quietly about their business in an understated but professional manner that rises to the top of their field. In the autumn of 1982 that was very much the case at Ballydoyle when two colts arrived. Both horses were sired by *Northern Dancer*, both seemed like they had the requisite looks and conformation to develop into top-class horses, but when it came to how high they would soar, they were furlongs apart.

The first horse to step off the lorry was a colt out of *Sex Appeal*, which is exactly what he had. The colt was beautiful to look at and had the walk and presence that horsemen associate with a high-class champion. The second horse to follow him into Ballydoyle was an entirely different model. His mother, *Fairy Bridge*, was a talent in her own right, but the bonny colt resembled his father, *Northern Dancer*, much more. He was gifted with a long blaze that ran down his face and was just like his sire in his conformation.

When the colts settled into their routine and began to show their first signs of ability, it was the first colt that impressed the most. He would take your breath away on the lush gallops of Ballydoyle. The second colt also impressed, but not quite as much as his stablemate.

That first colt would be named *El Gran Senor*, after *Northern Dancer*'s trainer Horatio Luro, and dazzled Vincent O'Brien and racing fans alike in his two-year-old campaign. His classy win in the 1983 Dewhurst Stakes copper-fastened a juvenile season that was without defeat and placed the colt as one of the best two-year-olds O'Brien had trained up to that point in his career.

The second colt, *Sadler's Wells,* didn't show the same dashing brilliance as *El Gran Senor*. However, he displayed enough ability in his first season at the track to be placed high up the end-of-season classifications, and was looked upon as

Sadler's Wells, champion sire a record fourteen times in Great Britain and Ireland, at Coolmore Stud. *Courtesy of Coolmore Stud*

a horse that would feature in the following season's Classics. Bred by Robert Sangster's Swettenham Stud, *Sadler's Wells* was the first foal from *Fairy Bridge*, the champion filly purchased by Sangster for the bargain price of $40,000.

Both *El Gran Senor* and *Sadler's Wells* emerged from winter quarters in the Gladness Stakes at the Curragh in April 1984. Unsurprisingly *El Gran Senor* was the stable favourite and he didn't disappoint, comfortably beating *Sadler's Wells*. *El Gran Senor* headed off to the 2000 Guineas in Newmarket, which he won in spectacular fashion from one of the best fields ever assembled for the race. 'The Senor' defeated *Chief Singer*, *Lear Fan* and *Rainbow Quest*. In the months that followed Newmarket, *Chief Singer* took the St James's Palace Stakes (Group 2) and Sussex Stakes (Group 1) over a mile and the July Cup (Group 1) over six furlongs. *Lear Fan*, who later became a very successful stallion, won the Prix Jacques le Marois (Group 1) over a mile at Deauville in France. *Rainbow Quest*, who became one of the best stallions in England, won the Prix de l'Arc de Triomphe at Longchamp in France and the Coronation Cup at Epsom in England.

It was gold-plated form, but *El Gran Senor* came up short in his very next race. O'Brien sent the colt to contest the Epsom Derby and said, 'He could be the best horse that I've trained.' Unfortunately for O'Brien and *El Gran Senor* supporters, the colt lost by the narrowest of margins, failing by a short head to pass *Secreto*, trained by O'Brien's son David, who was just starting out in his training career.

While *El Gran Senor* was battling for his trainer's affections, *Sadler's Wells* moved on from his defeat in the Gladness Stakes to Leopardstown to contest the Derrinstown Stud Derby Trial Stakes over 10 furlongs. After he won his trial in convincing fashion, O'Brien stepped *Sadler's Wells* back down in distance for the Airlie/Coolmore Irish 2000 Guineas at the Curragh. Despite having been defeated only once in his career, *Sadler's Wells* was sent off at 10/1 and was also disregarded by stable jockey Pat Eddery, who elected to ride *Capture Him*. It was a decision that Eddery would regret. Always racing handily and close to the pace under George McGrath, *Sadler's Wells* fought off challenges from *Procida* and *Secreto* to win his first race at the highest level.

Having been all set to line up in the St James's Palace Stakes at Royal Ascot, the colt was rerouted to France to tackle the Prix du Jockey Club (French Derby) at Chantilly. Despite leading into the straight, *Sadler's Wells* stamina began to fail in the closing stages and he was passed by *Darshan*, himself a horse blessed with supreme stamina. *Sadler's Wells* had to settle for third place.

Sadler's Wells was kept on the go after his French Derby defeat. The Eclipse Stakes run at Sandown Park is traditionally one of the summer's most eagerly contested races. Run over 10 furlongs and (usually) on good, fast summer ground, the Eclipse offers the chance for the top three-year-olds to come together against the very best of the older generation.

Having won the Eclipse the previous year with *Solford*, Vincent O'Brien, Robert Sangster and Pat Eddery were hopeful that *Sadler's Wells* would be able to hold off the challenge of the high-class mare *Time Charter*, a previous winner of the 1000 Guineas, King George and English Champion Stakes. This time *Sadler's Wells* was ridden by Eddery, who elected to keep things simple, waiting behind his rivals and the strong early pace set by *Society Boy*. Two furlongs out Eddery set *Sadler's Wells* alight and the colt dug deep, accelerated past *Society Boy* and held on from the fast-finishing *Time Charter*, who was considered by some as an unlucky loser in second place. Victory in the Eclipse was all the more noteworthy given the hectic schedule that *Sadler's Wells* kept during his three-year-old season.

Something that both professionals and punters noticed during the final two furlongs was *Sadler's Wells'* slightly awkward head carriage. Watching the tape back, one can see him straining his head to the right when Eddery gives him the call and asks him to win the race. Traditionally an unusual head carriage is a sign that the horse may not be the bravest in the world. *Sadler's Wells* proved to be the exception to that rule. He was in fact straining every sinew he had to get to the front and stay there.

That battling quality stood to *Sadler's Wells* as he continued his busy summer and lined up in the King George VI and Queen Elizabeth Stakes at Ascot. He once again ran a superb race, only being defeated by the previous year's Derby winner, *Teenoso*, with the likes of *Tolomeo*, *Time Charter*, *Sun Princess* and *Darshan* all behind him.

It seemed that a busy campaign had caught up with *Sadler's Wells* when he produced a below-par effort in the Benson and Hedges Gold Cup (now the Juddmonte International) at York. But just two weeks later, and back on home soil for the first time since his Irish 2000 Guineas win, he bounced back to his very best form. Developed by Joe McGrath before his death and run at Leopardstown as the Joe McGrath Memorial Stakes before being transferred to the Phoenix Park in 1984, the Phoenix Champion Stakes (now the Irish Champion Stakes) provided *Sadler's Wells* with the opportunity to regain his winning thread following a number of defeats.

Over 10 furlongs *Sadler's Wells* was challenged by a number of top-class horses including the Irish Oaks winner *Princess Pati*, *Flame of Tara* and the French raider *Seattle Song*. Settled in second place by Pat Eddery, *Sadler's Wells* travelled behind *Princess Pati*, who set a scorching early gallop in the hands of Pat Shanahan. As in the Eclipse, Eddery moved *Sadler's Wells* into a challenging position two furlongs from home, and despite the best efforts of Cash Asmussen and *Seattle Song*, *Sadler's Wells* would not be denied his win. He held on by three-quarters of a length to record his third victory at the highest level. Victory in the Phoenix Champion Stakes took his winnings for the season to £384,114. At the time, this was the fourth-highest single-season total for any horse trained in Britain or Ireland, behind *Troy* (£408,424 in 1979), *Tolomeo* (£400,000 in 1983) and *Shergar* (£386,410 in 1981).

Sadler's Wells, ridden by Pat Eddery, wins the inaugural running of the Phoenix Champion Stakes in 1984. *Courtesy of Pat Healy Photography*

Following his victory at the Phoenix Park, *Sadler's Wells* was pointed towards Paris and the Prix de l'Arc de Triomphe. However, the long campaign finally took its toll and he trailed in a disappointing eighth behind the eventual winner *Sagace*. After that dispiriting run in the Arc, *Sadler's Wells* retired to stud with a record of six wins from eleven starts. He was also crowned the leading miler in France at the end of his racing career.

While *Sadler's Wells* was beginning his stud career at Coolmore, his former stablemate *El Gran Senor* was winging his way to America, where he would begin his own stud career following early retirement due to a hoof problem, which arose after his win in the Irish Derby. With a fee set at $200,000, it was widely expected that *El Gran Senor* would become the next super stallion after his own sire, *Northern Dancer*. However, the handsome colt was sub-fertile and was a bitter disappointment at stud, while *Sadler's Wells* would go on to have a far more successful career.

When *Sadler's Wells* retired to stud in 1984, nobody at Coolmore or in the wider racing world could have dreamt of what was about to unfold, although he did have a lot going for him when he made the small move from Ballydoyle. His three Group 1 wins in the Irish 2000 Guineas, Coral Eclipse and the Phoenix Irish Champion Stakes showed that he had toughness, class and a sharp turn of foot – all of which made him a sought-after first-season sire. His pedigree also made him an attractive commercial proposition. His sire, *Northern Dancer*, was well established as a world leader.

Sadler's Wells maternal side was also full of classy performers. His dam, *Fairy Bridge*, was a full sister to the top-class racehorse *Nureyev*, who was first past the post in the 1980 2000 Guineas, but was subsequently disqualified from first place and was placed last following a bumping match with another horse in the final 2 furlongs of the race. *Fairy Bridge* was a very successful broodmare, both before and after she produced *Sadler's Wells*. She foaled *Tate Gallery*, a winner of the National Stakes at the Curragh, as well as *Fairy King*, who went on to be a successful stallion at stud.

Sadler's Wells retired to stud with a fee of £125,000 and had an enviable first book of mares. His first crop of foals did not disappoint, with *Prince Of Dance* capping a wonderful first season when he dead-heated with *Scenic*, another son of *Sadler's Wells*, in the Dewhurst Stakes. John Magnier said of *Sadler's Wells*:

> He has been a phenomenon. As an individual, he was always outstanding. His mother [*Fairy Bridge*] was brilliant, and as a yearling both M. V. [Vincent O'Brien] and Micky Rogers were both very high on him.
>
> But I remember discussing him, during his two-year-old days, with Pat Eddery, who wasn't so upbeat at that stage. He went on to win the Irish 2000 Guineas and the Eclipse.
>
> *El Gran Senor* was half-a-stone better than him as a racehorse, but when he retired to stud any fool could see he was going to make it. He [*Sadler's Wells*] got good mares and made the most of them, siring the Dewhurst Stakes dead-heaters *Scenic* and *Prince Of Dance* from his first crop. We have been very lucky to have *Sadler's Wells* and *Danehill* together at the same time.[1]

When his first crop entered their three-year-old season, there were six Group 1 winners, a remarkable return for any stallion, let alone one who was just starting out in his stud career.

The standout colts in that first crop were *Old Vic* and *In The Wings*. *Old Vic* was purchased by Sheikh Mohammed and went into training at Warren Place, Newmarket, under the watchful gaze of Sir Henry Cecil. The colt carried off two Derby wins in his Classic season, with dominant performances in the Prix du Jockey Club at Chantilly and at the Curragh in the Irish Derby, where he was ridden by the American superstar Steve Cauthen.

In The Wings proved to be equally talented. Like *Old Vic*, *In The Wings* was owned by Sheikh Mohammed, but the Sheikh decided to send him to the master French trainer André Fabre. *In The Wings* was less precious than *Old*

---

1   http://www.telegraph.co.uk/sport/horseracing/2300332/John-Magnier-hails-Sadlers-Wells.html

Vic and his two- and three-year-old seasons were ones of quiet nurturing. He remained undefeated for those two years until he came unstuck in his final race as a three-year-old, when he disappointed in the Prix de l'Arc de Triomphe.

It would be as a four-year-old that *In The Wings* showed his true merit. He kicked off with a Group 1 win in the Prix Ganay at Longchamp in April 1990, before displaying his class with a deeply impressive performance in the Coronation Cup at Epsom in June. He displayed his longevity and class when he landed the Breeders' Cup Turf at Belmont Park under crack American jockey Gary Stevens in October.

Both horses became successful sires, with *Old Vic* siring the 2005 Cheltenham Gold Cup winner, *Kicking King*, as well as Grand National winners *Comply or Die* and *Don't Push It*. *In The Wings* fathered the globe-trotting superstar *Singspiel* along with champion staying hurdler *Inglis Drever*, who won three renewals of the World Hurdle at the Cheltenham Festival in 2005, 2007 and 2008.

Sadler's Wells' second crop proved to be as talented as his first. Much was expected of *Salsabil* when she made her debut at Nottingham Racecourse in September 1989 and she didn't disappoint, winning by an easy three lengths. That proved to be the start of a hugely successful racing career. *Salsabil* bookended her juvenile career with a win in France's most prestigious two-year-old fillies' race, the Prix Marcel Boussac, run on Arc day at Longchamp, before heading into winter quarters.

Having made her seasonal debut in the Fred Darling Stakes at Newbury, *Salsabil* produced a top-class performance to land the 1000 Guineas at Newmarket the following May, before making a huge jump up in distance by landing the Epsom Oaks a month later. With two Classic wins against her own sex, *Salsabil* was set an even bigger challenge when her owner, Sheikh Hamdan Al Maktoum, pitched her against the colts in the Budweiser Irish Derby at the Curragh. She faced top-class opposition in the shape of *Quest for Fame* and *Blue Stag*, who had come first and second in the Epsom Derby. The highly touted *Belmez* was also in the line-up, yet *Salsabil* dug deep to fend off the boys and became one of only two fillies in the modern era to win the Irish Derby.

Success in the Prix Vermeille next time out set her up for a tilt at the Prix de l'Arc de Triomphe, but she ran a disappointing race and was subsequently retired to stud. Her name lives on with the Salsabil Stakes run at Navan Racecourse every April.

Those early successes with *Old Vic*, *In The Wings* and *Salsabil* put *Sadler's Wells* among the leading stallions of his generation. Unlike many other sires that experience a lull following initial success, *Sadler's Wells* continued to shine as a sire of top-class racehorses. The likes of *Opera House* (Coronation Cup, Eclipse Stakes, King George VI and Queen Elizabeth Stakes), *Barathea* (Irish 2000 Guineas, Breeders' Cup Mile) and *Carnegie* (Prix de l'Arc de Triomphe, Grand Prix de Paris) kept his name in lights, but it wasn't until one of his foals began to jump hurdles that *Sadler's Wells* entered a different league.

The Cheltenham Festival is the last place you would expect the result of a mating between *Sadler's Wells* and *Betty's Secret* to make his name. But that's exactly what *Istabraq* did. As a half-brother to the Derby winner *Secreto*, who denied *Sadler's Wells'* stablemate *El Gran Senor* the 1984 Epsom Classic, much was expected of *Istabraq* when he was sent to English trainer John Gosden. Gosden's assistant trainer John Durkin persuaded legendary jumps owner J. P. McManus to buy *Istabraq* as a hurdling prospect. The intention was that Durkin would train the horse for McManus. Sadly, however, Durkin was struck down with leukaemia and it was decided to send the horse to Aidan O'Brien until John recovered sufficiently to train him. In the end, John Durkin never recovered and passed away in January 1998.

Istabraq justified the belief that John Durkin had in him by winning that year's Champion Hurdle at Cheltenham, where there was barely a dry eye at the track, such was the emotion of that day. That first Champion Hurdle was followed by two further victories before he was robbed of the chance to become the first horse in history to win four consecutive Champion Hurdles in a row when an outbreak of foot and mouth disease in 2001 forced the cancellation of that year's festival.

Istabraq returned the following year, but time had caught up with the legendary horse and he was taken out of the race by his regular jockey, Charlie Swan, before the third hurdle. He retired to his owner's home in Martinstown, County Limerick, where he has enjoyed his retirement since.

The exploits of *Istabraq* brought a lot of headlines for *Sadler's Wells*, but it was his propensity to sire top-class flat horses that cemented his status as the best stallion in the world. In 1999 a son of his won the French and Irish Derbies with such ease that people were talking of the colt as a new wonder horse. Owned by Michael Tabor, who was strengthening his links with John Magnier and Coolmore Stud at this time, *Montjeu* confirmed that he was a horse of rare brilliance by topping up those wins at Chantilly and the Curragh with a gritty success at the Arc at the end of his three-year-old campaign.

His exploits at four, however, saw him ranked alongside some of the best horses the world has ever seen. An easy win in the Tattersalls Gold Cup in May 2000 was bettered only by a brilliant display in the King George VI and Queen Elizabeth Diamond Stakes, where he didn't have to work very hard to defeat crack Group 1 horses in the shape of *Fantastic Light* and *Daliapour*. Despite disappointing in the Arc that October, *Montjeu* retired to Coolmore Stud a champion and became a sire of lasting merit, producing four Epsom Derby winners before his untimely death in 2012.

The successes of *Montjeu* and his siblings had pushed demand for *Sadler's Wells'* progeny through the roof. This was reflected when Coolmore made the decision in 2000 to make his covering fee private. Before this decision was made, *Sadler's Wells* was standing at a fee of £150,000. One can only speculate as to how much his fee was increased, but it would be fair to say a few extra punts were added. Indeed, his fee remained private up to his retirement in 2008 due to declining fertility.

Montjeu, Sadler's Wells and *Galileo*.
Three of the best stallions in the modern era, at Coolmore Stud.
Courtesy of Coolmore Stud

Having sired horses of the calibre of *Montjeu*, it was amazing to think that at the start of the 2001 flat season, *Sadler's Wells* had yet to sire a winner of the Epsom Derby. That changed a number of months later when *Galileo* stormed home under Michael Kinane to fill in a notable omission on *Sadler's Wells'* stallion CV. Another son of his, *High Chaparral*, gave *Sadler's Wells* a second Epsom Derby winner the following season when he outstayed his stablemate *Hawk Wing* under a tactically astute Johnny Murtagh.

With three of his best sons standing alongside him at Coolmore, *Sadler's Wells* began to cement his legacy as a sire of sires. *Montjeu, Galileo* and *High Chaparral* all became top-class sires in their own right, with many of their progeny making their way to Ballydoyle for their racing careers.

There is no doubt that without *Sadler's Wells*, Coolmore Stud would not be in the position it is today. During his stud career, *Sadler's Wells* sired more than seventy Group 1 winners, including the four-time Ascot Gold Cup hero *Yeats*, as well as 230 stakes winners. His record of fourteen sires' championships in Great Britain and Ireland may never be equalled, although if there is a stallion that could match that feat it might be his son *Galileo*. He also secured three sires' championships in France and one in North America.

Not only was he a prodigious sire of top-class colts, *Sadler's Wells* also sired top-class fillies, who in turn went on to be successful broodmares. From 2005 to 2011 *Sadler's Wells* was champion broodmare sire in Great Britain and Ireland, as his daughters made their own impact. One of his best daughters was the 2001 Epsom Oaks winner *Imagine*, who went on to be a Group 1 winning producer when she foaled the *Danehill* colt *Horatio Nelson*.

Sadler's Wells passed away in his paddock at Coolmore Stud on 26 April 2011. His handler had noticed that he wasn't himself for a few days previously, and when John Magnier returned to the stud farm, having been away on business, he was informed that the great horse wasn't at his best. Magnier went down to the paddock to see *Sadler's Wells* and stayed with his stallion during his last hours.

In the immediate aftermath of his death, tributes poured in. John Magnier said of his loss:

> *Sadler's Wells* was the most unbelievable stallion we could ever have wished for. He brought Coolmore to a completely different level. We have a lot to be grateful to him for and are delighted to have four of his very best sons standing here.[2]

Christy Grassick, general manager of Coolmore Stud, echoed Magnier's sentiments, saying:

---

2   http://www.ownerbreeder.co.uk/2011/05/tribute-to-sadlers-wells/

He was undoubtedly the best sire Europe has ever seen, and through his sons *Galileo*, *Montjeu*, *High Chaparral* and *Yeats*, along with grandsons *Hurricane Run* and *Rip Van Winkle*, he has left a wonderful legacy at Coolmore and his influence looks set to continue for many years to come. We all feel privileged to have been involved with such a special horse.[3]

The impact of his death was felt right across the racing and breeding world. Kirsten Rausing, herself a successful breeder, paid tribute to *Sadler's Wells* in *Thoroughbred Owner & Breeder* magazine:

Sadler's Wells was more than a legend. He formed the basis of Coolmore's enormous success but in so doing also formatted the European and, to an extent, worldwide development of the thoroughbred breed in the late 20th century. His influence in the thoroughbred industry will, of course, be everlasting, equalled so far only by *St Simon* in the 19th century and by his own sire, *Northern Dancer*, contemporarily.

All modern thoroughbred breeders will be grateful to have lived through the *Sadler's Wells* era. All of us lucky enough to have seen and touched the great horse will forever remember him.

Andrew Caulfield, a respected pedigree expert, said:

Superlatives are greatly overused in the world of sport, but no one could begrudge their being used about *Sadler's Wells*, with his phenomenal record of 14 sires' championships in the space of 15 years. No stallion has come close to such dominance in Britain and Ireland – not even the legendary stallions which operated during the much less competitive eras of the 18th and 19th centuries.[4]

---

3 http://www.racingpost.com/news/horse-racing/legendary-sire-sadlers-wells-dies-aged-30/
   849178/#newsArchiveTabs=last7DaysNews
4 http://www.ownerbreeder.co.uk/2011/05/tribute-to-sadlers-wells/

Sadler's Wells, in bronze, standing at the entrance to Coolmore Stud.
Courtesy of Coolmore Stud

The esteem in which *Sadler's Wells* was held was exemplified when HRH Queen Elizabeth II wrote a handwritten letter to Coolmore to thank the stud for her recent visit and mentioned the passing of *Sadler's Wells*. She had a number of horses by *Sadler's Wells* and it is said that she was extremely disappointed that she missed the opportunity to visit the stallion before his passing in 2011.

When a stallion passes away, tradition dictates that he be buried in the graveyard at Coolmore Stud. This would not suffice for *Sadler's Wells* and it was decided that he would be preserved exactly the way he was before he passed away. The finest taxidermist was sought for him and he now stands proudly in Coolmore's private gallery, where a whole wing is dedicated to his achievements on and off the race track. His deeds at stud will never be forgotten. An empire was built on the strength of his success as a stallion. *Sadler's Wells* was indeed 'the daddy of 'em all'.

DANEHILL

As day breaks over Coolmore's Australian base in the Hunter Valley, the warm sun bounces off a statue of a horse that redefined the Australian breeding industry for generations to come. The statue looks over the 8,000-acre farm that was once his domain. In much the same way that *Sadler's Wells* redefined the breeding landscape in Europe, this horse had an impact on the southern hemisphere breed that was not seen before and will, doubtlessly, not be seen again.

When one utters the name *Danehill*, breath is quickly taken away for two reasons – the impact that he had during his stallion career and the regret that his early death in 2003 caused. The breeding and racing worlds were only beginning to scratch the surface of *Danehill's* stallion supremacy when he was taken sooner than expected. Then again, all the good ones are, aren't they?

Bred by Prince Khalid Abdullah and his Juddmonte Farms, *Danehill* was a relatively successful racehorse. However, it was his deeds at stud that ensure his name will echo down through the generations. *Danehill*, who was foaled in March 1986, was sent to the stables of Jeremy Tree with the hope that he would develop into a Classic-type horse during his three-year-old season. While he failed to fulfil those Classic aspirations (he finished third in the English 2000 Guineas and fourth in the Irish equivalent), he made his mark on the 1989 flat season with wins at Royal Ascot in the Group 3 Cork and Orrery Stakes (now renamed the Group 1 Diamond Jubilee Stakes) and the Group 1 Haydock Sprint Cup, where he showed an impressive change of pace to land the Group 1 prize that saw him crowned as the champion sprinter of his generation. That prize secured *Danehill's* place at stud. Along with his race record, which included four wins from nine starts, *Danehill's* pedigree also ensured that he would be given ample opportunity to pass on his ability to the next generation.

A grandson of *Northern Dancer*, *Danehill* was sired by *Danzig*, who was a wonderfully gifted horse but only raced three times, owing to injuries. He went on to have a much more successful career at stud, becoming champion sire in America for three consecutive years from 1991 to 1993.

Nowadays Juddmonte has its own very successful breeding operation, but back in 1989 no such farm was in existence, so once the horse went to stud Coolmore became involved. *Danehill* would spend the first chapter of his stallion career as a 'shuttle stallion'. This meant that *Danehill* spent the northern-hemisphere breeding season at Coolmore and the southern-hemisphere season at Arrowfield Stud in Australia.

The shuttle-stallion concept was something relatively new when *Danehill* retired to stud. The generally held principle was that a stallion would cover somewhere in the region of forty mares in a breeding season and that would be his maximum. John Magnier and Coolmore Stud could see the potential in stallions doing a 'double shift' rather than lazing about in their spacious paddocks.

Two of the founding stallions at Coolmore, *Danehill* and *Sadler's Wells*, say hello to each other. *Courtesy of Coolmore Stud*

The advantages were numerous. Not only would the stallion master earn more income through covering fees, but the chance of siring a horse of comparable ability would be increased dramatically. With more of the stallion's stock on the ground, crop sizes would be increased and more talented horses would race and win, which would in turn drive up demand for the stallion's offspring. *Danehill* was a pioneer for this shuttle-stallion concept.

While *Be My Guest* and *Sadler's Wells* were dominating the breeding scene in Europe, *Danehill* was causing a revolution in the southern hemisphere. He became champion sire in Australia for the first time in 1995 and went on to claim that title a further eight times. His success in Australia did not come without its costs, however. Because he was enjoying so much success, demand for his services was increasing.

In 1996 Coolmore decided to set up camp permanently in Australia and settled on a stunning property in New South Wales. Located on more than 8,000 acres, including 5,000 acres of irrigated river flats and undulating paddocks, Coolmore Australia has become one of the bedrocks of the Australian thoroughbred industry over the last twenty years. Careful management has ensured that the land continues to provide the optimal conditions for the growth and development of thoroughbreds of the highest quality. The pastures at Coolmore Australia have been shown by agronomic studies to be among the highest quality in Australia.

The land occupied by Coolmore in Australia has a history that dates back much further than twenty years, however. Settled in 1824 by George Bowman and established as Arrowfield, the property has a precedent of producing racehorses of the highest quality for more than a hundred years. The 1920 Melbourne Cup winner *Poitrel*, champion racehorse and sire *Heroic* and high-class galloper *Manfred* are examples of some of the successful racehorses bred during the first quarter of the twentieth century at what is now known as the Coolmore Australia property.

Coolmore has a strong affinity with the Australian bloodstock industry dating back to the advent of the shuttle-stallion concept. This began in the late

1970s and early 1980s with the likes of *Mount Hagen* travelling to the Kelly's Newhaven Park Stud and *Godswalk* taking up seasonal residence at Colin Hayes' Lindsay Park Stud. The venture developed apace and within little more than a decade, the Coolmore-owned shuttler *Last Tycoon* earned champion Australian sire honours for the 1993–94 season.

Having established its own base, it was natural that Coolmore would want to stand *Danehill* there. However, there was a small problem. Arrowfield Stud (which has no connections to Bowman's Arrowfield) was in no mood to just hand over the southern hemisphere breeding rights to Coolmore. A very intense bidding war began between the two organisations before Coolmore eventually came out on top. The final fee of AU$24 million was a record price and ensured that *Danehill* was the most expensive stallion in Australian history at that time.

Danehill continued to thrive in Australia. He sired the high-class *Redoute's Choice* from one of his early crops. *Redoute's Choice* went on to become champion sire of Australia in the 2005–06 season. *Danehill* also sired the horse who is now leading the way for the *Danehill* line in Australia, *Fastnet Rock*. A hugely imposing and talented horse, *Fastnet Rock* has become the leading sire in Australia, having sired more than twenty-one individual Group 1 winners, including *First Seal, Wanted, Irish Lights, Magicool, Qualify, Diamondsandrubies, Amicus, Rock Classic, Lone Rock, Atlantic Jewel, Driefontein, Mosheen, Planet Rock, Rock 'n' Pop, Foxwedge, Sea Siren, Nechita, Super Cool, Albany Reunion, Your Song* and *Atlante*.

Despite his phenomenal success in Australia, *Danehill* wouldn't have quite the same impact in Europe during his first number of seasons at stud. He did sire the Irish 2000 Guineas and Irish Derby winner *Desert King*, along with Phoenix Stakes winner *Danehill Dancer*, but it wasn't until a mating with the *Be My Guest* mare *Offshore Boom* that *Danehill's* prodigious ability was fully appreciated. That tryst with *Offshore Boom* produced *Rock Of Gibraltar*, who won a record seven consecutive Group 1 races in 2001 and 2002. That period also saw *Danehill* sire the likes of *Mozart* (champion sprinter in 2001) and the Epsom Derby winner *North Light* (2004).

The rise of *Danehill* coincided with the re-emergence of Ballydoyle as a training powerhouse. Aidan O'Brien, who was installed as Coolmore's trainer in 1996, trained a whole host of *Danehill's* best offspring, including *Rock Of Gibraltar* and *Mozart*, but also *Holy Roman Emperor, Oratorio, Peeping Fawn*, the brilliant *George Washington, Duke Of Marmalade* and *Dylan Thomas*.

Those final two horses were perhaps the best sons of *Danehill* ever to race. They also exemplified the very best attributes that *Danehill* passed on to his stock. Both horses were remarkably tough. *Dylan Thomas* ran in an incredible ten Group 1 races over two seasons, winning six of them, including the 2007 Prix de l'Arc de Triomphe. He retired to stud with an official rating of 131, which made him the joint highest-rated son of *Danehill*.

Duke Of Marmalade also proved to be made of steely stuff when he came back from a near career-ending injury, which hampered his two- and three-year-old

Dylan Thomas, a brilliant six-time Group 1 winner and now a successful stallion, at Coolmore. *Courtesy of Coolmore Stud*

A wonderful-looking horse, *Rock Of Gibraltar* was one of *Danehill*'s best sons.
Courtesy of Coolmore Stud

campaigns, to win five Group 1 races in a row during the 2008 season, including the Prince of Wales's Stakes, King George and the Juddmonte International. The toughness and durability that *Dylan Thomas* and *Duke Of Marmalade* showed on the racetrack was consistent with what *Danehill* put into his stock.

Aside from the latent ability, what characterised *Danehill*'s stock was their remarkable temperament. Australian newspaper *The Form* said of the stallion in 2001:

> We saw *Danehill* again on Tuesday. He was one of twelve stallions Coolmore proudly displayed to a media contingent, and probably the most inauspicious of the dozen megastars. Quite frankly, if you weren't told he was *Danehill* you could be forgiven for wondering why this horse was so special. He doesn't look like a superstar and just stood before the onlookers totally unfazed by the attention. That's probably the reason behind the phenomenon.

That testament to his bombproof temperament was echoed by the then Coolmore Australia farm manager, Peter O'Brien (no relation to Aidan O'Brien), who, in an interview in 2003, paid tribute to *Danehill*'s wonderfully placid nature:

> He'd swagger in, did what he had to do and come back out again. He never expended any excess energy. It's what a lot of his offspring have inherited. Obviously he covered a lot of mares but he put condition on in the breeding season.[1]
>
> Certainly the advance in veterinary techniques assisted his durability. In the old days a stallion would cover mares when they came in season every second day. You find a stallion would cover 40 mares but the actual time he covered would be quite similar to a stallion who did the same job on 100 mares nowadays.[2]

---

1   Putting on condition refers to when a horse begins to gain weight and reach their natural weight as a stallion.
2   http://www.smh.com.au/articles/2003/06/26/1056449369802.html

However, just as things seemed to be going so well for *Danehill* and the Coolmore team, disaster struck. The morning of 13 May 2003 began like any other. *Danehill* was taken from his box at Coolmore Stud and led the short distance to his paddock, where he would be taken by his handler to consume grass.

Feeling very content with himself, *Danehill* playfully reared up, but that moment of fun soon turned to horror as *Danehill* slipped, fell awkwardly and suffered a femoral artery bleed. Despite having access to some of the best veterinary care in the world, the stallion was not able to recover from the injury he sustained. *Danehill* passed away in his paddock at just seventeen years of age. In the vast majority of cases stallions live well into their twenties, so to lose *Danehill* at such a young age was a hammer blow for everyone connected with the horse.

The news of *Danehill*'s death sent shock waves throughout the entire breeding industry. Peter O'Brien perhaps summed it up best when he said that losing the stallion was like losing a member of the family:

> Basically he was just being hand-grazed by the groom that looks after him all the time. He just reared over and slipped. A freak accident, nobody's fault. Unfortunately it happened to the best. Unusual for the horse, he's so quiet. Everybody here was devastated. In Australia, for Coolmore it was like losing a member of the family.[3]

As was the case with *Sadler's Wells*, the hope when *Danehill* retired to stud was that one day one of his sons would take over his mantle and carry on his legacy. While *Sadler's Wells* had the benefit of living thirteen years longer than his stud mate, *Danehill* managed to produce his own stallion sons, in both the northern and southern hemisphere.

---

3   *Ibid.*

The expectation when *Rock Of Gibraltar* retired to stud in 2002 was that he would be the next *Danehill*, and while he became a relatively successful stallion, siring the likes of *Society Rock*, *Mount Nelson*, *Eagle Mountain*, *Prince Gibraltar* and *Raydara*, it was his unheralded stud companion in Coolmore who proved to be *Danehill's* most effective son. Having started with a bargain-basement fee of £4,000, *Danehill Dancer* established himself as one of the most important stallions of this century.

A dual Group 1 winner as a two-year-old, *Danehill Dancer* retired to stud without a lot of fanfare and it became obvious that if he was going to be a success at stud, he would have to do it the hard way, without access to many top-class mares, something that's usually needed if a stallion is going to become a success at stud. He proved more than up to the challenge, displaying a rare ability to upgrade the mare he was covering, which in essence means that a mare would produce a better class of foal having visited *Danehill Dancer* as opposed to another stallion.

One of his best progeny came from his early crops, in the shape of the bull-like *Choisir*, who travelled all the way from Australia to take Royal Ascot by storm in 2003, winning the Group 1 Golden Jubilee Stakes and the Group 2 King Stand Stakes before just being beaten in the July Cup that season by the lightning-quick *Oasis Dream*.

Choisir's international success put *Danehill Dancer* in a new light, and his star continued to rise in the years that followed. He became a vitally important cog in the Coolmore operation, siring the likes of *Again* (Moyglare Stud Stakes, Irish 1000 Guineas), *Alfred Nobel* (Phoenix Stakes), *Lillie Langtry* (Coronation Stakes and Matron Stakes), *Planteur* (Prix Ganay), *Steps in Time* (Coolmore Classic), *Unaccompanied* (Spring Juvenile Hurdle and Istabraq Festival Hurdle), *Dancing Rain* (Epsom Oaks), *Speciosa* (English 1000 Guineas) and *Legatissimo* (English 1000 Guineas, Nassau Stakes and Matron Stakes).

His best son was perhaps *Mastercraftsman*, who jousted with *Sea The Stars* in the unforgettable flat season of 2009. *Mastercraftsman* won four Group 1 races for the Coolmore operation during his racing career and has gone on, like his sire and grandsire, to become a successful stallion in his own right, siring the likes of *Kingston Hill* (Racing Post Trophy and English St Leger) and *The Grey Gatsby* (Prix du Jockey Club and Irish Champion Stakes).

Danehill Dancer retired from stallion duties in 2014 owing to declining fertility. He was the champion sire of Great Britain and Ireland in 2009 and champion two-year-old sire on three occasions, and has certainly left his hoofprints on the breed.

While *Danehill Dancer* was doing his best to carry on his sire's legacy in the northern hemisphere, another son of *Danehill, Redoute's Choice*, was flying the flag for *Danehill* in the southern hemisphere. *Redoute's Choice* retired to stud in 2000 following a glittering career on the racetrack, which saw him win multiple Group 1s, including the Caulfield Guineas, Blue Diamond Stakes, the Manikato Stakes and the CF Orr Stakes. It was at stud, however, that his work for the *Danehill* legacy really began. He became champion first-season sire in 2004, champion two-year-old sire in 2005 and outright champion sire in 2006. He also went on to claim a further two sires' titles in 2010 and 2014. By 2016 *Redoute's Choice* had sired over a hundred stakes winners and twenty-seven Group 1 winners, including *Miss Finland, Lankan Rupee, Musir, Melito, Lotteria, God's Own, Snitzel, Stratum, Fashions Afield, Nadeem, Undoubtedly, Bradbury's Luck, Samantha Miss* and *Cheeky Choice*.

Redoute's Choice has developed into a noted sire of sires too. Six of his sons have also sired Group 1 winners: *Not a Single Doubt* (*Miracles of Life, Always Certain*); *Stratum* (*Streama, Southern Lord, Crystal Lily*); *Snitzel* (*Sizzling, Shamus Award*); *Duelled* (*Shootoff*); *Fast 'N' Famous* (*Quintessential*); and *Bradbury's Luck* (*Luckygray*).

While *Redoute's Choice* has strong claims to be *Danehill's* best sire son in Australia, another son is also staking a claim for that prestigious title. The champion sprinter of Australia in 2005, *Fastnet Rock*, who stands at Coolmore's Australian base in the Hunter Valley, has quickly gilded a stellar reputation of

Danehill at stud. His death in 2003 was a tremendous loss. *Courtesy of Coolmore Stud*

his own, becoming an influential sire in both Australia and Europe. The 2015 Epsom Oaks winner *Qualify*, who defeated another granddaughter of *Danehill*, *Legatissimo*, in the dying strides of that Classic, is just one of eighteen Group 1 winners from his first six crops. His success down under earned *Fastnet Rock* a ticket to Coolmore's head office in County Tipperary, where he has sired a number of high-class horses from limited books of mares. Along with *Qualify*, *Fastnet Rock* has thrown the likes of *Cougar Mountain*, *Fascinating Rock* and *Smuggler's Cove*, and there is great expectation that he will develop into a dominant stallion in Europe in the same way that he has in Australia.

Another son of *Danehill* to earn rave reviews at stud is the Juddmonte-bred *Dansili*. A Group 1 performer on the track, *Dansili* has, like *Danehill Dancer*, risen to the upper echelons of the breeding industry due to the outstanding deeds of his first crop of runners. His first six crops included seven Group 1 winners. At a time when his stud fee never rose above £12,500, this made breeders sit up and take notice of *Dansili*. As with *Danehill Dancer*, the richness of *Dansili's* stock became much deeper as the quality of his mares improved. *The Fugue*, *Rail Link*, *Harbinger*, *Zoffany*, *Passage of Time*, *Fallen For You*, *Miss France* and *We Are* are just some of the high-class horses that have been sired by *Dansili*, and he can be expected to carry on the *Danehill* name with distinction for many years to come.

Not only did *Danehill* sire top-class colts that developed into high-class sires, he also sired a whole host of brilliant daughters that played a huge role in *Danehill* becoming a noted broodmare sire. Perhaps his most famous daughter is the Juddmonte-owned mare *Kind*, the dam of the immortal *Frankel*, a horse considered by many to be the finest racehorse of any generation. *Frankel* is just one of fourteen stallions at stud out of a *Danehill* mare. *Teofilo*, *Intense Focus* and *Siyouni* are just three more examples of stallions that have sired black-type winners, having come from a *Danehill* mare.[4]

4   Black type refers to when a horse wins or is placed in a Group 1/2/3 or listed race on the flat. Black type is important for fillies as it adds value to their mating careers.

The on-track merits of *Frankel* were another ringing endorsement for the now much-vaunted *Galileo–Danehill* cross. The concept of mating a *Danehill* mare with the world's leading stallion, *Galileo*, is one that has reaped huge benefits. Amazingly, *Galileo* sired the 2011 winners of the English and Irish 2000 Guineas and the French 1000 Guineas, all of which came from a *Danehill* mare. The potency of this cross remains as strong as ever. In August 2015 the cross provided the winner of the Grade 1 Secretariat Stakes (*Highland Reel*) and the first past the post in the Beverly D. Stakes at Arlington Park (*Secret Gesture*).

Danehill was given the ultimate accolade after his death when he was buried standing up in the graveyard at Coolmore Stud, where the likes of *Montjeu, High Chaparral, George Washington, Fairy King* and *Be My Guest* all rest. He is currently the most successful sire of all time. In total *Danehill* was the sire of 2,008 runners: 1,545 were winners (76.9 per cent), 349 were stakes winners (17.4 per cent) and 232 were stakes placed (11.6 per cent). His progeny have won more than AU$375 million and have included eighty-nine Group/Grade 1 winners among his 349 stakes winners. *Duke Of Marmalade* (foaled in Ireland and exported to Australia) was from one of *Danehill*'s last foal crops, which comprised ninety-six live foals in 2003. *Danehill* has 114 sons and fifty-six grandsons at stud in Australia up to 2016, plus 459 daughters who are broodmares.

As the sun passes over Coolmore's Hunter Valley base and another day is consigned to the record books, *Danehill* remains imposing, glistening in bronze, surveying his life's work, and when you take a step back and take in his vantage point, you realise just what a phenomenon he was. He was taken far too early from this earth, but his name will echo down the generations and people will forever speak in hushed tones about *Danehill*. Whoever listens to these stories for the first time will not believe them, but those of us lucky enough to have been around to see *Danehill* in action will just smile and nod. 'Oh he was real, all right,' we will say. 'He was the real deal.'

Famous Group 1 Winners Sired by Danehill

Aquarelliste (FR): Prix Ganay, Longchamp; Prix Vermeille-Hermitage Barriere, Longchamp; Prix de Diane Hermes, Chantilly

Arena (AUS): Victoria Derby, Flemington; Guineas, Rosehill; sire

Artiste Royal (IRE): Charles Whittingham Memorial Handicap, Hollywood Park; Clement L Hirsch Memorial Turf Championship, Santa Anita

Aussie Rules (USA): Poule d'Essai des Poulains, Longchamp; Turf Mile Stakes, Keeneland; sire

Banks Hill (GB): Coronation Stakes, Royal Ascot; Prix Jacques Le Maurois, Deauville; Breeders' Cup Filly & Mare Turf, Belmont Park

Blackfriars (AUS): Victoria Derby, Flemington; sire

Cacique (IRE): Manhattan Handicap, Belmont Park; Man O'War Stakes, Belmont Park; sire

Catbird (AUS): Golden Slipper Stakes, Rosehill; sire

Champs Elysees (IRE): Northern Dancer Turf Stakes, Woodbine; Hollywood Turf Cup Stakes, Hollywood Park

Clodovil (IRE): Gainsborough Poule d'Essai des Poulains, Longchamp; sire

Dane Ripper (AUS): Australian Cup, Flemington; Cox Plate, Moonee Valley; Manikato Stakes, Moonee Valley; Stradbroke Handicap, Eagle Farm

Danehill Dancer (IRE): Phoenix Stakes, Leopardstown; National Stakes, Curragh

Danish (IRE): Queen Elizabeth II Challenge Cup Stakes, Keeneland

Danske (NZ): Couplands Bakeries NZ 2000 Guineas, Riccarton Park; sire

Danzero (AUS): Golden Slipper Stakes, Rosehill; sire

Desert King (IRE): National Stakes, Curragh; Irish Derby, Curragh; Irish 2000 Guineas, Curragh; sire

Dress To Thrill (IRE): Matriarch Stakes, Hollywood Park

Duke Of Marmalade (IRE): International Stakes, Newmarket; King George VI and Queen Elizabeth Stakes, Ascot; Prince of Wales's Stakes, Ascot; Gold Cup, Curragh; Prix Ganay – Anniversaire Air Mauritius, Longchamp; sire

Dylan Thomas (IRE): Irish Champion Stakes, Leopardstown (twice); Irish Derby, Curragh;

King George VI and Queen Elizabeth Stakes, Ascot; Prix de l'Arc de Triomphe – Lucien Barrière, Longchamp; Prix Ganay, Longchamp; sire

Echelon (GB): Matron Stakes, Leopardstown

Elvstroem (AUS): CF Orr Stakes, Caulfield; Caulfield Cup, Caulfield; Underwood Stakes, Caulfield; Victoria Derby, Flemington; Dubai Duty Free, Nad Al Sheba; sire

Exceed And Excel (AUS): Dubai Racing Club Cup, Caulfield; Newmarket Handicap, Flemington; sire

Fastnet Rock (AUS): Oakleigh Plate, Caulfield; Lightning Stakes, Flemington; sire

Flying Spur (AUS): All Aged Stakes, Randwick; Australian Guineas, Flemington; Golden Slipper Stakes, Rosehill; sire

George Washington (IRE): Phoenix Stakes, Curragh; National Stakes, Curragh; Queen Elizabeth II Stakes, Ascot; 2000 Guineas, Newmarket; sire

Grey Lilas (IRE): Netjets Prix du Moulin de Longchamp, Longchamp

Ha Ha (AUS): Golden Slipper Stakes, Rosehill; Flight Stakes, Warwick Farm

Holy Roman Emperor (IRE): Phoenix Stakes, Curragh; Prix Jean-Luc Lagardère-Grand Criterium, Longchamp; sire

Horatio Nelson (IRE): Prix Jean-Luc Lagardère-Grand Criterium, Longchamp

Indian Danehill (IRE): Prix Ganay, Longchamp; sire

Intercontinental (GB): Breeders' Cup Filly & Mare Turf, Belmont Park; Matriarch Stakes, Hollywood Park

Kissing Cousin (IRE): Coronation Stakes, Royal Ascot

Laisserfaire (AUS): Cape Flying Championship, Kenilworth (twice); Sprint, Newmarket; South African Fillies & Mares Sprint (twice), Scottsville

Landseer (GB): Poule d'Essai des Poulains, Longchamp; Keeneland Turf Mile Stakes, Keeneland; sire

Light Jig (GB): Yellow Ribbon Stakes, Santa Anita

Luas Line (IRE): Garden City Breeders' Cup Stakes, Belmont Park

Lucky Owners (NZ): Hong Kong Mile, Sha Tin; sire

Merlene (AUS): Golden Slipper Stakes, Rosehill; Sires' Produce Stakes, Randwick

Mountain High (IRE): Grand Prix de Saint-Cloud, Saint-Cloud; sire

Mozart (IRE): July Cup, Newmarket; Nunthorpe Stakes, York; sire

North Light (IRE): Derby Stakes, Epsom Downs; sire

Nothin' Leica Dane (AUS): Victoria Derby, Flemington; Spring Champion Stakes, Randwick; sire

Oratorio (IRE): Baileys' Irish Champion Stakes, Leopardstown; Coral Eclipse Stakes, Sandown Park; Prix Jean-Luc Lagardère-Grand Criterium, Longchamp; sire

Peeping Fawn (USA): Audi Pretty Polly Stakes, Curragh; Blue Square Nassau Stakes, Goodwood; Darley Irish Oaks, Curragh; Darley Yorkshire Oaks, York

Promising Lead (GB): Pretty Polly Stakes, Curragh

Punctilious (GB): Yorkshire Oaks, York

Redoute's Choice (AUS): Blue Diamond Stakes, Caulfield; CF Orr Stakes, Caulfield; Caulfield Guineas, Caulfield; Manikato Stakes, Moonee Valley; sire

Regal Rose (GB): Cheveley Park Stakes, Newmarket

Rock Of Gibraltar (IRE): Dewhurst Stakes, Newmarket; Irish 2000 Guineas, Curragh; 2000 Guineas, Newmarket; St James's Palace Stakes, Royal Ascot; Sussex Stakes, Goodwood; Grand Criterium – Lucien Barrière, Longchamp; Netjets Prix du Moulin de Longchamp, Longchamp; sire

Rumplestiltskin (IRE): Moyglare Stud Stakes, Curragh; Prix Marcel Boussac, Deauville, Longchamp

Simply Perfect (GB): Fillies' Mile Stakes, Ascot; Falmouth Stakes, Newmarket

Spartacus (IRE): Phoenix Stakes, Curragh; Gran Criterium, Milan; sire

The Duke (AUS): Hong Kong Mile, Sha Tin

Tiger Hill (IRE): Grosser Dallmayr Preis Bayerisches Zuchtrennen, Munich; Grosser Preis von Baden (twice), Baden-Baden; sire

Wannabe Grand (IRE): Cheveley Park Stakes, Newmarket

Westerner (GB): Gold Cup, York; Prix du Cadran, Longchamp, (twice); Prix Royal-Oak (twice), Longchamp; sire

THE NEW SYNDICATE

Irish Champions Weekend 2015. Another Group 1 day at the Curragh has come to an end and there is a familiar sight as one scans the race card. Three Group 1 races are run on the second day of Irish Champions Weekend, a bold new concept in Irish racing, and the three big prizes have fallen to the same group of gentlemen. The Group 1 Moyglare Stud Stakes, the Vincent O'Brien Goffs National Stakes and the Palmerstown House Estate Irish St Leger have all gone the way of the Coolmore operation. The three winning horses, *Minding*, *Air Force Blue* and *Order Of St George* are trained at Ballydoyle by Aidan O'Brien and owned by John Magnier, Derrick Smith and Michael Tabor. It's another

The connections of *Gleneagles* after the colt's win in the 2015
St James's Palace Stakes at Royal Ascot. *Courtesy of Racing Post*

Derrick Smith (third from the left), the third member of the Coolmore triumvirate,
with his family at the races. *Courtesy of Racing Post*

Group 1 day at the office for the owners who have come to dominate the landscape of global flat racing over the last two decades.

Even with all the success that the Coolmore triumvirate has enjoyed over the last number of years, it is a phenomenal day. *Minding* carried the purple and white silks of Derrick Smith to victory, *Order Of St George* sported the blue silks with orange disc of Michael Tabor, while *Air Force Blue* carried the famous navy colours of Mr and Mrs John Magnier. It was the perfect Group 1 hat-trick.

While some may think that the Coolmore ownership have their fair share of luck on their side, days like this are the result of years of planning and forethought. Skill, judgement and horsemanship are the key ingredients, with one man leading the way with his vision. To all and sundry, since the passing of Vincent O'Brien, he is known as 'The Boss'. He is the man who has changed Coolmore from a small stud farm in County Tipperary into a global behemoth that stretches across three continents and stands proudly as the leading producer of champion racehorses in the world.

At the races, John Magnier is easy to spot. Sporting his navy overcoat, blue shirt with white collar and his trademark Panama hat, Magnier drifts quietly around the track, his eyes always scanning, taking everything in and not missing a thing. To watch him at the races is something magical. Yet if you asked the majority of people to pick this phenomenally talented and successful businessman out of a line-up, they would struggle. But that is the way John Magnier likes it.

Having enjoyed outstanding success with Vincent O'Brien and Robert Sangster in the early stages of Coolmore's development, Magnier was ready to re-establish Coolmore as a global force when he handpicked Aidan O'Brien to continue the work that M. V. O'Brien had carried out at Ballydoyle before him. The selection of O'Brien was classic Magnier – his ability to see the great potential in front of him. When it comes to business, Magnier tends to get what he wants.

Depending on who you talk to, there are two versions of John Magnier. People who know the man speak of his warm and caring nature, of a man who takes great care of his employees and will help people along the way. Others would have you believe that Magnier is a cold-blooded and ruthless businessman whose sole interest is making money, lots of it. They say he strikes fear into the hearts of mere mortals and will stop at nothing to make sure that he and his associates are taken care of. If you put the two sides together, you have an image of a man with angel's wings and devil's horns. The truth, as with most things, lies somewhere in the middle.

There is no doubt that Magnier is a brilliant businessman with a tough streak. A 2015 *Irish Independent* profile estimated his net worth at €950 million. While the majority of that fortune has come from the success of the likes of *Sadler's Wells*, *Danehill*, *Galileo*, *Montjeu* and *High Chaparral* at Coolmore Stud, Magnier has made fortunes from other investments as well, proving that he is not just a one-trick pony. He owns a stake, along with his Coolmore partners, in the ultra-exclusive Sandy Lane Hotel in Barbados, along with having substantial shares in the Barchester chain of nursing homes in the United Kingdom and a share in the Mitchells & Butlers pub chain. Magnier has also made huge profits

The Coolmore team in 2015 celebrating another success at Royal Ascot.
Courtesy of Racing Post

from investments with Devro and Salamander Energy, and from his stake in Manchester United FC, which he and his business partner, J. P. McManus, sold to the current owners, the Florida-based Glazer family. The selling of those shares is what Magnier is best known for outside the horse-racing world.

In the early 2000s Magnier encouraged the Manchester United manager of the time, the legendary Sir Alex Ferguson, to pursue his love of racehorses by becoming involved with a number of horses at Ballydoyle. One of these horses was *Rock Of Gibraltar*, who became a star on the track, winning seven Group 1 races in succession. With Magnier strengthening his power behind the scenes at Manchester United, it seemed that Ferguson and Magnier were set for a very happy and successful future.

However, when *Rock Of Gibraltar* retired to stud, their friendship imploded. Ferguson claimed that he was entitled to half of *Rock Of Gibraltar's* earnings as a stallion. Magnier disagreed, and the two became embroiled in a conflict that had Manchester United, the world's biggest soccer club, teetering on the brink of disaster. Ferguson issued legal proceedings against Coolmore but, in a feud that lasted six months, he blinked first and backed down, accepting the Coolmore owner's proposal, which was an offer of one nomination to the stallion, the same deal that Aidan O'Brien and then stable jockey Mick Kinane received. Magnier eventually sold his 28.89 per cent stake in the football club to Malcolm Glazer, who became the new owner, something which still rankles with a huge section of Manchester United supporters. The *Rock Of Gibraltar* affair showed that Magnier wasn't a person to be messed with, even if your name is Sir Alex Ferguson.

Back at his day job, Magnier continued to be a runaway success. With *Sadler's Wells* and *Danehill* providing the majority of the ammunition, Coolmore began to dominate the European racing scene, and Magnier's famous all-navy colours sailed past the winning post at tracks like Ascot all the way to Santa Anita in California. *Galileo, Hawk Wing, Pour Moi, Giant's Causeway, George Washington, Declaration of War* and the never-to-be-forgotten *Yeats* are just some of the famous horses that have carried the Magnier silks to Group 1 glory.

Magnier proved that he could not only breed a champion racehorse, but also that, like Vincent O'Brien, he had an eye for spotting a future star. He purchased the likes of *Hurricane Run, Starspangledbanner* and *Haradasun*, as well as the brilliant Australian champion *So You Think*, who landed five Group 1 races in Europe in 2011–12 to supplement the five he won down under.

The scale of Magnier's and Coolmore's dominance can be seen in the impact they have had on both the Epsom and Irish Derbies over the last two decades. Both races, run over 1 mile 4 furlongs in June, have come to represent the ideal test for a horse with Classic aspirations. Each race offers a unique test of a horse's ability to stay the distance and handle different types of ground and track configurations. The strength of thoroughbred talent residing at Coolmore is indicated by the fact that thirteen of the seventeen winners of the Epsom Derby – the blue riband of the turf – between 1998 and 2015 were sired by Coolmore stallions (*High Estate,*

Fairy King, Grand Lodge, Sadler's Wells (two), *Danehill, Montjeu* (four) and *Galileo* (three)). Their record in the Irish Derby, run at the Curragh, is equally impressive. Since 1998 Magnier has owned or part-owned the winner of twelve runnings of the Group 1 race, with four of his Epsom Derby winners (*Galileo, High Chaparral, Camelot* and *Australia*) bagging the English and Irish Derby double.

Magnier's passion for horses is easy to understand. The Magnier family has been involved with horses for a very long time. The tradition began in the 1850s with Thomas Magnier, who offered the services of his stallions to local breeders in the Blackwater Valley in County Cork. One of those stallions was the renowned *Edlington*, whose fee was the not-inconsiderable sum of £3. Their interest continued throughout the last century, most notably with *Cottage*, who sired the mighty *Cottage Rake*. Trained by Vincent O'Brien, *Cottage Rake* landed three Cheltenham Gold Cups (1948–50).

Cottage set the standard that continued with the sensational sire *Deep Run*. *Deep Run* dominated the National Hunt sires tables in Britain and Ireland for Coolmore's National Hunt wing like no other before or since. He won fourteen consecutive sires' championships (1979/80–1992/93), and Cheltenham highlights for his progeny included *Golden Cygnet* winning the Supreme Novices' Hurdle in a faster time than the Champion Hurdle, the brilliant *Dawn Run* adding the Gold Cup to her Champion Hurdle success, *Deep Sensation* landing the Queen Mother Champion Chase, and the victories of the full brothers *Morley Street* and *Granville Again* in the Champion Hurdle.

Since *Deep Run*'s domination of the 1980s and 1990s there have been multiple champion sires such as *Be My Native* (2000/01, 2001/02, 2002/03 and 2003/04) and *Supreme Leader* (2004/05 and 2005/06). The current star National Hunt stallions include *Oscar* (sire of 2012 Champion Hurdle winner *Rock On Ruby*, 2010 Queen Mother Champion Chase winner *Big Zeb* and 2014 Cheltenham Gold Cup winner *Lord Windermere*), *Flemensfirth* (sire of 2010 Cheltenham Gold Cup winner *Imperial Commander*) and *Milan* (sire of 2014 Champion Hurdle winner *Jezki*).

The influence of *Sadler's Wells* on National Hunt racing has been, and will continue to be, immense. Not only did he sire the brilliant three-time Champion Hurdle winner *Istabraq* (1998–2000) but his sons *Montjeu, Oscar* and *Milan* have all sired winners of the race, while a grandson sired the 2010 winner *Binocular*. The 2012 Cheltenham Gold Cup went to *Synchronised*, also a son of *Sadler's Wells*, while the 2005 winner *Kicking King* and 2014 winner *Lord Windermere* are by two of his numerous top-class National Hunt sire sons.

As with most successful business people, Magnier's attention to detail is laser-like. Nothing happens at Coolmore without his say-so. He was involved in the design of the state-of-the-art horseboxes that ship his valuable stallions to Australia for their second breeding season. He also expects a strong work ethic from his employees – two security men were dismissed for not working when they should have been. Despite this, Magnier receives unconditional loyalty from all his staff. Some, like Paul Shanahan, have worked their way from the bottom right to the very top of the Coolmore organisation. Magnier provides opportunities and allows the people around him to flourish. His circle of trusted confidants is small. Along with Shanahan, Demi O'Byrne and Timmy Hyde are just two of a handful of people whom Magnier consults about business matters. It's a tight-knit but hugely successful group.

Magnier is also not afraid to make tough decisions if they are in the best interest of his organisation. When *George Washington* was proving to be less than fertile in his first season at stud in 2007, Magnier made the instant decision to retire to stud his most promising three-year-old, *Holy Roman Emperor*, to fill the gap. It was a decision Aidan O'Brien begged Magnier to reconsider, but with no success, and *Holy Roman Emperor* was whisked away to Coolmore to begin his stallion career.

While he does have a ruthless side to him, there is no doubting that there are compassion and empathy behind Magnier's steely brown eyes. In an interview with the *Racing Post* in 2001, Stan Cosgrave of Moyglare Stud, a highly successful breeding operation in its own right, said of Magnier:

He's always been a big man who thought on the grand scale. Even when he wasn't going that well, he would think big. You'd never see John Magnier in a small car.

I remember when they had a bad case of virus abortion down at Fermoy [one of Coolmore's sister stud farms] and had 20 or 30 mares up in slings and God knows what breaking loose. Well, he came through that and I thought then, 'he'll come through anything'.

He has a terrific team and they are mainly horsemen, not academics, and he looks after them. He has a natural touch with people and I can think of loads of folk he has done good turns for down the years. You always got a fair deal; if a foal died or was born crooked he would always do something for you. People remember that sort of thing.

He is not a showman, never one to boast. And the outstanding thing about him is the number of people who have worked for him who become millionaires. I've known men with 40 or 50 mares who employ people who come out after a lifetime's service just the same as they went in.

With John it's different. He was always encouraging his people to take shares and make a few bob. A lesser man would resent his employees doing that because he'd think they were trying to get level with him. Not Magnier. Nobody ever gets head-hunted out of Coolmore because nobody else would look after them so well ... Those who criticise Coolmore because of its size should remember that it is just a reflection of how the supermarkets and banks have gone. That is business nowadays.

While many people have good things to say about John Magnier, one person you won't hear talking about him is the man himself. Magnier is notoriously wary of the media and detests giving interviews. He once said, 'I don't like talking to the press, it only sounds like bragging.'[1]

On the rare occasions that he does make himself available, his insights are illuminating. In the brilliant documentary *The Young Prince of Ballydoyle*,

---

1   http://news.bbc.co.uk/sport2/hi/front_page/3434311.stm

'The Boss', John Magnier (centre), in deep thought at the Tattersalls yearling sale.
Courtesy of Tattersalls

Magnier explained his breeding philosophy, something which has stood the test of time over the last fifty years. 'Breed the best to the best,' he said, simply. 'That's the first thing that you have to do. Then luck and environment has a lot to do with it. What I have found is that most of the good horses come from the same people. We are lucky in Ireland that we have some of the best horse people in the world.'

By Magnier's side as Coolmore re-emerged as a dominant force in flat racing was Michael Tabor. During the Coolmore debrief after another successful Group 1 win, Tabor's distinctive laugh can be heard as the team celebrate another top-level victory. The laugh, which booms from the winner's enclosure, is one of tremendous satisfaction, of a job well done, of another successful gamble paying off. That lure of a gamble is something that has always resonated with Tabor.

The son of a glass manufacturer, Tabor was first bitten by the gambling bug at his local dog track. It was there, at the now-defunct Hendon Stadium, that Tabor became infatuated with the duels that took place between punters and bookmakers. Tabor turned that infatuation into a business by establishing his own chain of bookmakers, Arthur Prince, in 1967, the year in which *Foinavon* won the Aintree Grand National at 100/1.

Tabor's quest for a fuller understanding of the racing game saw him become not only a successful bookmaker but a feared punter too. His successes allowed him to expand his interest into ownership. His first horse, *Tornado Prince*, won a novice hurdle at Ascot in 1974, before going on to win a further six times. Tabor was hooked.

Having successfully built up his bookmaking business, Tabor subsequently sold his Arthur Prince chain for a reputed £27 million in 1995, which gave him the capital to expand his ownership interests. It was around the time that Tabor was selling his business that J. P. McManus introduced him to John Magnier. It was a meeting that changed both men's lives forever.

Tabor's first big horse was the deeply talented American racer *Thunder Gulch*. Having bombed out when running in Tabor's silks for the first time, *Thunder Gulch* recovered to win the Kentucky Derby of 1995, giving his enthusiastic owner his highest-profile winner on the world stage at the time. Although *Thunder Gulch* failed to land the second leg of the American Triple Crown (the Preakness Stakes), having been drawn out wide in stall 11, he went on to win the third leg (the Belmont Stakes).

Having enjoyed a stellar racing career, *Thunder Gulch* was on the verge of being sold to Japan at the end of his career. Tabor's wife, Doreen, was against the idea, and thanks to John Magnier, who purchased 50 per cent of the colt, *Thunder Gulch* remained with Tabor and took up stud duties at Coolmore's American base in Ashford, Kentucky, where he became a noted sire.

Buoyed by the initial success of *Thunder Gulch*, Tabor and Magnier grew closer. Both men had a lot to gain from working together. At the time, Magnier was looking to re-establish Coolmore/Ballydoyle as a global powerhouse after a lean period in the late 1980s and early 1990s, while Tabor was looking to add to the success he had already enjoyed with his Kentucky Derby winner. It seemed like a match made in heaven, and so it proved. The pair teamed up to pay

600,000 gns for a *Sadler's Wells* colt who went into training with the legendary Newmarket trainer Sir Michael Stoute. The colt, named *Entrepreneur*, landed the 1997 English 2000 Guineas for the pair. It was the tipping point for Tabor. Two years later, in 1999, the extraordinary *Montjeu* carried his silks to victory in the Irish and French Derbies as well as in the Prix de l'Arc de Triomphe, as he stamped himself as one of the most gifted middle-distance horses of his generation.

Michael Tabor: The man who helped bring Coolmore back to the top of world racing.
Courtesy of Racing Post

Tabor bagged his first Epsom Derby winner just two years later, in 2001, when *Galileo* winged his way home to re-establish Coolmore as a dominant player in the world of flat racing. Although Tabor had a half share in *Galileo*, the son of *Sadler's Wells* did all his running in the colours of John and Sue Magnier. But Tabor didn't have to wait long to toast an Epsom Derby winner in his own colours. A mere twelve months later, *High Chaparral* galloped his way into the history books, winning the first of his two Derbies (he followed up at the Curragh four weeks later) by defeating his stablemate *Hawk Wing*. That victory must have been extra sweet for Tabor considering that *Hawk Wing*, who was an outstanding racehorse and went on to win a huge amount of prize money, was one of the few horses in which he didn't take a 50 per cent stake. (Normally Magnier and Tabor take an equal 50 per cent share in the horses they own, but on occasion, they can own a horse by themselves.)

In an interview with Julian Muscat in July 2012, Tabor explains that it wasn't the first time an opportunity like that slipped through his fingers. He also missed the boat when it came to the outstanding juvenile and successful sire *Holy Roman Emperor*:

> I had a lovely foal out of my mare [the Grade 1 winner] *Circle of Life* and John had a home-bred foal that turned out to be *Holy Roman Emperor*. He suggested we went 50–50 on each foal, but I declined.
>
> *Holy Roman Emperor* now looks like making a very good stallion and mine was an also-ran, but that's life. I was offered the opportunity, which I didn't accept, but you can't win them all. Not in this game.
>
> For reasons that none of us can remember, John didn't come into *Rags to Riches* with Derrick [Smith] and me. To this day, John still wonders why. She was a standout yearling [she fetched $1.9 million] and, of course, she gave us an unforgettable day when she won the Belmont Stakes [in 2007].
>
> My role within Coolmore is very simple. You're running a business, you know what your income is, and you treat it as such. As partners, Derrick and I discuss things with the team, and, in the main, you have to go along with them because they have a proven expertise. To be honest, it's a pleasure just to listen to them. They always say why they are doing this, or breeding this mare to that stallion. I'm not an expert on that side of it, but I find it fascinating. And it's mind-boggling to see the foals and yearlings which result from that planning.

The Belmont Stakes victory for *Rags to Riches* also marked another very important turning point for the Coolmore partners as it saw the first Classic winner involving Derrick Smith, who is the final member of the new Coolmore triumvirate. Smith, who had a long-standing friendship with Michael Tabor from their days in the betting jungle, came into the Coolmore fold in 2004 and has enjoyed remarkable success in the intervening years with the likes of *Camelot, Australia, Fame And Glory, Marvellous, Mastercraftsman, Minding, So You Think, St Nicholas Abbey, Alfred Nobel* and *Leading Light,* all carrying his now-famous colours of purple and white to Group 1 glory.

The bookmaking firm Ladbrokes was where Smith cut his teeth. He enjoyed a successful twenty-four-year stint with the company, working his way up from the firm's racetrack pitches to become its head of trading. Having left Ladbrokes, Smith indulged his fondness for a bet while acting as a property consultant, a role which allowed him to make the move to Barbados and reacquaint himself with Tabor, who spends the winter months there.

With their other business ventures going exceptionally well, Smith, Magnier and Tabor began to team up on the racecourse. The seeds for this budding partnership came when Smith stood side by side with both Magnier and Tabor as *High Chaparral* and *Hawk Wing* fought out that memorable finish to the 2002 Epsom Derby, pulling twelve lengths clear of the third horse home, *Moon Ballad*.

Smith was hooked, and soon his purple and white silks would become a familiar sight on English and Irish racecourses. One of the best horses, in the early years, to carry the Smith colours was *Mastercraftsman*. The steel-grey son of *Danehill Dancer* was a top-class horse for Smith and the Coolmore partners. Having landed two Group 1s as a two-year-old, *Mastercraftsman* bagged Classic glory for Smith when he won the 2009 Irish 2000 Guineas at the Curragh, before seeing off the best milers around at the St James's Palace Stakes at Royal Ascot in June of that year.

He also, unsuccessfully, butted heads with *Sea The Stars* on two occasions that season, going down narrowly to that superstar in the Juddmonte International at York before placing third behind *Sea The Stars* and *Fame And Glory* in the Irish Champion Stakes at Leopardstown that September. The colt has gone on to be a huge success at stud, siring the likes of French Derby and Irish Champion Stakes winner *The Grey Gatsby*.

It wasn't until *Camelot* sauntered his way down the straight at Epsom in 2012 that Smith could finally revel in a Derby winner wearing his silks. Amazingly, a horse carrying Smith's colours had finished in the runners-up berth on four occasions before *Camelot* righted the situation. That June day at Epsom proved to be one of the all-time highs for Smith, as *St Nicholas Abbey* also carried his colours into the hallowed winner's enclosure when landing the Coronation Cup. The victory for *Camelot* at Epsom provided Smith with his hundredth Group 1 victory, a remarkable achievement considering the relatively short time he has been involved in racing. *Camelot* ranks alongside *Australia* as the most talented horse to have carried Smith's colours to date.

While *Camelot* landed the 2000 Guineas along with the Epsom Derby, before narrowly failing to land the Triple Crown in 2012, *Australia* was an entirely different model of a thoroughbred, but no less talented. A son of *Galileo* and out of the brilliant dual Oaks winner *Ouija Board*, *Australia* was bred to be special. Having sauntered away with a Group 3 on Irish Champion Stakes day in 2013, *Australia* arrived for the 2014 Epsom Derby as the raging-hot favourite, having run an excellent prep race a number of weeks earlier in the 2000 Guineas at Newmarket. Ridden by Joseph O'Brien, *Australia* cruised through the race and fought off the persistent challenge of *Kingston Hill* (owned by Smith's son, Paul) to give his owner a second Derby winner. *Australia* proved himself a top-class three-year-old with further victories in the Dubai Duty Free Irish Derby and the Juddmonte International Stakes, before going down by the narrowest of margins to *The Grey Gatsby* in the Irish Champion Stakes. The colt was retired to Coolmore following a hoof injury and his first foals were on the ground in 2016.

In a 2012 interview with the *Racing Post*, the leading trade paper in Britain and Ireland, Smith revealed that the roots of Coolmore's success over the last twenty years go back to one individual:

> All of us benefit from the time John spent with Vincent O'Brien. Sometimes Sue [Magnier's wife] will say something about her father, and John will pick it up and tell us about the way Vincent did things. There's plenty of pedigree there.
>
> John has fantastic people around him and he never stops asking them questions. But at the end of the day, if you had to pick one man, he is probably the best judge.

In fact it was John [who] first brought up the idea to target the Triple Crown with *Camelot* soon after Christmas in Barbados. I must admit if it was down to me, I'd probably have chosen the Derrinstown Derby Trial and on to Epsom, but John pushed for it.

He is the commercial man of the operation, and after what happened to *St Nicholas Abbey* in the [English 2000] Guineas two years ago [he was defeated when a red-hot favourite], I thought we must have a special horse because John wanted him to do a special thing.

When Smith's *Leading Light* landed the 2013 Ladbrokes St Leger at Doncaster, this secured his place in the annals of racing history, as he became one of the few owners in history to win every Classic race in England and Ireland. After *Leading Light* had been unsaddled, Smith modestly said to the waiting press, 'That is the full set of Classics. I've now won every one in England and Ireland. All ten. I never thought I'd win one.'

When *Order Of St George* landed the 2015 Irish St Leger on Irish Champions Weekend, Derrick Smith led the horse into the winner's enclosure. As the music blared and the public announcer did his best to whip up a frenzy, there was a quiet sense of satisfaction within the victorious party. Smith handed over the reins to the horse's handlers and took his spot beside his fellow owners. Smiles and laughter were the order of the day – no shouting from the rooftops, no flying dismounts or over-the-top celebrations, just a sense of satisfaction at a job well done.

As *Order Of St George* was led back for a well-deserved wash down, the focus panned back to his owners – a group of men, not only rich in the monetary sense of the word but filled with a richness born out of their love of the horse. It is sometimes easy to forget that when you strip away all the money, prestige and success of the Coolmore operation, the people there are just like you and me – lovers of horses.

AIDAN O'BRIEN

The hand on the clock ticks past 8 a.m. and another work morning at Ballydoyle begins. As each of the fifty horses and work riders that make up the first lot warm up in the huge covered ride, their boss is waiting for them. Unlike the Vincent O'Brien era, when a stiff upper lip was favoured, the current master of Ballydoyle has a warm greeting for all his members of staff.

Aidan O'Brien greets each staff member by name, a prodigious feat of memory, if nothing else. But that's how the show rolls at Ballydoyle: 160 individual greetings each and every morning. When John Magnier appointed Aidan O'Brien as the successor to Vincent O'Brien, there was an huge amount of pressure placed upon O'Brien's young shoulders. Yes, he had made a spectacular start to his training career, but could he bring that success to the unforgiving world of high-level flat racing?

Aidan Patrick O'Brien was born on 19 October 1969 in Wexford, Ireland. His father, Dennis, was a farmer and a small-scale trainer of point-to-point horses. Point-to-point races are the breeding ground for the next generation of National Hunt stars, and Mr O'Brien had a degree of success with Aidan at his side, training 140 winners. Young Aidan learned at his father's bootstraps and soon developed his own love of the horse. His career began in the respected yard of P. J. Finn's in County Kildare. However, O'Brien spent just twelve months there before making the move to one of the top racing yards, not just in Ireland, but in the entire racing world.

At the time, Jim Bolger was beginning his rise to become one of the world's leading trainers. From his base in Coolcullen, County Kilkenny, Bolger has moulded some of the finest people in racing. Along with Aidan O'Brien, the likes of Paul Carberry and the record-setting Tony McCoy served their apprenticeships under Bolger. The trainer was a famously hard taskmaster, but O'Brien warmed to the routine at Bolger's. He spent three very successful years with Bolger before leaving in 1993. Later, Bolger said, 'I would have done anything to keep Aidan, except marry him!'

O'Brien's departure was the beginning of an extraordinary journey that continues to this very day. His new wife, Annemarie, who was a champion National Hunt trainer the previous season and an accomplished rider in her own right, retired from the training ranks and passed her licence on to Aidan. He hit the ground running and combined his own riding career with his training at the new yard he had created, Piltown. O'Brien became champion Irish National Hunt trainer in the 1993–94 season and went on to lift the title for another five successive seasons. He landed his first Grade 1 in his third season holding a licence when *That's My Man* won the Royal Bond Novice Hurdle at Fairyhouse in December 1995. He rounded off that calendar year with a second Grade 1 when he saddled *Double Symphony* to win the Denny Gold Medal Chase at Leopardstown.

It wasn't long before O'Brien gained the attention of racing fans further afield. *Urubande* gave the young trainer his first winner at the Cheltenham Festival when he dug deep for his jockey Charlie Swan to nab the Royal and Sun Alliance Novices' Hurdle at the 1996 showpiece. The pair teamed up again soon after to give O'Brien his second Grade 1 on English soil, winning the Martell Aintree Hurdle.

O'Brien's phenomenal success at his first training base, Piltown, put his name up in lights and it wasn't long before he was attracting the attention of the most influential name in flat racing. Since Vincent O'Brien had retired from training in 1994, the Ballydoyle stables had lain idle. John Magnier approached Aidan O'Brien with a proposition. O'Brien was offered the chance to move into Ballydoyle and train for Magnier and his associates, as Magnier tried to get the Coolmore/Ballydoyle axis back on the road again. It was a bold move for Magnier to make, given O'Brien's youth, but it was also a calculated move given the huge amount of success O'Brien had achieved in his career to date.

O'Brien accepted his offer, but rather than give up his yard at Piltown, he combined his horses at that yard with the horses at Ballydoyle, which gave him even more horses to run both over the jumps and on the flat. Speaking to *The Sunday Times* in the spring of 2008, O'Brien admitted how lucky he was to be able to walk into a yard like Ballydoyle:

> We were just lucky to be here and to be training in the place that Dr O'Brien has set up. He set it up from scratch; it's only just maturing now. Generations of time and work went into this place, with the team of people working for the boss man, John and Sue, and the people who are with him now, Michael [Tabor] and Derrick [Smith]. The boss is an unbelievable man. He's got such vision, he's a big-picture man, but he understands horses and people like no other man I know. We're lucky to be around at the same time as him.

The move to Ballydoyle proved to be a hit from the outset. With Christy Roche as his stable jockey, O'Brien took aim at the biggest flat races in Britain and Ireland, proving that he could handle the pressure that came with training in such a legendary yard.

His first top-class horse on the flat was a *Danehill* colt named *Desert King*. Racing in the blue and orange silks of Michael Tabor, *Desert King* gave O'Brien his first taste of Group 1 glory on the flat when he took the National Stakes at the Curragh in 1996. *Desert King* carried his excellent two-year-old form into his Classic season, giving his young trainer a brace of Classic wins in 1997, with dominant displays in the Irish 2000 Guineas and Irish Derby. He later went on to sire the record-breaking *Makybe Diva*, who landed three consecutive Melbourne Cups.

Magnier's faith in O'Brien had been justified. Emboldened by his selection of trainer, Magnier, with Tabor, began to target the big yearling sales across the world and, just like he had with M. V. O'Brien, put the horses into training at Ballydoyle. Soon the sight of regally bred horses from Ballydoyle became commonplace once again on the racetracks of England, Ireland and France.

While O'Brien was exploring new avenues in flat racing, he maintained a very close link with the National Hunt world in the shape of the charismatic *Istabraq*. The *Sadler's Wells* gelding had come to O'Brien following the illness and untimely passing of John Durkin. *Istabraq's* owner, J. P. McManus, took a chance in the 2002 Champion Hurdle, when he allowed the horse to run, even though it appeared time had caught up with him. Sadly *Istabraq* couldn't recapture the brilliance he had shown earlier in his career and failed to finish the race.

King of Kings gave O'Brien his first taste of Classic glory in England when he won the 2000 Guineas in 1997. It was a first success but would not be the last, as O'Brien snared the 1 mile Group 1 a further six times with *Rock Of Gibraltar* (2002), *Footstepsinthesand* (2005), *George Washington* (2006), *Henrythenavigator* (2008), *Camelot* (2012) and *Gleneagles* (2015).

Victory with *King of Kings* was also noteworthy because of the jockey who rode the colt. At that time Michael Kinane was considered as the best big-race jockey in the world and had ridden *Vintage Crop* to victory in the Melbourne Cup of 1993, along with a host of other Group 1 winners, for trainers all around the world. In bringing *King of Kings* to victory, Kinane and O'Brien laid the foundations of what became one of the most successful trainer/jockey partnerships of our generation. Kinane signed on to be Ballydoyle's No. 1 jockey following the retirement of another top-class jockey, Christy Roche.

With Kinane's ice-cool ability in the saddle and O'Brien's skill at getting horses to peak on the day that mattered most, the duo looked like they were a match made in heaven. The colt that really cemented their partnership was a flashy chestnut who had his own way of doing things, a horse who loved nothing more than to stare other horses in the eye and dare them to pass him, before pulling out what was required and winning with the minimum of fuss. *Giant's Causeway* was well named because he was as tough as the cliffs he was named after. Nicknamed 'The Iron Horse', he was masterfully guided by O'Brien through tough race after tough race during a three-year-old campaign that would have broken lesser horses.

Aidan O'Brien, a study of concentration at Ballydoyle. *Courtesy of Coolmore Stud*

Following defeats in the English and Irish 2000 Guineas, *Giant's Causeway* picked up the first Group 1 win of his three-year-old career by a narrow margin in the St James's Palace Stakes at Royal Ascot, before going on to land the Coral Eclipse, Sussex Stakes, Juddmonte International and Irish Champion Stakes, as he lit up the summer of 2000. His career ended on a heartbreaking note, however, when he failed by the narrowest of margins to land the Breeders' Cup Classic on his first start on dirt, going down by a flared nostril to the American star *Tiznow*. Debate raged over whether it was an error or a better horse that defeated *Giant's Causeway*, but the colt had given his all and was retired to stud, where he went on to be a classic sire, fathering the likes of *Footstepsinthesand*, who won the English 2000 Guineas for Ballydoyle in 2005.

While many trainers would rue the loss of a champion like *Giant's Causeway*, O'Brien had a ready-made replacement in the shape of *Galileo*. The imposing son of *Sadler's Wells* had made a sparkling debut in October 2000 and had safely negotiated his way through his prep races as O'Brien readied him for the 2001 Epsom Derby.

It is strange to think, given all the success O'Brien has enjoyed in his career, that in 2001 the Epsom Derby was still a notable gap on his CV. He had run a number of well-fancied runners before *Galileo*, but all had disappointed. In 2001 that completely changed.

Coolly ridden by Michael Kinane, *Galileo* delivered on all the expectations placed on him by routing his rivals to give O'Brien his first Derby success and, in the process, continued the legacy of Ballydoyle and Vincent O'Brien. The younger O'Brien was furthering a tradition of excellence in much the same way that the horses from Ballydoyle were. The 2001 campaign also saw O'Brien become the first Irish trainer to be the champion trainer in England since Vincent O'Brien achieved the feat in 1971.

Aidan O'Brien receiving feedback from his work riders at Ballydoyle.
Courtesy of Coolmore Stud

Galileo's excellent three-year-old season, which saw him add two further Group 1s to his résumé in the Irish Derby and King George, was topped by an unbelievable crop of two-year-olds that O'Brien handled brilliantly. *Johannesburg, Hawk Wing, Rock Of Gibraltar* and *High Chaparral* were all Group 1 winning juvenile colts that year as O'Brien broke the world record for Group 1 winners in a season, which was previously held by the American Hall of Fame trainer D. Wayne Lukas.

His twenty-three wins at the highest level showed that O'Brien had a rare talent for training racehorses and keeping them sound and healthy, so that they enjoyed their racing throughout long and arduous campaigns. The fruits of O'Brien's labour came to a head in the following season when *High Chaparral* led *Hawk Wing* home in the Epsom Derby to give Ballydoyle a 1–2 in the world's most famous race. Ridden by Johnny Murtagh and Mick Kinane respectively, the pair pulled an incredible fourteen lengths clear of the third horse, *Moon Ballad*, who subsequently won the world's richest horse race, the Dubai World Cup, the following March.

Rock Of Gibraltar, who raced in the colours of former Manchester United manager Sir Alex Ferguson, made his own headlines in 2002 by winning five Group 1s in a row, following on from the two that he had won during his two-year-old season. Those victories saw the colt break *Mill Reef*'s record of consecutive Group 1 wins. His racing career ended in a narrow defeat in the Breeders' Cup Mile, before he retired to stud in 2002.

O'Brien's star continued to shine brightly over the next couple of seasons. A new stable jockey in the shape of Kieren Fallon helped O'Brien land the first two Classics of 2005, when *Footstepsinthesand* and *Virginia Waters* brought both Newmarket Classics back to Ballydoyle.

It was also during that period that O'Brien began to sculpt the career of the greatest long-distance horse of the modern generation. Having missed the 2004 Derby, *Yeats* began the 2005 season with a lot to prove. Victory in that season's Coronation Cup went some way to restoring his lofty reputation, after he missed out on running in the Epsom Derby, but it was O'Brien's foresight to run the horse over a longer distance the following season that allowed *Yeats* to write his name in history. The year 2006 saw the horse capture the first of a remarkable four straight Ascot Gold Cups, a feat so stunning, so barely believable, that a statue of him now stands in the parade ring at Ascot saluting his achievements.

While *Yeats* was setting records of his own, the crop of horses trained by O'Brien during that time was something exceptional. *George Washington*, perhaps the most charismatic horse ever to emerge from Ballydoyle, gave O'Brien another 2000 Guineas win in 2006, while *Dylan Thomas* gave his trainer his first and, to date, only win in the Prix de l'Arc de Triomphe in 2007, under an inspired ride from Kieren Fallon. Following the departure of Fallon from the Ballydoyle hot seat after a number of off-track incidents at the end of 2007, O'Brien teamed up with Johnny Murtagh for the 2008 campaign. It would be a season that neither would forget.

Henrythenavigator, a super-slick miler sired by *Kingmambo*, kicked things off for the pair by defeating future Derby winner *New Approach* in the 2000 Guineas at Newmarket. It was the start of a record-breaking season that saw O'Brien train a further twenty-two Group/Grade 1 winners, breaking the record he had set back in 2001. O'Brien swept all before him in Ireland as he captured every one of the Classic races run during that season, something that had not been achieved since 1935. He also equalled the record number of winners at a single Royal Ascot meeting when he saddled six winners, the same number as his predecessor at Ballydoyle. (In the 2016 meeting he would break this record with seven winners.) It was a remarkable feat of training, to say the very least.

By 2012 O'Brien was universally recognised as the best trainer in the world, and during that season he trained one of the very best horses to have passed through his hands at Ballydoyle. Given the name *Camelot* by Sue Magnier, the beautiful son of *Montjeu* bridged a ten-year Epsom Derby gap for O'Brien, when he devoured the opposition to give his trainer another slice of history. As O'Brien's son Joseph, who by then had risen to become Ballydoyle's No. 1 jockey, rode *Camelot*, the pair became the first father/son trainer/jockey combination to win the Derby. They repeated the feat two years later with *Australia*.

Camelot followed up his success at Epsom with a gritty display in the Dubai Duty Free Irish Derby at the Curragh. The race was run on unbelievably soft ground and it was only thanks to the good grace of the Coolmore team that the colt was allowed to take his chance, as the heavy ground did not suit *Camelot* at all. That success gave O'Brien a remarkable tenth win in the race following on from *Desert King* (1997) *Galileo* (2001), *High Chaparral* (2002), *Dylan Thomas* (2006), *Soldier Of Fortune* (2007), *Frozen Fire* (2008), *Fame And Glory* (2009), *Cape Blanco* (2010) and *Treasure Beach* (2011). He landed his eleventh success in the race two years later when *Australia* waltzed to victory in 2014. *Camelot* was also the first of three straight Epsom Derby winners that O'Brien trained, along with *Ruler Of The World*, ridden by Ryan Moore, and the aforementioned *Australia*.

O'Brien's magic touch does not just apply to colts. The trainer also has an innate understanding of fillies. *Peeping Fawn*, *Alexandrova*, *Imagine*, *Shahtoush*, *Lillie Langtry*, *Sophisticat*, *Misty For Me*, *Homecoming Queen*, *Virginia Waters*, *Ballydoyle*, *Minding*, *Found* and *Diamondsandrubies* are just some of the highly talented fillies O'Brien has trained to Group 1 glory.

His handling of *Peeping Fawn* is a testament to that ability. At the start of the 2007 flat season, *Peeping Fawn* was a well-bred wannabe who had yet to display her ability on the racetrack. When she did make her belated debut in the April of her three-year-old campaign, she lacked racecourse experience and finished third behind the Jim Bolger-trained *Ezima* at Navan Racecourse. In fact, the penny didn't drop for *Peeping Fawn* until her fourth race, when she finally got off the mark, landing a 1 mile maiden race at Naas. Having finally secured her first win, O'Brien pressed on with *Peeping Fawn*, pitching her straight into Group 1 company at the Curragh next time out. Given her relative lack of experience, *Peeping Fawn* ran a super race to place third behind the English 1000 Guineas winner *Finsceal Beo*.

Ballydoyle being ridden by Joseph O'Brien on the way to the start at the Curragh.
Courtesy of David Betts

O'Brien kept *Peeping Fawn* working and the filly appeared a month later in the Epsom Oaks, when she narrowly failed to defeat the Sir Henry Cecil-trained *Light Shift*. Despite having packed six races into just three months of racing, O'Brien didn't let up on *Peeping Fawn*. The *Danehill* filly finally got her Group 1 prize when she won the Pretty Polly Stakes at the Curragh, before exacting her revenge on *Light Shift* when she reversed Epsom form and took the Darley Irish Oaks back to Ballydoyle.

O'Brien could see that *Peeping Fawn* still had more to give. The trainer sent her into battle twice more, at Goodwood in the Nassau Stakes and at York in the Yorkshire Oaks, and both times the filly cantered home unchallenged. In the hands of a lesser trainer, *Peeping Fawn* would have had little chance to show her talent, but with Aidan O'Brien she was allowed to develop naturally and rewarded that patience with four Group 1 prizes.

Along with being the outstanding trainer of his generation, O'Brien has also developed a reputation as a breeder of outstanding merit. As well as the seven-time Group 1 winner *Rock Of Gibraltar* (in partnership with his wife, Annemarie, and her father, Joe Crowley), O'Brien has continually bred a number of highly talented horses who have made their way to Ballydoyle. *Beethoven*, successful in the Dewhurst in 2009, was bred under O'Brien's Whisperview Trading banner. Other horses bred from O'Brien's vision include *Furner's Green, Perfect Truth, Palace* and *Kingfisher*. The 2015 Epsom Oaks winner *Qualify* is another horse to come from O'Brien's breeding programme. *Qualify* is a daughter of Coolmore stallion *Fastnet Rock* and is out of *Galileo* mare *Perihelion*, who raced for Ballydoyle in 2007 and 2008.

While many people are quick to point out the huge potential that is given to O'Brien each season, the simple fact is that he is a trainer of unique ability. Just like Vincent O'Brien, Aidan O'Brien has made an indelible mark on horse racing in the time he has been training. Yet while he sits at the top of his profession, one can't help but wonder if he will remain at Ballydoyle for the duration of his training career. In 2015 there were strong rumours that up-and-coming trainer David O'Meara was set to take over from O'Brien at Ballydoyle, with O'Brien and his family expected to relocate back to the family's yard at Piltown, which has been upgraded over the years.

While one can't imagine the powers that be at Coolmore would easily wave goodbye to Aidan O'Brien, the trainer did hint in the winner's enclosure at Royal Ascot 2015 that a changing of the guard was taking place at Ballydoyle:

> I'm just a small part of a very big team, and privileged to be able to play a part. I'm getting older now and the younger lads are coming on. I'm watching more and going with the flow. I'm 45 and it's great to see younger people coming along and taking responsibility. I just stand at the top of the gallops and watch the work, which is good for me, and a lot less pressure …
>
> [The children] are all getting older and bigger and know a lot about everything and it's a big team. They are grabbing it and I'm not stopping them,

I'm giving it. I might live a bit longer then. Anything they want, they can have it, and I'm very happy to be sitting in the back seat, believe me.

We [O'Brien and his wife Annemarie] have done this for 20 years, hard graft day in and day out. Maybe next year at Ascot we might be able to stay here an odd night. That's the reality, we're over and back every day, we never stay anywhere. Maybe shortly we might be able to start doing stuff like that, living normal lives. I've never seen any of the cities that we go to; I go racing and go back home.[1]

Total dedication to his craft, a singular focus on winning and a work ethic second to none are just some of the reasons why Aidan O'Brien is the best trainer in the world today. Enjoy him while you can, because talent like his is something that comes along but once in a generation.

'Every night we say our prayers, we say a Rosary and we thank God for how lucky we are,' O'Brien said in an interview with *The Sunday Times* on 11 April 2008. He continued:

How lucky we were that the day has gone by, and be thankful for it, how lucky we are to be in the position we are in, thank God for our health. Every night. We never take it for granted. That never happens. I hope that doesn't sound strange, but I'm so grateful for everything.

You must remember, first, where I was reared, and all the things that went into giving me the attitude I have and the way I'm made up came from my parents. And I knew the way they struggled to give us everything. Then to work for someone like Jim Bolger, how lucky I was to meet Annemarie, and then to get married to someone like Annemarie, and to have the success we had, and to have four great healthy kids, and then to get the job here. It's unbelievable. It's been an unbelievable journey.

An unbelievable journey that is far from over.

---

1   http://www.theguardian.com/sport/2015/jun/16/aidan-obrien-st-james-palace-royal-ascot

The master and his horse. Aidan O'Brien sizes up *Bondi Beach* after his win in the 2015 Curragh Cup. *Courtesy of David Betts*

A. P. O'BRIEN MAJOR WINS

Republic of Ireland

Irish 1000 Guineas (6): *Classic Park* (1997), *Imagine* (2001), *Yesterday* (2003), *Halfway To Heaven* (2008), *Misty For Me* (2011), *Marvellous* (2014)

Irish 2000 Guineas (10): *Desert King* (1997), *Saffron Walden* (1999), *Black Minnaloushe* (2001), *Rock Of Gibraltar* (2002), *Henrythenavigator* (2008), *Mastercraftsman* (2009), *Roderic O'Connor* (2011), *Power* (2012), *Magician* (2013), *Gleneagles* (2015)

Irish Champion Stakes (7): *Giant's Causeway* (2000), *High Chaparral* (2003), *Oratorio* (2005), *Dylan Thomas* (2006, 2007), *Cape Blanco* (2010), *So You Think* (2011)

Irish Derby (11): *Desert King* (1997), *Galileo* (2001), *High Chaparral* (2002), *Dylan Thomas* (2006), *Soldier Of Fortune* (2007), *Frozen Fire* (2008), *Fame And Glory* (2009), *Cape Blanco* (2010), *Treasure Beach* (2011), *Camelot* (2012), *Australia* (2014)

Irish Oaks (5): *Alexandrova* (2006), *Peeping Fawn* (2007), *Moonstone* (2008), *Bracelet* (2014), *Seventh Heaven* (2016)

Irish St Leger (3): *Yeats* (2007), *Septimus* (2008), *Order Of St George* (2015)

Matron Stakes (1): *Lillie Langtry* (2010)

Moyglare Stud Stakes (7): *Sequoyah* (2000), *Quarter Moon* (2001), *Necklace* (2003), *Rumplestiltskin* (2005), *Misty For Me* (2010), *Maybe* (2011), *Minding* (2015)

National Stakes (10): *Desert King* (1996), *King of Kings* (1997), *Beckett* (2000), *Hawk Wing* (2001), *One Cool Cat* (2003), *George Washington* (2005), *Mastercraftsman* (2008), *Power* (2011), *Gleneagles* (2014) *Air Force Blue* (2015)

Phoenix Stakes (14): *Lavery* (1998), *Fasliyev* (1999), *Minardi* (2000), *Johannesburg* (2001), *Spartacus* (2002), *One Cool Cat* (2003), *George Washington* (2005), *Holy Roman Emperor* (2006), *Mastercraftsman* (2008), *Alfred Nobel* (2009), *Zoffany* (2010), *Pedro The Great* (2012), *Dick Whittington* (2014), *Air Force Blue* (2015)

Pretty Polly Stakes (4): *Peeping Fawn* (2007), *Misty For Me* (2011), *Diamondsandrubies* (2015), *Minding* (2016)

Tattersalls Gold Cup (6): *Black Sam Bellamy* (2003), *Powerscourt* (2004), *Duke Of Marmalade* (2008), *Fame And Glory* (2010), *So You Think* (2011, 2012)

Australia

Cox Plate (1): *Adelaide* (2014)

Canada

Canadian International (2): *Ballingarry* (2002), *Joshua Tree* (2010)

France

Critérium International (3): *Mount Nelson* (2006), *Jan Vermeer* (2009), *Roderic O'Connor* (2010)

Critérium de Saint-Cloud (4): *Ballingarry* (2001), *Alberto Giacometti* (2002), *Fame And Glory* (2008), *Recital* (2010)

Grand Prix de Paris (2): *Scorpion* (2005), *Imperial Monarch* (2012)

Poule d'Essai des Poulains (4): *Landseer* (2002), *Aussie Rules* (2006), *Astronomer Royal* (2007), *The Gurkha* (2016)

Poule d'Essai des Pouliches (1): *Rose Gypsy* (2001)

Prix de l'Arc de Triomphe (1): *Dylan Thomas* (2007)

Prix Ganay (2): *Dylan Thomas* (2007), *Duke Of Marmalade* (2008)

Prix Jacques Le Marois (1): *Excelebration* (2012)

Prix Jean-Luc Lagardère (7): *Second Empire* (1997), *Ciro* (1999), *Rock Of Gibraltar* (2001), *Hold That Tiger* (2002), *Oratorio* (2004), *Horatio Nelson* (2005), *Holy Roman Emperor* (2006)

Prix Lupin (1): *Ciro* (2000)

Prix Marcel Boussac (4): *Rumplestiltskin* (2005), *Misty For Me* (2010), *Found* (2014), *Ballydoyle* (2015)

Prix Maurice de Gheest (1): *King Charlemagne* (2001)

Prix Morny (3): *Orpen* (1998), *Fasliyev* (1999), *Johannesburg* (2001)

Prix du Moulin de Longchamp (1): *Rock Of Gibraltar* (2002)

Prix Royal-Oak (1): *Yeats* (2008)

Prix de la Salamandre (1): *Giant's Causeway* (1999)

United Kingdom

1000 Guineas (3): *Virginia Waters* (2005), *Homecoming Queen* (2012), *Minding* (2016)

2000 Guineas (7): *King of Kings* (1998), *Rock Of Gibraltar* (2002), *Footstepsinthesand* (2005), *George Washington* (2006), *Henrythenavigator* (2008), *Camelot* (2012), *Gleneagles* (2015)

Ascot Gold Cup (7): *Yeats* (2006, 2007, 2008, 2009), *Fame And Glory* (2011), *Leading Light* (2014), *Order Of St George* (2016)

Champion Hurdle (3): *Istabraq* (1998, 1999, 2000)

Coronation Cup (7): *Yeats* (2005), *Scorpion* (2007), *Soldier Of Fortune* (2008), *Fame And Glory* (2010), *St Nicholas Abbey* (2011, 2012, 2013)

Coronation Stakes (2): *Sophisticat* (2002), *Lillie Langtry* (2010)

Dewhurst Stakes (4): *Rock Of Gibraltar* (2001), *Beethoven* (2009), *War Command* (2013), *Air Force Blue* (2015)

Eclipse Stakes (5): *Giant's Causeway* (2000), *Hawk Wing* (2002), *Oratorio* (2005), *Mount Nelson* (2008), *So You Think* (2011)

Epsom Derby (5): *Galileo* (2001), *High Chaparral* (2002), *Camelot* (2012), *Ruler Of The World* (2013), *Australia* (2014)

Epsom Oaks (6): *Shahtoush* (1998), *Imagine* (2001), *Alexandrova* (2006), *Was* (2012), *Qualify* (2015), *Minding* (2016)

Fillies' Mile (4): *Sunspangled* (1998), *Listen* (2007), *Together Forever* (2014), *Minding* (2015)

Golden Jubilee Stakes (1): *Starspangledbanner* (2010)

International Stakes (5): *Giant's Causeway* (2000), *Duke Of Marmalade* (2008), *Rip Van Winkle* (2010), *Declaration of War* (2013), *Australia* (2014)

July Cup (3): *Stravinsky* (1999), *Mozart* (2001), *Starspangledbanner* (2010)

King George VI and Queen Elizabeth Stakes (3): *Galileo* (2001), *Dylan Thomas* (2007), *Duke Of Marmalade* (2008)

Lockinge Stakes (1): *Hawk Wing* (2003)

Middle Park Stakes (4): *Minardi* (2000), *Johannesburg* (2001), *Ad Valorem* (2004), *Crusade* (2011)

Nassau Stakes (2): *Peeping Fawn* (2007), *Halfway To Heaven* (2008)

Nunthorpe Stakes (2): *Stravinsky* (1999), *Mozart* (2001)

Prince of Wales's Stakes (2): *Duke Of Marmalade* (2008), *So You Think* (2012)

Queen Anne Stakes (3): *Ad Valorem* (2006), *Haradasun* (2008), *Declaration of War* (2013)

Queen Elizabeth II Stakes (3): *George Washington* (2006), *Rip Van Winkle* (2009), *Excelebration* (2012)

Racing Post Trophy (7): *Saratoga Springs* (1997), *Aristotle* (1999), *High Chaparral* (2001), *Brian Boru* (2002), *St Nicholas Abbey* (2009), *Camelot* (2011), *Kingsbarns* (2012)

St James's Palace Stakes (7): *Giant's Causeway* (2000), *Black Minnaloushe* (2001), *Rock Of Gibraltar* (2002), *Excellent Art* (2007), *Henrythenavigator* (2008), *Mastercraftsman* (2009), *Gleneagles* (2015)

St Leger (4): *Milan* (2001), *Brian Boru* (2003), *Scorpion* (2005), *Leading Light* (2013)

Sun Chariot Stakes (1): *Halfway To Heaven* (2008)

Sussex Stakes (4): *Giant's Causeway* (2000), *Rock Of Gibraltar* (2002), *Henrythenavigator* (2008), *Rip Van Winkle* (2009)

Yorkshire Oaks (3): *Alexandrova* (2006), *Peeping Fawn* (2007), *Tapestry* (2014)

GALILEO

There is a moment when a foal is born in which the mind flashes forward. It rushes to certain times and places and one wonders, could this foal be the one? For every foal born, there come dreams that for two years remain unbroken, until that foal takes to the racetrack. That's where the majority of dreams end. Only a few will go on to fulfil the expectations of their owners. Then there are a precious few that soar higher than anyone dared to hope. In that bracket lies the most phenomenal stallion of his generation: *Galileo*.

Galileo, the world's best sire. *Courtesy of Coolmore Stud*

One can only imagine the expectations that were quietly expressed when *Galileo* was born on 30 March 1998. Born to outstanding parents, he was better placed than the majority of foals to succeed when he hit the racetrack. His father was the great *Sadler's Wells*, who had already sired the likes of *In The Wings, Old Vic, Salsabil, King's Theatre* and *Istabraq*, before mating with the 1993 Prix de l'Arc de Triomphe winner *Urban Sea*. It was a coming together that tipped the horse-racing world on its axis.

Urban Sea was no slouch herself. A huge, flashy chestnut mare, she performed with distinction on the racetrack. She ran twenty-three times, winning on eight occasions, with her most memorable victory coming when she powered clear in the autumnal sunshine in Paris to land the Prix de l'Arc de Triomphe under Éric Saint-Martin, son of the legendary French jockey Yves Saint-Martin. That performance saw her crowned as the European Champion Older Mare of that season.

Much was expected from *Urban Sea* when she retired to stud, and she didn't disappoint. A mating with another Arc winner, *Lammtarra*, produced a filly called *Melikah*, who went on to capture the Pretty Polly Stakes and was placed in the Epsom Oaks and the Irish equivalent in what was a truncated racing career. Her first visit to *Sadler's Wells* naturally raised expectations. Born with a narrow white blaze running down his face and one distinctive white sock on his near hind leg, *Galileo* arrived into the world with a pedigree dripping with potential.

Named after the Italian astronomer, physicist, engineer, philosopher and mathematician Galileo Galilei, the equine *Galileo* made his way to Ballydoyle at the end of his yearling year in 1999 with a big reputation. It was up to Aidan O'Brien and his team to cut and polish the rough diamond before unleashing him on the world.

While many of Coolmore's champions enjoy a busy two-year-old campaign, *Galileo* had a very quiet introductory year at Ballydoyle. He settled into his routine without much fuss and began to show signs that he might just have the ability to go with his first-class pedigree and looks. Leopardstown Racecourse in south County Dublin was where he made his racecourse debut, in October 2000. Such a meeting rarely catches the headlines, although the top trainers in Ireland do use these types of meetings to start their more backward horses. It gives the trainers a chance to look under the bonnet with a view to the horse's

Galileo and Mick Kinane winning the 2001 Irish Derby. *Courtesy of Racing Post*

Classic season the following year. Despite facing two runners each from the leading stables of John Oxx and Jim Bolger, *Galileo* was sent off the even-money favourite to make a winning debut in the navy colours of Sue and John Magnier.

During the race, which was run on unsuitably soft ground, *Galileo* travelled with supreme class and when Michael Kinane, his regular rider, asked him to put the race to bed, *Galileo* pulled away from his rivals with contemptuous ease to win by fourteen lengths from *Taraza* and *American Gothic*. It was a performance that oozed class, and seasoned observers said *Galileo* was the kind of horse that could make the winter nights very short indeed.

Having wintered well and grown into his muscular frame, *Galileo* kicked off his three-year-old campaign in the Ballysax Stakes back at Leopardstown. The Ballysax has become one of the more traditional starting points for Coolmore's potential Derby horses, and in 2001 *Galileo* was sent off at the prohibitive odds of 1/3 to maintain his record. Again he travelled with unmistakable ease to win by three and a half lengths. Back in second was his stablemate *Milan*, who later won that year's English St Leger, and behind him was the Dermot Weld-trained *Vinnie Roe*, who made history by becoming the first horse to win a Classic race four years in a row when he landed consecutive runnings of the Irish St Leger from 2001 to 2004. The die was cast.

In May 2001 *Galileo* made his third trip to Leopardstown for his final prep before the Epsom Derby, when he lined up in the Derrinstown Stud Derby Trial. Ridden this time by Ballydoyle stalwart Seamus Heffernan, *Galileo* produced a more workmanlike performance than was expected, with Heffernan pushing him out to take the race from the John Oxx-trained *Exaltation* by one and a half lengths. Despite not impressing everyone with his performance, *Galileo* was cut to 5/1 by the majority of bookmakers and travelled to Epsom as the main hope to give Ireland back-to-back winners of the Classic following *Sinndar*'s win in 2000.

It is hard to comprehend now, but it had been nineteen long years since Coolmore had stood in that famous winner's enclosure at Epsom when *Golden Fleece* powered home under Pat Eddery. In 2001 it was the turn of *Galileo* and

Mick Kinane to seize their place in equine history. It wouldn't be a cakewalk for the pair, however. Sent off 11/4 joint favourite with *Galileo* was the Michael Stoute-trained *Golan*, who had been a clear-cut winner of the 2000 Guineas at Newmarket the previous month. There was also the Godolphin-trained, dual Group 1 winner *Tobougg*, who was looking to give his rider Frankie Dettori his first taste of Derby glory.

After the stalls shot open, *Galileo* was beautifully positioned as the field climbed through the punishing first half mile of Epsom's famous switchback course. Coming down and turning into the famous Tattenham Corner, *Galileo* was still travelling easily and was waiting for Kinane to send the signal to go and grab the race that he was destined to win. Two furlongs out Kinane and *Galileo* ranged alongside the early pacesetters, and then it happened, that moment when a good horse suddenly becomes a great horse.

Kinane asked *Galileo* to quicken and win the race. The colt lowered his head, stretched out his limbs and his Rolls Royce engine powered him forward clear of *Golan* to score by a comprehensive three and a half lengths. It was a performance of concrete excellence, copper-fastened by a change of speed that ensured *Galileo* joined the likes of *Sir Ivor*, *Nijinsky*, *The Minstrel* and *Golden Fleece* as one of the top-class horses trained in Ballydoyle in winning the most important Classic there is. It was also a performance that caught the eye of the Timeform organisation, the opinion of which is treated with reverence by many in horse racing. They gave *Galileo* a rating of 130 and placed his Derby win as the best they had seen in ten years.

Despite his breathtaking Derby performance, there was no chance for *Galileo* to rest on his laurels. The Irish Derby at the Curragh Racecourse was immediately nominated as his next target. Traditionally Irish Derby day is the most glamorous in the Irish racing calendar. People from all walks of life converge on the lush pastures of the Curragh in County Kildare, some to watch the action and others to be seen at the prestigious event.

The 2001 Irish Derby, then sponsored by Budweiser, saw *Galileo* sent off as the raging-hot 4/11 favourite to confirm his Epsom superiority over *Golan*. For *Galileo* supporters it was a race they could simply sit back and enjoy. Confidently ridden by Mick Kinane, who was, remarkably, looking for his first Irish Derby win at the seventeenth attempt, *Galileo* cruised through the race and recorded his second Group 1 victory in just three weeks, defeating the Italian Derby winner *Morshdi* by four lengths.

After he had taken on and defeated his fellow three-year-olds, the time had come for *Galileo* to step out of his own age bracket and take on the very best of the older generation. His first clash came in the King George VI and Queen Elizabeth Diamond Stakes at Ascot in July, a race widely regarded as the midsummer championship race of Europe. Lying in wait for *Galileo* was *Fantastic Light*, a brilliantly tough and classy older horse who was sure to give the Coolmore horse a tough test in his first race in open company.

It promised to be a race to savour. *Galileo* was the blue-blooded, dual Derby winner seemingly without any chinks in his armour. Owned by Coolmore's fiercest rivals, the Dubai stable of Godolphin, *Fantastic Light* was a seasoned globe-trotting superstar with a wicked turn of pace that had carried him to victories all around the world.

The race did not disappoint. It was run at a furious pace even by Group 1 standards, and both *Galileo* and *Fantastic Light* travelled exceptionally well as the field swung into the final straight. Unfortunately for supporters of *Fantastic Light*, *Galileo* and Mick Kinane (who was granted an injunction from the High Court in Ireland to ride in the race, after receiving a riding ban) nipped up the inside of the pacesetters, while Frankie Dettori and *Fantastic Light* were forced a couple of lengths wider than *Galileo*. The pair joined forces two furlongs out and battled headlong to the finishing post. A hundred yards from the line, the petrol gauge ran empty for *Fantastic Light* and *Galileo* pulled away to win. The performance drew gasps of admiration from the crowd. Both horses and their respective jockeys had given their all. Little did anyone know that, just six weeks later, we would be treated to another show-stopping duel.

The Irish Champion Stakes, run at Leopardstown in September, has become a season-defining race over the last twenty years. Run over 10 furlongs, it provides horses that have showcased their ability over the shorter 1 mile trip or the longer 1 mile 4 furlongs the chance to show that they have the perfect mix of speed and stamina, both qualities that breeders crave. The 2001 event was billed as *Galileo* v *Fantastic Light*: the rematch. *Galileo* may have defeated *Fantastic Light* in the King George, but there were plenty of people who questioned his ability to step back to 10 furlongs effectively.

As a spectacle, the 2001 Irish Champion Stakes didn't disappoint. In front of 17,000 spectators, on a sun-kissed afternoon at Leopardstown, *Galileo* and *Fantastic Light* thrilled the crowd with another power-packed duel. As was the case at Ascot, *Galileo*'s stablemate *Ice Dancer* set a blazing gallop, but rather than follow him, *Fantastic Light*'s pacesetter *Give The Slip* sat back and refused to chase the Coolmore hare. Two furlongs from home *Ice Dancer* came back to the pack. In what proved to be a race-winning move, *Give The Slip*, who had *Fantastic Light* on his tail, took up the running and moved off the rail, ensuring that *Fantastic Light* started his finishing effort first and expended less energy than *Galileo*. It was Ascot all over again, but this time in reverse. *Galileo* and *Fantastic Light* locked horns down the Leopardstown straight but, try as they might, Kinane and *Galileo* could not pass Frankie Dettori and *Fantastic Light*, who won by a neck.

In the immediate aftermath, Aidan O'Brien blamed himself for *Galileo*'s defeat. Speaking to reporters he said:

> They [Godolphin] read it brilliantly tactically, but we just didn't get our tactics right on the day. Our pacemaker *Ice Dancer* went off in front, but their pacemaker *Give The Slip* didn't follow him. He was content to go his own way and we sort of ended up with two races, and in *Galileo*'s race there wasn't the 100% 10-furlong gallop we'd hoped for. In his two Derbies and in the King George, *Galileo* was ridden far closer to the pace. Today we had him too far back.[1]

---

1   http://www.theguardian.com/sport/2001/sep/10/horseracing

While it was commendable of O'Brien to shoulder the blame for the defeat of *Galileo*, a few things were not right with his dual Derby champion. During the race, Mick Kinane felt that *Galileo* was not travelling with the same zest he had shown in the earlier part of his three-year-old campaign. It was suggested that a number of strongly run races on fast ground could have emptied *Galileo*, and it seemed that in the final furlong he was beginning to feel the strain of his earlier exertions.

The defeat marked the end of *Galileo's* unbeaten record. He attempted to gain a measure of revenge seven weeks later in the Breeders' Cup Classic in America, but he could never get to grips with the dirt surface and he trailed in a disappointing sixth. After that race it was announced that *Galileo* would retire to stud to stand alongside his sire, *Sadler's Wells*.

A number of awards flowed *Galileo's* way after his retirement was confirmed. He was crowned the European Champion Three-Year-Old and earned himself an overall Timeform rating of 134, which placed him at the very top of his generation.

When *Galileo* arrived to stud at Coolmore, expectations were understandably high. His racecourse performances were among some of the most captivating over the previous twenty years, and the hope was that he would be able to pass on some of his ability to his offspring. Despite his being a triple Group 1 winner, *Galileo's* fee for his first season at stud was set at a somewhat modest €32,500. Considering his achievements on the track, the fee allowed both the top-end breeders and the more modest ones to gain access to one of the best-bred sires in the stud book. Breeders took the hint, and soon a high-class book of mares was prepared for *Galileo's* first season in the covering barn.

While a choice book of mares may give a stallion an advantage in their first season at stud, it does not guarantee success. There have been countless stories of champion racehorses who have failed to become top-class stallions at stud, including the famous American racehorse *Cigar*, who was a little short on lead when he went to stud and could never reach the heights he did when he was a racing superstar.

Fortunately for Coolmore, *Galileo* had no such problems and he took to his new job with all the professionalism he had shown when he was in training at Ballydoyle. Foals were born and there was a buzz of expectation when *Galileo's* first yearlings came up for auction.

Top prices of €1,530,000, €1,050,000 and €635,000 were given for a number of yearlings by *Galileo*. The consensus was that his first-crop foals were extremely well put together and showed the same sort of temperament their father had shown. *Galileo* was doing something very important. He was 'stamping' his stock. This is something breeders, owners and trainers all like to see. *Galileo* was passing on his looks and his temperament to his yearlings. All that was needed now was for his first runners to have the same kind of ability. And it didn't take long for his first crop to demonstrate that they could really run.

For any stallion, siring a Group 1 winner in their first crop is considered a resounding success. In 2006 *Galileo* sired not just one Group 1 winner, but two. Even more impressive was the fact that these two Group 1 winners came in Classic races, traditionally the hardest races to win in a calendar year. *Nightime* got the ball rolling for *Galileo* when she powered clear of her rivals to win the Irish 1000 Guineas at the Curragh in the May of that year. That September the Jeremy Noseda-trained *Sixties Icon* landed the English St Leger at Doncaster. The race was a remarkable success for *Galileo*, because, along with the winner, he also sired the second and third home in the shape of *The Last Drop* and *Red Rocks* – the latter would go on to become a millionaire winner of the Breeders' Cup Turf in America.

The quality of *Galileo's* first crop was mirrored by a horse of outstanding ability in his second crop. When *Teofilo*, named after the Olympic boxer Teófilo Stevenson, landed a maiden at the Curragh on Irish Oaks day in 2006 for his trainer Jim Bolger, it began an undefeated juvenile campaign which saw him win the most prestigious two-year-old races in Ireland (the National Stakes) and England (the Dewhurst Stakes). His unbeaten five-race campaign saw him crowned the leading juvenile of his generation and showcased *Galileo's* ability to sire not just outstanding three-year-olds, but also fast, precocious and brilliantly talented two-year-olds.

By any standards, it was a remarkable start at stud, and it was only the beginning. In July 2007 a huge, imposing chestnut landed the same maiden that *Teofilo* had won twelve months previously. *New Approach*, remarkably, completed the same five-race unbeaten sequence as *Teofilo*. Unlike *Teofilo*, who was unable to race at three owing to a niggling injury that would end his racing career, *New Approach* carried on where he left off at two and gave *Galileo* his first winner of the Epsom Derby, when he held off *Tartan Bearer* to score for Bolger and jockey Kevin Manning.

It was only seven years previously that *Galileo* had stood in that same winner's enclosure. *New Approach*'s win elevated *Galileo* to a rarefied position. He became one of the few stallions in history to have sired the winner of the Epsom Derby having also won the race himself. *New Approach* helped *Galileo* become that season's champion sire in Great Britain and Ireland: it was the first time he had won this accolade. Coolmore's blueprint of breeding an outstanding racehorse, retiring him and then making him a champion sire had never been better demonstrated.

The same year that *Galileo* secured his first sires' championship, one of his foals developed into perhaps the greatest horse the world has ever seen. Born to the *Danehill* mare *Kind*, and bred by the globally successful Juddmonte Stud Farm, *Frankel* came into the world on 11 February 2008. Named after one of Juddmonte's most successful trainers, Bobby Frankel, who had passed away due to cancer, *Frankel* was sent to another legend of the turf in the shape of Sir Henry Cecil. The young *Frankel* displayed some signs of fiery temperament when he first entered Cecil's legendary Warren Place stables in Newmarket, but with careful management he began to show more than a hint of potential before he made his debut at Newmarket's July Course in August 2010.

Frankel went on to complete an unbeaten two-year-old campaign with wins in the Royal Lodge Stakes at Ascot and the Dewhurst Stakes at Newmarket, but it is what he did as a three-year-old that will live for ever. His performance in the 2011 QIPCO 2000 Guineas at Newmarket was jaw-dropping. *Frankel* led from the outset and proceeded to rip the hearts out of his rivals, running them ragged from start to finish and winning by six lengths. It was a truly sensational performance and one that many experts said would never be equalled.

Frankel continued to set racecourses alight, and when he retired in the autumn of 2012, he carried off an unbeaten fourteen-race record and was ranked by Timeform as the best racehorse that has ever run. With a rating of 147, *Frankel* was rated higher than some of the best horses that have ever graced the Turf, including the likes of *Sea Bird II* (foaled in 1962), *Brigadier Gerard* (foaled in 1968) and *Tudor Minstrel* (foaled in 1944).

As the quality of *Galileo's* offspring increased, so did the number of breeders wanting to send their mares to him. In the world of supply and demand, this was the dream scenario for Coolmore. After he had started off his stud career at a modest fee, *Galileo's* price began to take off just as quickly as his offspring were shooting away from their opposition. It wasn't long before Coolmore Stud listed *Galileo's* stud fee as private. There have only been a handful of stallions throughout the last hundred years that have been listed as private. *Galileo's* sire, *Sadler's Wells*, along with his grandsire, *Northern Dancer*, were among the select band of stallions whose fee was not published to the general public. While estimates suggest that *Galileo's* covering fee could be somewhere in the region of €300,000, the fact that it has remained private for a number of years now would suggest that if you have to enquire, *Galileo* may be out of your price range.

Teofilo, New Approach and *Frankel* may have put *Galileo's* name up in lights, but it is at Ballydoyle, Coolmore Stud's training centre, that *Galileo* has continued to excel. *Soldier Of Fortune*, a runaway winner of the Irish Derby in 2007, was one of the first headline horses by *Galileo* to enter the care of Aidan O'Brien and his team. The likes of *Cape Blanco*, a Group/Grade 1 winner in both Ireland and America, *Treasure Beach* and *Rip Van Winkle* continued to bag Group 1 wins for *Galileo* and Ballydoyle, but it wasn't until a golden chestnut horse, who debuted at the Curragh in the summer of 2013, that *Galileo*'s link with Ballydoyle became gold-plated.

Given the name of *Australia* by the Coolmore team, the *Galileo* colt out of the 2004 Epsom Oaks winner *Ouija Board* displayed a level of performance that was in keeping with his regal pedigree. Having demolished then Epsom Derby favourite *Free Eagle* in a Group 3 race at Leopardstown in his two-year-old career, *Australia* lined up for the 2014 Investec Derby at Epsom with destiny in front of him. Ridden with supreme confidence by Coolmore's stable jockey Joseph O'Brien, *Australia* powered clear of his rivals to become that rarest of rare horses: one who was sired by a Derby winner, born to an Oaks winner and won the Derby.

Victory for *Australia* at Epsom also provided *Galileo* with his second consecutive Derby winner following *Ruler Of The World*'s gutsy win in 2013 under Ryan Moore. *Australia* proved his class with an easy win in the Dubai Duty Free Irish Derby the same month, before treating his rivals with contempt in the Juddmonte International Stakes at York Racecourse in August 2014.

A heartbreakingly narrow loss to *The Grey Gatsby* in the QIPCO Irish Champion Stakes the following month would be the final act for *Australia* on the racecourse, as an injury sustained on the gallops at Ballydoyle brought his racing career to a premature end. The colt took up stallion duties alongside *Galileo* at Coolmore and it was no great surprise to see him line up beside his sire in Tipperary.

Australia's deeds on the racetrack in 2014 helped *Galileo* to his sixth sires' championship, following on from wins in 2008, 2010, 2011, 2012 and 2013, and while he has a fair way to go to match the number of championships that *Sadler's Wells* won, if any horse can do it, it's *Galileo*.

While his sons may garner the majority of headlines, it should not be forgotten that *Galileo* has also enjoyed tremendous success with his fillies who have raced. *Nightime*, who was *Galileo*'s first Classic winner, led the way, and she has been followed by the likes of *Lush Lashes*, who became the first horse

Ruler Of The World, ridden by Ryan Moore, sprinting away with the 2013 Epsom Derby.
Courtesy of Ian Headington

ever to win €1 million on her racecourse debut when she landed the 2007 Goffs Million at the Curragh. *Maybe, Found, Tapestry, Together Forever, Galikova, Misty For Me, Marvellous, Lily of the Valley, Golden Lilac, Was, Minding, Romantica, Great Heavens, Allegretto, Altano, Seventh Heaven* and *Igugu* have all won Group/ Grade 1s for their sire.

In 2014, with the likes of *Teofilo, Rip Van Winkle* and *New Approach* all siring Group 1 winners from their early racing crops, *Galileo* had begun to develop a reputation as a sire of sires, something that puts him right alongside his own sire *Sadler's Wells* in terms of influential stallions at stud. Writing in the *Thoroughbred Daily News* (TDN) at the beginning of 2014, noted US commentator Bill Oppenheim recorded that *Galileo* had claimed his:

… third consecutive title as the TDN Leading North American and European Sire. Having won that title in 2012 and 2013 with progeny earnings of $13.4 million and $14.3 million … *Galileo* set his own record this year, with progeny earnings over $18.6 million. These included thirty-eight black-type winners, sixty-six black-type horses, twenty-five Group winners, fifty Group horses, and eight Group 1 winners … In ten crops of racing age, *Galileo* has sired 151 black-type winners (average fifteen a crop), 264 black-type horses (twenty-six per crop), ninety-five Group stakes winners, 183 Group stakes horses (eighteen per crop), and forty-one Group 1 winners.

Such is the clamour for sons and daughters of *Galileo* that in 2013 Sheikh Joaan Al Thani, who races his horses under the Al Shaqab banner, paid a world-record price of 5 million gns for a sister to the 2012 Epsom Oaks winner *Was*. The filly, who was placed in the care of France's leading trainer André Fabre, was named *Al Naamah*, but she failed to live up to the promise of her price tag, finishing down the field in the 2015 Epsom Oaks.

The year 2015 saw *Galileo*'s latest star performer grace the racecourse. *Gleneagles* started the 2015 campaign as something of an underwhelming favourite for the first Classic of the season, the QIPCO 2000 Guineas at Newmarket in May. It wasn't that he was a bad horse – a Group 1 win in the National Stakes at the Curragh the previous September was testament to his ability. It was the fact that when he got to the front, he would pull himself up rather than extend away from his rivals. It meant that his winning distance would always be quite narrow and give the impression that *Gleneagles* was a good horse rather than a champion.

However, in the 2000 Guineas, with his new jockey, Ryan Moore, aboard, *Gleneagles* emerged from the pack to score a decisive victory and give *Galileo*'s offspring their second win of the famous race, following *Frankel* in 2011. Having completed the English/Irish Guineas double, with victory at the Curragh in the same month, *Gleneagles* headed to Royal Ascot in June and put up another imperious performance to land the St James's Palace Stakes and confirm himself as the one of the best mile horses *Galileo* has sired.

Gleneagles was *Galileo's* forty-sixth individual Group 1 winner, a remarkable achievement given the shortness of his stud career, and helped him win his seventh sires' championship. In analysing this career, it is amazing to see just how many top-class horses he has sired. Up to the end of 2015, *Galileo* had sired twenty-nine horses rated 120 or higher by Timeform. Given the fact that 120 is generally considered as the starting point for a good Group-level horse, the preponderance of horses in the category by one sire clearly demonstrates *Galileo's* impact since he retired to stud.

Highland Reel was another top-class horse sired by *Galileo*.
Courtesy of David Betts

Not only have his sons and daughters made a great contribution to the industry, but *Galileo* has also made a huge amount of money for his owners. If one assumes that his private fee is €300,000, and if he covers 200 mares a year, *Galileo* makes €60 million per covering season. And while he enjoys the very best of surroundings, it doesn't cost €60 million to keep *Galileo* fed and watered.

Now if we think that he could have another ten or twelve years siring champions, we are looking at one of the most valuable animals anywhere in the world, perhaps ever. In the same way that his namesake changed the way we think, the equine *Galileo* changed the landscape of racehorse breeding. Sometimes dreams do become reality.

The bronze statue of *Galileo* at Coolmore.
Courtesy of Coolmore Stud

Montjeu

He came, he dazzled and in the blink of an eye he was gone. For three magical seasons from 1998 to 2000, there was no horse in the world that stirred the emotions quite like *Montjeu*. Even saying his name now, sixteen years after his retirement and four years after his premature death in 2012, conjures up many wonderful memories and reminds us why the sport of horse racing is the passion we have chosen. While many horses hint at potential greatness, there can be no doubt that *Montjeu* had it. Be it his gorgeous turn of foot that he would unleash at the deep end of his races, or his ability, no matter what the speed of the race was, to simply cruise along as if he were out for a stroll on the streets of Paris on a cool autumn day, he was undoubtedly a champion. He did what he wanted, when he wanted to do it. And when he decided that the viewing public was worthy of seeing the fullness of his talents, *Montjeu* was a remarkable sight. One could argue that there hasn't been a middle-distance horse since the great *Nijinsky* to have the talent, confidence and swagger of *Montjeu*.

Unlike the vast majority of their horses, *Montjeu* wasn't born into the Coolmore family. Although he was sired by *Sadler's Wells*, *Montjeu* was out of the Prix de Lutèce winner *Floripedes*. The colt was bred in Ireland by Sir James Goldsmith, who named him after his château outside Autun in France. Unfortunately Goldsmith died in 1997, before the colt began racing, and his ownership was transferred to a holding company owned by Laure Boulay de la Meurthe, mother of two of Goldsmith's children. The colt was sent into training with John E. Hammond at Chantilly. Hammond was, by 1998, established as one of the finest trainers in Europe.

Having spent time learning at the bootstraps of the brilliant French trainer André Fabre, Hammond struck out on his own in 1988. He trained his first top-class racehorse soon after, when he guided the brilliant *Suave Dancer* to glory in the 1991 Prix de l'Arc de Triomphe. In a fantastic racing career, the colt also won the Prix Greffulhe, the Prix du Jockey Club and the Irish Champion Stakes, and finished second in the Irish Derby and the Prix Lupin. Hammond was the trainer of other top-class performers such as *Dear Doctor* (winner of the Arlington Million), *Dolphin Street* (Prix de la Forêt), *Sought Out* (Prix du Cadran), *Cherokee Rose*, who won both the Haydock Sprint Cup and the Prix Maurice de Gheest, and *Nuclear Debate*. One can only imagine what Hammond thought when *Montjeu* stepped off the box at his Chemin des Aigles stables in Chantilly in 1998.

For a horse of his size and scope, not a lot was expected of his two-year-old campaign. Under the watchful gaze of Hammond and his experienced staff, *Montjeu* began to show speckles of talent on the gallops, along with a lot of highly charged energy, which is known as 'temperament' in the horse-racing world. Having too much temperament has been the undoing of countless horses throughout the centuries, but having just the right amount can turn an ordinary horse into something exceptional. Finding that balance would be the key for *Montjeu*.

Having won two ordinary races in his two-year-old season, *Montjeu* was brought into the Coolmore fold after Demi O'Byrne, who purchased the vast majority of Coolmore's horses at the sales, saw the colt winging his way to victory in his second race, the Prix Isonomy, by three-quarters of a length from *Spadoun* at Chantilly. *Spadoun* enhanced the form soon after by running away with the Group 1 Critérium de Saint-Cloud.

Montjeu made his reappearance as a three-year-old in the silks of Michael Tabor, who, along with John Magnier, purchased a half share in the colt. The Group 2 Prix Greffulhe has become one of the traditional starting points for French horses with middle-distance Classic aspirations. Ridden by the American jockey Cash Asmussen, *Montjeu* won snugly by a length from the Aga Khan's *Sendawar*. It wasn't known at the time, but *Montjeu* had brushed aside a colt that would win three Group 1 races over a mile during the 1999 season.

Sendawar bagged the Poule d'Essai des Poulains (French 2000 Guineas), the St James's Palace Stakes at Royal Ascot and the Prix du Moulin de Longchamp, yet *Montjeu* had treated him with contempt. It was just a taste of things to come.

Having won his trial for the Prix du Jockey Club (French Derby) when landing the Prix Lupin at the scarily believable odds of 1/10, *Montjeu* arrived for his shot at Classic glory as the red-hot favourite to give his new owners a first victory in the French Derby. The imposing colt didn't disappoint. Having been held up at the back of the field by Asmussen, *Montjeu* seized control of the race at the top of the Chantilly straight and powered away from his rivals to seal victory in the manner of a colt right out of the top drawer. His victory over *Nowhere To Exit* and *Gracioso* had all the experts purring about what they had seen.

Three weeks later the Irish racing public got to feast their eyes on *Montjeu* for the first time as John Hammond sent the colt to contest the Budweiser Irish Derby at the Curragh. Ridden, once again, by Cash Asmussen, *Montjeu* travelled with ease, and when he was asked to break away from his rivals and win his race inside the final furlong, the response was immediate and he sprinted away from the high-class *Daliapour*. It was another deeply impressive display, and Asmussen claimed he had five kilos to spare over his rivals.

Having landed back-to-back Derbies, *Montjeu* was given a traditional French-style summer break, with the Prix de l'Arc de Triomphe at Longchamp in October his main end-of-season objective. He bagged the Prix Niel, widely considered the prime Arc trial for three-year-old French horses, in workmanlike style, winning by a head from *Bienamado* with new jockey Michael Kinane, who was Coolmore's retained jockey at the time.

Lying in wait for *Montjeu* in the Arc was crack Japanese horse *El Condor Pasa*, who was looking to become the first horse from the Land of the Rising Sun to win the most prestigious 1 mile 4 furlong Group 1 race in Europe. Trainer John Hammond takes up the story:

His final work prior to running in the Arc was on the famous Piste des Reservoirs (a straight mile) at Chantilly. He was due to work five furlongs on his own, and by coincidence, as we were waiting, one of his main rivals, *El Condor Pasa*, went by us very, very quickly. I have never seen a horse work more impressively. *Montjeu* then came smoothly by leaving nothing like the same impression. Hence, when in the race *El Condor Pasa* kicked well clear at the head of the straight with *Montjeu* boxed in ten lengths behind, I would, had I possessed them, have lowered my binoculars.

Even when he finally got clear, it still looked impossible. It was the one time he needed racing guts to match his brilliance and he put his head down (yes he occasionally did!) and in the truest sense of the expression gave all watching a real horse race. That they drew six lengths clear of the third, with the fourth another five lengths back, with a bunch of Group 1 winners yet further behind, shows what a truly fantastic contest it was.[1]

It was a performance of class coupled with an unquenchable desire not to be beaten. It looked for the entire world that *El Condor Pasa* could not be caught, yet when Kinane pulled *Montjeu* out and encouraged the horse to quicken up, the colt battled like a true champion. In the aftermath of their victory, Kinane referred to *Montjeu* as the 'best mile-and-a-half horse that I have ever sat on'.

Despite an unexpected defeat next time out, when he was favourite for the Japan Cup, *Montjeu* was kept in training as a four-year-old with the aim of securing back-to-back wins in the Prix de l'Arc de Triomphe, something that had not been achieved since *Alleged* in 1977 and 1978.

The Tattersalls Gold Cup at the Curragh was selected as the starting point for *Montjeu's* four-year-old campaign. If his owners were hoping for an easy reintroduction, they would be disappointed, as the likes of *Greek Dance* and *Mutafaweq* were ranged against him. In the race, however, *Montjeu* was simply in a different league from his rivals. In a performance that had to be seen to

---

1 http://www.johnhammondchantilly.com/news/montjeu/ (accessed 2015)

Montjeu, ridden by Cash Asmussen, wins the 1999 Budweiser Irish Derby
in breathtaking style. *Courtesy of Racing Post*

be believed, *Montjeu* and Mick Kinane simply sauntered past his four rivals,
seemingly expending little energy, to win from *Greek Dance*. A dazzlingly
impressive performance had scribes reaching for the dictionaries to find new
superlatives to describe what they had just seen. The star of the show returned
to Chantilly and continued to enhance his reputation with another breathtaking
display, this time in the Grand Prix de Saint-Cloud, where he was reunited with

old ally Cash Asmussen, as Mick Kinane was retained to ride at the Irish Derby meeting, which took place on the same day as the Grand Prix.

It didn't matter who rode *Montjeu* that day as he was, once again, head and shoulders above the opposition. Speaking after dismounting, Asmussen said to the waiting press, 'The last time I went so fast, I was landing in a Concorde at New York!'[2]

Asmussen was watching from the stands when *Montjeu* made his next race-course appearance in the fiftieth edition of the King George VI and Queen Elizabeth Diamond Stakes at Ascot in July 2000. Paired up again with his big-race jockey, Mick Kinane, who was struggling with a back injury, *Montjeu* was sent off the 1/3 favourite to make his first appearance on English soil a winning one. For the brave punters who took the long odds on *Montjeu*, there were a number of anxious moments before the race, when the colt would not be coaxed into the parade ring where the other six runners had already gathered. John Hammond, once again, takes up the story:

> All the other runners had gone in, and even with a lead he had produced his stubborn best at the opportune moment; ears pinned back and teeth bared, he was having nothing of it. He was being led around by Didier Foloppe, my marvellous head man and *Montjeu*'s daily rider, who was making a rare visit to the races. With an understanding look between us, I legged him up in his immaculate navy-blue suit, tie, and polished shoes, and he rode him into the paddock. If I have one regret about *Montjeu*'s career, it was that no one took a photo of this magic moment. It would have meant much more than any of the winning photo shots.
>
> The race itself was a direct contrast to the preliminaries. Never has it been won more easily.

And never has a truer statement been uttered. *Montjeu* was simply jaw-

---

2   http://www.racingpost.com/horses/horse_home.sd?horse_id=503034#topHorseTabs=horse_
    stories&bottomHorseTabs=horse_form

dropping in the 2000 King George. Despite having the likes of *Fantastic Light* and *Daliapour* ranged against him, *Montjeu* blew his six rivals away with a performance that had people comparing him to the equally brilliant *Nijinsky*, a horse that, like *Montjeu*, won this midsummer Group 1 contest without having to come out of first gear.

It looked to the entire world that *Montjeu* would go through the rest of his career undefeated. However, the King George proved to be his zenith. A proposed match race with the other great champion of the time, *Dubai Millennium*, failed to come to fruition, and *Montjeu* was pointed towards the first Sunday in October and the chance to defend his Prix de l'Arc de Triomphe title. Having scraped home in his trial race, the Prix Foy, *Montjeu* was a pale shadow of his former self, finishing a bitterly disappointing fourth to dual Derby winner *Sinndar*, who scooped the prize for Irish duo Johnny Murtagh and trainer John Oxx.

Montjeu was given the chance to end his career on a high note in the English Champion Stakes, which was run at Newmarket before its transfer to Ascot. Like *Nijinsky* in 1970, *Montjeu* blew out in the Champion Stakes, running another below-par race behind the Aga Khan-owned *Kalanisi*.

In a final attempt to give *Montjeu* the send-off that a colt of his talent deserved, his owners at Coolmore sent him to contest the 2000 Breeders' Cup Turf at Churchill Downs. However, the colt had nothing left to give and trailed in a disappointing seventh, once again behind his Champion Stakes conqueror *Kalanisi*.

Following those three defeats, *Montjeu* was retired to Coolmore Stud in 2000 with a rating of 137, which placed him in the highest echelons. When he retired, the perception was that his stock would need time to develop. If a buyer was looking for a champion two-year-old, perhaps they would be looking elsewhere. There was also the question of temperament. As he showed quite markedly in the King George at Ascot, *Montjeu* was very much his own man, and the worry among breeders at the time was how much of his temperament he would pass on to his offspring. It also didn't help *Montjeu* that sons of *Sadler's Wells* didn't have a very impressive record at stud at that time.

Whatever expectations Coolmore may have had for *Montjeu* and his first crop, it is safe to say he surpassed them all. Despite a slow start in 2004, his first crop blew into life in the second half of the flat season, with many beautifully bred colts and fillies winging their way home to win their respective maiden races and filling each set of owners with hope for the future.

Father and son, *Sadler's Wells* (right) and *Montjeu* (left), enjoy a quiet moment at Coolmore.
Courtesy of Coolmore Stud

One such horse was *Motivator*, who was trained by Michael Bell in New-market and owned by the Royal Ascot Racing Club, a veritable who's who of racing and non-racing folk. Foaled from the *Gone West* mare *Out West*, *Motivator* became his sire's first Group 1 winner when he scooted home in the 2004 edition of the Racing Post Trophy, the final Group 1 of the season run in England for juveniles and an excellent pointer to the following season's Classic races. It was a deeply impressive performance and gave the Royal Ascot Racing Club hope that they had a very serious horse on their hands.

Having wintered well and scored convincingly in his prep race for the Epsom Derby, *Motivator* was sent off the short-price favourite to land the blue-riband race of the English flat season. Ridden by Johnny Murtagh, who was chasing his third Derby success in five years, *Motivator* travelled like the best horse in the race and he accelerated away from his rivals to win by an impressive five lengths. Back in second place was the French raider *Walk in the Park*, who was also sired by *Montjeu*. By any standards, it was a phenomenal start to a stud career.

That day at Epsom proved to be *Motivator*'s brightest day in the sun. In his next time out, the 2005 Coral Eclipse, he was turned over at short odds by *Oratorio* and an inspired Kieren Fallon. The same pair exacted more pain on *Motivator* in their next clash, at Leopardstown in the Irish Champion Stakes, when they came with a withering late run to scoop the Group 1 prize.

Motivator's career ended with a respectable fifth place in the Prix de l'Arc de Triomphe before a planned trip to the Breeders' Cup was cut short when the colt picked up an injury on the gallops. He was retired to stud where he has gone on to sire the phenomenal mare *Treve*, who made history when she became the first horse since *Alleged* to win back-to-back runnings of the Arc in 2013 and 2014.

During the summer of 2005, when *Motivator* was running away with the Epsom Derby, two other sons of *Montjeu* were enhancing their sire's reputation with their own on-track displays. Since he had won two minor events as a juvenile, much was expected of *Hurricane Run* when the winter wraps were taken off by his trainer, André Fabre. Bred by German owners Gestüt Ammerland, *Hurricane Run* was the mirror image of his sire in looks and the way that he was built, possessing the same intelligent expression that his father had and carrying himself in the same way.

Not only did he have the same looks as his father, *Hurricane Run* also possessed a similar level of ability. Having enjoyed a luckless trip to the French Derby, *Hurricane Run* came to the Curragh for the Irish Derby looking for Classic revenge. After Coolmore had purchased a controlling stake in the colt, *Hurricane Run*, ridden by Kieren Fallon, who at that point was Coolmore's retained rider, mowed down the opposition to score victory, snugly, from yet another son of *Montjeu*, *Scorpion*, who would bag two Group 1s himself before the season's end, winning the Grand Prix de Paris in July and the English St Leger at Doncaster in September. *Scorpion* also landed the Coronation Cup at Epsom as a four-year-old.

Just like his sire, *Hurricane Run* ran in the Arc at the end of the season. Having won the Prix Niel, he emulated his father by winning the Prix de l'Arc de Triomphe in sensational style. They looked to be in trouble turning for home but *Hurricane Run* and Fallon enjoyed a dream run up the far-side rail, and with the colt displaying an electric turn of pace, they raced away to score from the high-class stayer *Westerner*, with the previous year's champion *Bago* back in third place. It was a victory that secured *Hurricane Run* horse-of-the-year honours. The colt was voted European Horse of the Year at the prestigious Cartier Awards and was the world's top-ranked horse for 2005 and the world's top-ranked long-distance horse according to the World Thoroughbred Racehorse Rankings.

Coolmore turned down the opportunity to retire *Hurricane Run* at the end of his brilliant three-year-old career and kept him in training with the hope of adding more lustre to an already glittering CV. His four-year-old campaign was eerily similar to *Montjeu*'s. He kicked off with a facile success in the Group 1 Tattersalls Gold Cup at the Curragh, before tenaciously landing the King George at Ascot, with Belgian jockey Christophe Soumillon in the plate. That victory at Ascot saw *Hurricane Run* become the first horse to win the King George/Arc double since *Montjeu*. Like father, like son.

As was the case with *Montjeu*, *Hurricane Run*'s career tailed off after Ascot. He ended his career with defeats in the Arc and the English Champion Stakes before being retired to Coolmore, where he sired the likes of Ormonde Stakes winner *Memphis Tennessee*, Prix Penelope winner *Don't Hurry Me*, Prix du Lys winner *Kreem* and Futurity Stakes winner *First Cornerstone*.

The extraordinary impact of *Montjeu*'s first crop (with a total of six Group 1 winners) had breeders flocking to Coolmore to breed their mares to *Montjeu*. He continued to make a deep impact on the racetrack with his offspring displaying the same high level of ability as their father. *Authorized* became his sire's second winner of the Epsom Derby when he gave his jockey Frankie Dettori his first win in the race at the fifteenth attempt, in 2007. The colt, trained by Peter Chapple-Hyam, emulated *Motivator* by winning the Racing Post Trophy at two, before going on to win the Epsom Classic. *Frozen Fire*, meanwhile, provided his sire with his first win in the Irish Derby in 2008 when he won one of the roughest editions of the race that has been run at the Curragh.

Another son, *Fame And Glory*, gave *Montjeu* back-to-back winners of the Irish Derby when he put in a truly dominant display at the Curragh in 2009. The colt had previously finished a close second to *Sea The Stars* at Epsom on his previous run. *Fame And Glory* proved to be one of *Montjeu*'s best and most versatile sons. Having had the speed to win a 1 mile 2 furlong Group 1 as a two-year-old, *Fame And Glory* had the class and the stamina to win the Ascot Gold Cup, run over 2 miles 4 furlongs, as a five-year-old. He retired to Coolmore's National Hunt wing (along with their flat stallions, Coolmore also stands a number of horses that will produce horses that run over hurdles and fences) as the winner of five Group 1 races.

While *Fame And Glory* enjoyed a long and successful career, two of *Montjeu*'s most gifted sons had their careers cut short before they had the chance to show off the depth of their talent. *Montmartre* was a brilliant winner of the Grand Prix de Paris in 2008 and looked sure to take a high rank among the best of horses of his generation. A winner of three of his five starts, *Montmartre* displayed a rare brand of exhilaration when running away with the Longchamp Group 1. It was a performance of such merit that he usurped his owner's other start horse, *Zarkava*, as the favourite for the Prix de l'Arc de Triomphe. However, due to a recurring injury, he would not make it to the Arc. At the time of his forced retirement, *Montmartre*'s trainer, Alain De Royer-Dupré, said of his charge, 'It is very sad, but we had no option. *Montmartre* was one of the exceptional horses to have passed through my hands.' *Zarkava* went on to win the Arc in comfortable style.

Like *Montmartre*, *Pour Moi* was another son of *Montjeu* cruelly denied the chance to fulfil his substantial potential. Described by his legendary trainer André Fabre as 'a great horse with great acceleration', *Pour Moi* arrived at Epsom for the 2011 Derby as something of an unknown quantity. The favourite for the race was the Queen's *Carlton House*, trained by Sir Michael Stoute, who was bidding to give the monarchy a famous Derby win. *Pour Moi* had impressed a number of onlookers with his win in his prep race, the Prix Greffulhe, at Saint-Cloud, but there were doubts that he or his inexperienced rider, Mickael Barzalona, could handle all that Derby day threw at them.

The doubters were soon silenced. In a ride of sheer audacity, Barzalona held *Pour Moi* up at the back as the field swung for home and bided his time until he unleashed *Pour Moi* with a perfectly timed run to get up in the shadows of the post from 25/1 outsider *Treasure Beach*, who was given a textbook ride by Colm O'Donoghue. Barzalona's enthusiasm very nearly got the better of him as he stood bolt upright in the stirrups before he and *Pour Moi* had crossed the finish line. It was an extraordinary moment that very nearly cost the young jockey the biggest win of his career.

Victory at Epsom confirmed *Pour Moi* as a horse of rare brilliance, but it would be the last time we would see him on a racecourse. The colt suffered an overreach in preparation for the Prix de l'Arc de Triomphe and was immediately retired to Coolmore, where he has gone on to make a promising start to his stud career.

Coolmore may have cursed its luck when *Pour Moi* was forced to retire, but it was soon gifted with one of the most versatile and brilliant horses that has come around in the last twenty years. Named *Camelot* by Sue Magnier, the *Montjeu* colt swept everything aside in a devastating five-race sequence that saw him narrowly fail to become the first colt to win the English Triple Crown (2000 Guineas, Derby, St Leger) since *Nijinsky* in 1970. Perhaps the fastest son of *Montjeu* ever, *Camelot* supplemented a win in the Racing Post Trophy at two with a gritty success in the 2000 Guineas at Newmarket to become the first offspring of *Montjeu* to win a Group 1 at 1 mile or less. He gave *Montjeu* an incredible fourth winner of the Epsom Derby with his regular jockey Joseph O'Brien aboard, before grinding out a win in atrocious conditions in the Irish Derby.

Camelot then failed by three-quarters of a length to win the Triple Crown when he couldn't catch the Godolphin-trained *Encke*. It was a heartbreaking defeat and one that remains a source of disappointment at Coolmore/Ballydoyle, particularly because *Encke* was one of the horses involved in the doping scandal that rocked the Godolphin operation in 2013.

Montjeu was not only the premier Derby sire in the world, he was also the sire of one of, if not the greatest, National Hunt horses to race in Ireland. *Hurricane Fly* was an institution. When time was called on his career in August 2015, *Hurricane Fly* had amassed an extraordinary list of wins, beating the record for most Grade 1 races won in a career. Trained by champion Irish trainer Willie Mullins and ridden primarily by champion Irish jump jockey Ruby Walsh, *Hurricane Fly* won twenty-two Grade 1 races in a remarkable racing career. The Irish Champion Hurdle (five times), Punchestown Champion Hurdle (four times), December Festival Hurdle (four times), Champion Hurdle (twice), Morgiana Hurdle (three times), Hatton's Grace Hurdle, Royal Bond Novice Hurdle, Future Champions Novice Hurdle and the Herald Champion Novice Hurdle all fell the way of *Hurricane Fly* in a career that will not be forgotten by those of us lucky enough to have seen him race.

Montjeu's sons may have garnered the majority of headlines during his stud career, but now his daughters are beginning to make an impact on the breed as broodmare sires. Classic winner *Legatissimo* provided *Montjeu* with his first Classic success as a broodmare sire when the David Wachman filly landed the 2015 QIPCO 1000 Guineas for Coolmore. She proved herself a filly of the highest class with further wins in the Nassau Stakes at Glorious Goodwood and the Coolmore Matron Stakes at Leopardstown on Irish Champions Weekend. The cross of a *Danehill*-line sire with a *Montjeu* mare is one that is most attractive to breeders and could become increasingly important as the years progress.

Unfortunately for breeders and racing fans alike we will never know just how good *Montjeu* would have been as a sire. In early 2012, just as *Camelot* was preparing for his tilt at the 2000 Guineas, *Montjeu* was put to sleep at Coolmore Stud. A short statement read:

Montjeu may no longer be with us but his legacy shall remain for decades.
Courtesy of Coolmore Stud

Montjeu, the highest-rated racehorse ever by the great *Sadler's Wells*, has died this morning at Coolmore Stud after a short illness, which was due to complications from an overwhelming septicaemia.

He was just sixteen. It was a shuddering blow for everyone connected with Coolmore and showed just how fickle the horse-racing industry can be. *Montjeu* was one of four pillars of Coolmore, along with *Sadler's Wells*, *Danehill* and *Galileo*. Only *Galileo* remains alive.

Even in death, *Montjeu* continues to live on in our hearts and minds. His brilliant son *St Nicholas Abbey* lit up racetracks from 2009 to 2013, until he met with a tragic end. The horse fractured a leg on the gallops at Ballydoyle and despite the best efforts of the vets' team and the will of the horse, he died due to complications from colic surgery after a seven-month battle to save his life. He was laid to rest beside his sire at Coolmore, where his legacy will live on, just like the memories he gave us all.

As for *Montjeu*, he was a once-in-a-generation phenomenon.

Becoming a Champion
the Coolmore Way

'Breed the best to the best and hope for the best' is one of the oldest maxims in the world of breeding champion horses. Yet given Coolmore Stud's penchant for breeding champion after champion for the last five decades, perhaps the phrase should now read 'Breed the best to the best and get the best.' The process of breeding a champion is as inexact a science as one could possibly think of. Take for instance the 2015 Epsom Derby, Coral Eclipse, Irish Champion Stakes and Prix de l'Arc de Triomphe winner *Golden Horn*. His owner, Sir Anthony Oppenheimer, has spent a lifetime breeding his own horses and it was only in 2015 that he bred a horse worthy to stand alongside the likes of *Nijinsky*, *Sea The Stars* and *Frankel* as one of the finest thoroughbreds to have graced a racecourse.

Yet while *Golden Horn* was a one-off for his owner, Coolmore, unlike the vast majority of other big stud farms, consistently produces champion racehorses year after year. In turn, the horses we see on the track today will retire to Coolmore's base in County Tipperary to produce the next wave of champion horses, and the virtuous circle will continue. When mating plans are being decided, Coolmore is looking into its crystal ball to see which matings will throw up its next Derby or Guineas winner. It's all about looking to the future and trying to find the next *Galileo*, *Montjeu* or *Australia*.

As foals are born, then weaned from their mothers and make the transition to yearlings and eventually two-year-old racehorses, the dream remains very much intact. It is only when they run that the dream is at risk of ending. For a Coolmore colt, there is an established race programme that Aidan O'Brien has used over the course of his training career to identify his best juveniles for the season ahead. Given the number of regally bred horses at his disposal, the job of sifting through his crop of youngsters begins at the turn of each year, with the horses being put through very light paces in the February or March of their two-year-old campaign.

Traditionally O'Brien and Coolmore will begin to run their prospective 2000 Guineas horses at the beginning to middle of the flat season, with their future Derby horses coming out in the second half of the season. Indeed the 2013 Epsom Derby winner, *Ruler Of The World*, didn't make his debut until the spring of his three-year-old season and only had two runs before winning the Derby. The 2015 season's champion two-year-old, *Air Force Blue*, made his debut on Irish Guineas weekend at the Curragh at the end of May. Every maiden race at the Curragh is noteworthy given its reputation as Ireland's premier flat-racing course, and *Air Force Blue* put in a striking display, leading from the front and winning with a degree of authority under Ryan Moore.

Once a horse has shed their maiden tag it is time to step them up in class, with Royal Ascot in the middle of June offering the perfect opportunity to see the level of ability a horse possesses. Coolmore traditionally targets the 7 furlong Group 2 Coventry Stakes, run on the opening day of Royal Ascot, as the platform to run in its most exciting two-year-olds. In 2015 *Air Force Blue* put in a commendable performance, finishing second to the Mark Johnston-trained *Buratino*.

It is not unusual for Coolmore to come up short in the Coventry, as it is a race that comes quite early in a juvenile's career and many colts do not have the necessary experience to handle Royal Ascot at that stage. Indeed *Rock Of Gibraltar*, who turned into a world-class champion, was defeated in the Coventry back in 2001.

Following on from Royal Ascot, the Curragh on Irish Derby weekend is a meeting that Coolmore likes to use to test the water with the more highly regarded two-year-olds. The Railway Stakes has become something of a 'Coolmore benefit' over the last twenty years, with Aidan O'Brien training the winner of the 6 furlong contest an incredible twelve times up to 2015, when *Painted Cliffs* won for the master trainer. O'Brien has sent the likes of *Rock Of*

Gibraltar, *George Washington*, *Mastercraftsman* and *Holy Roman Emperor* to win the Railway Stakes before going on to Group 1 glory.

It is after the Railway Stakes that O'Brien and Coolmore take the biggest leap with their two-year-olds and begin to run some of them in Group 1 races, taking the Phoenix Stakes at the Curragh in August as the starting point. As is the case with the Railway Stakes, during O'Brien's tenure at Ballydoyle, Coolmore has had an enviable record in the 6 furlong Group 1, winning it a mind-boggling fourteen times up to 2015, when *Air Force Blue* landed his first win at the highest level.

The Phoenix is the perfect test for a high-achieving colt or filly and comes at the ideal time of the season, as horses have had a number of chances to gain racecourse experience and show their ability. It also allows Royal Ascot form to be tested, and traditionally the Coventry Stakes winner will look to double up at the Curragh. Following on from the Phoenix Stakes, Coolmore traditionally rests its star two-year-old, particularly if it wins the Phoenix Stakes, until the National Stakes, run over 7 furlongs at the Curragh on Irish Champions Weekend. This race is usually where Coolmore runs its highest-achieving two-year-old colt. When he won the 2015 National Stakes, *Air Force Blue* was following in a long line of Coolmore champions who have captured the Group 1 prize. *George Washington*, *Hawk Wing*, *Gleneagles*, *One Cool Cat* and *Mastercraftsman* are just some of the colts to have won the race for the Coolmore team.

After the National Stakes O'Brien and Coolmore may decide to tackle the Dewhurst Stakes at Newmarket, which is traditionally the race that crowns that season's leading two-year-old. Coolmore hasn't enjoyed much success in the Dewhurst in recent times, but it made its way back into the winner's enclosure in 2015, when *Air Force Blue* confirmed himself as the outstanding juvenile of his generation with a breathtaking success, to give the new Coolmore syndicate of Magnier, Tabor and Smith its fourth success in the race.

Not only is the Dewhurst the leading two-year-old race in Britain, but it is also a pointer towards the following season's 2000 Guineas, which is run at the same track. *Rock Of Gibraltar* took the 2001 Dewhurst before landing the 2000 Guineas in 2002. The immortal *Frankel* did the same in 2010/11, with *Dawn Approach* emulating those two colts in 2012/13.

Air Force Blue, ridden by Ryan Moore, was a brilliant winner of the 2015 Dewhurst Stakes at Newmarket. *Courtesy of Martin Lynch*

For Coolmore's Derby horses, the journey to the top takes that little bit longer. Before his untimely death in 2012, *Montjeu* was Coolmore's go-to Derby sire. He had sired three previous winners of the race (*Motivator, Authorized* and *Pour Moi*) before *Camelot* gave him his fourth success in the 1 mile 4 furlong Classic.

171

Each summer, traditionally in the months of July and August, Aidan O'Brien takes the wraps off a huge number of regally bred colts whose pedigrees all scream 'Epsom Derby winner'. As we all know, there can only be one horse to be first past the post, so the majority of horses will never make it to Epsom. Yet hope springs eternal until each horse proves that they don't belong in the Epsom shake-up.

Both O'Brien and Coolmore dislike testing their potential Derby horses as two-year-olds, which is why they won't have many runs as a juvenile. *Galileo* only had one run at two, *Camelot* had two, *High Chaparral* and *Australia* had three, while *Ruler Of The World* didn't run as a two-year-old. Coolmore likes its Derby horses to be brought along slowly, reaching their full potential in the first week of June on the Epsom Downs.

Having won their maidens, O'Brien will normally give his two-year-olds one or two more runs before putting them away for the winter so they can grow both physically and mentally. The Group 2 Beresford Stakes, run over 1 mile at the Curragh, is just one of the races to which Aidan O'Brien will send his prospective Derby horses. The race, which was won in 2008 by the legendary *Sea The Stars*, has a solid record of producing horses capable of competing at Group 1 level. Coolmore has annexed the race on the last five occasions with *Battle Of Marengo*, *David Livingston*, *Geoffrey Chaucer*, *Ol' Man River* and *Port Douglas*. The ill-fated *St Nicholas Abbey* also took the race for Coolmore in 2009.

In more recent times, the Breeders' Cup Juvenile Turf Stakes (formerly the Golden Fleece Stakes) has become a platform on which O'Brien likes to test his better class of horse. Run at Leopardstown on Irish Champions Weekend, the Group 3 contest gives O'Brien the chance to run his less experienced colts on a Group 1 day when the pressure is that much more intense and the crowd that much bigger. The merit of the race rose in 2013, when *Australia*, who developed into a dual Derby winner, sprinted away from the highly regarded (and at the time Epsom Derby favourite) *Free Eagle*. It was a brilliant performance and one that cemented *Australia*'s place at the head of the Epsom betting market, a position he retained before winning at Epsom.

The Group 1 Racing Post Trophy run at Doncaster in late October is a race that Coolmore likes to target with an eye on Epsom and the Curragh the following season. In 2011 *Camelot* took the 1 mile contest in such devastating style that many people claimed they had witnessed a wonder horse right before their eyes. The *Montjeu* colt went on to fulfil his promise with a dominant performance the following June at Epsom. In 2001 O'Brien and Coolmore gave *High Chaparral* his Group 1 debut there and the son of *Sadler's Wells* didn't disappoint, grinding out the victory from his stablemate *Castel Gandolfo*. *High Chaparral* proved himself one of the best horses of this century, winning a further five Group 1 races in his career, including two Derby victories and back-to-back successes in the Breeders' Cup Turf.

During the early part of their three-year-old campaigns, Coolmore's objective for their Derby challengers is to sort the wheat from the chaff. Aidan O'Brien fields a huge number of runners in the classic Derby trials, but if there is a trend to follow, it is worth paying close attention to the colts he runs at Leopardstown and Chester. The Ballysax and Derrinstown Stud Derby Trial Stakes at Leopardstown are Coolmore's go-to races for their leading Derby hopes. Both *Galileo* and *High Chaparral* took this route before winning at Epsom, while *Yeats* won both events before injury scuppered his chances of running at Epsom. Both races offer horses the chance to gain some valuable experience of running left-handed and have proved an excellent source of high-class performers down the years.

Having runners at Chester is a fairly new development for Coolmore and primarily came about when Kieren Fallon came on board as their retained jockey in 2005. That season saw Aidan O'Brien bring a number of horses to Chester's May meeting to give them valuable experience that only that tight track can offer. It was at Chester in 2013 that *Ruler Of The World* announced himself as a major Derby contender when he landed the Group 3 Chester Vase under Ryan Moore, before the pair went on to Derby glory at Epsom.

Following on from Epsom, Coolmore likes to target the Irish version at the

Curragh with its Derby horses. All five Ballydoyle Derby winners have lined up for the Irish Derby, with four of them winning, *Ruler Of The World* being the odd one out. Once the two Derbies have been run, things get really interesting. With Coolmore's business plan to produce stallions, the pressure is on to secure more Group 1 honours. Speed is the keyword in the bloodstock world at the moment, and what breeders really crave is a horse who has shown both speed and stamina at Group 1 level during their racing career. That's why so many horses are dropped down in distance after running in the Derby.

Races like the Coral Eclipse, Juddmonte International, the Irish and English Champion Stakes over 10 furlongs and the Prix de l'Arc de Triomphe over 12 furlongs are the races that Coolmore likes to target with its 12-furlong horses. Not only are they prestigious races to win in their own right, but they also look great on a prospective stallion's CV. It's why *Australia* campaigned over 10 furlongs after his two big-race wins at Epsom and the Curragh. By landing the 2014 Juddmonte International in such breathtaking style, *Australia* proved that not only did he have the stamina associated with a top-class Derby winner but he also had bundles of speed. He was seen as the ideal stallion prospect. Yet defeat next time out in the Irish Champion Stakes damaged that reputation and knocked a sizeable chunk off his stallion fee, which was set at €50,000 at the start of 2015. Losing to *The Grey Gatsby* meant *Australia* had to really prove he excelled at 10 furlongs. However, he was never afforded the chance as he was retired soon after.

The faster Coolmore colts are targeted for the 2000 Guineas, with the Irish 2000 Guineas, St James's Palace Stakes at Royal Ascot and the Sussex Stakes at Glorious Goodwood also on their hit list. Along with running their speedier horses in the 1 mile Classic, Coolmore has, over the last number of years, chosen the 2000 Guineas as the starting point for some of its Derby challengers. In 2012 The Syndicate took a brave route and elected to run their main Derby colt, *Camelot*, in the 2000 Guineas. It was a big gamble given that *Camelot's* sire, *Montjeu*, had up to that point never sired a Group 1 winner at 1 mile.

Throw in the fact that *Camelot* had the physique and pedigree to thrive over 1 mile 4 furlongs, and many were openly questioning Coolmore's decision to run their star colt at Newmarket. However, Coolmore's decision was vindicated when *Camelot* won the 2000 Guineas from *French Fifteen* before going on to Epsom to give Coolmore and Aidan O'Brien their first Derby victory in ten years, storming home in front of the David Lanigan-trained *Main Sequence* and his Coolmore stablemate *Astrology*. The Coolmore operation also chose to run *Australia* in the 2014 edition of the 2000 Guineas and almost struck gold again, with the *Galileo* colt narrowly losing out to *Night Of Thunder* and subsequent miler of the year *Kingman*.

While the Coolmore colts have a defined pattern of races in which they will appear, the fillies who run in the Coolmore livery have a somewhat more scattered schedule. Unlike the colts, for which Group 1 wins are the key barometer of a chance at a successful stud career, for a filly or a mare two words matter: black type. These two words hold as much weight for a prospective broodmare as a Group 1 does for a future sire. Black type, which will appear in the pedigree of a horse, is earned when a filly is placed at Listed, Group 3, Group 2 or Group 1 races. To be placed in these races indicates that the horse has above-average ability.

Races like the Group 1 Moyglare Stud Stakes run at the Curragh on Irish Champions Weekend, the Fillies' Mile and the Cheveley Park Stakes (both Group 1s), along with the Prix Marcel Boussac on Arc day, are key juvenile contests for two-year-old fillies. The 1000 Guineas and Oaks (English, Irish and French), the Coronation Stakes at Royal Ascot, the Falmouth Stakes at Newmarket and the Matron Stakes at Leopardstown on Irish Champions Stakes day are just some of the prestigious Group 1 races open to the better class of fillies.

From a breeding perspective, however, if a Group 1 win is not attainable, the next best thing a filly can do on the racecourse is to earn herself some black type. It is one of the key components of the bloodstock industry. This is one of the reasons that fillies are campaigned with more vigour than colts. From Royal Ascot right through to the Breeders' Cup meeting at the end of October, fillies can easily notch up five, six and sometimes even seven runs before the start of their three-year-old campaigns. Two fillies that raced with such fearlessness are the 2012 QIPCO 1000 Guineas winner, *Homecoming Queen*, and 2015 Investec Oaks winner, *Qualify*.

A daughter of *Holy Roman Emperor*, *Homecoming Queen* was highly tried as a juvenile; in fact, it took her eight runs to shed her maiden tag. Having finished unplaced in her first start as a three-year-old, *Homecoming Queen* took the Leopardstown 1000 Guineas Trial before springing a 25/1 shock, leading from start to finish and running away with the 1000 Guineas at Newmarket by nine lengths, with Ryan Moore aboard. It was a startling performance and one that wasn't to be repeated, as *Homecoming Queen* finished unplaced in her final two starts, before being retired to Coolmore.

Similarly to *Homecoming Queen*, *Qualify* was kept busy during her first season of racing, running a total of seven times and winning twice. A daughter of *Fastnet Rock*, *Qualify* finished last on her first start of 2015, behind *Legatissimo*, in the 1000 Guineas at Newmarket. Having finished unplaced in the Irish equivalent, *Qualify* was sent off at 50/1 for the Investec Oaks at Epsom. She defied those odds by producing one of the shocks of the season, running down *Legatissimo* in the closing stages to win her first Group 1 thanks, in the main, to a masterful ride from her jockey, Colm O'Donoghue. She tried to repeat her heroics next time out in the Dubai Duty Free Irish Derby, but could not make the impact that was expected of her, finishing in sixth place behind the impressive winner, *Jack Hobbs*.

Of all the horses Coolmore has owned in the past two decades, *Gleneagles* is perhaps the most fitting example of how they have perfected the breeding of a champion racehorse and (they hope) a champion sire of the future. The now-retired colt was a champion racehorse at two and three years of age. His pedigree is 100 per cent Coolmore. He was sired by *Galileo*, who had another phenomenal year in 2015, thanks not only to *Gleneagles* but also to the likes of *Ballydoyle* and *Minding*, both of whom won Group 1 races as juveniles.

Not only did *Gleneagles* have a great father, but his dam also had blue blood coursing through her veins. *You'resothrilling* wasn't the greatest horse to have ever graced a racetrack (she won two out of her seven races) but her breeding assured her a place at stud, regardless of showing ability as a race mare. Her brother, *Giant's Causeway*, played a major role in re-establishing the Coolmore/Ballydoyle operation as a global force in world racing. In his two seasons on the track, 'The Iron Horse' won five Group 1 races in a row and came agonisingly close to landing Coolmore's first Breeders' Cup Classic when he went down by a tiny margin to the teak-tough American horse *Tiznow* at Churchill Downs in 2000. He has subsequently gone on to become a champion sire in North America.

Thanks to her illustrious pedigree, *You'resothrilling* was given every chance to succeed at stud, and what better way for that to happen than to mate her with *Galileo*? She certainly hit the ground running. Her first tryst with *Galileo* produced the high-class filly *Marvellous*, who lived up to her name when she produced a devastating turn of foot to win the 2014 Irish 1000 Guineas at the Curragh for the Coolmore Syndicate, trainer Aidan O'Brien and jockey Ryan Moore. It was a tremendous performance from the filly and gave *You'resothrilling* the perfect start to her new career as a broodmare.

The following month, in June 2014, *Gleneagles* appeared for the first time when he made his racecourse debut over 7 furlongs at Leopardstown. Much was expected from the colt, but inexperience got the better of him and he could only finish fourth behind the Ger Lyons-trained *Convergence*. He made no mistake next time out at the Curragh, winning smoothly under Joseph O'Brien. That win kick-started a hugely successful season for *Gleneagles* as he won the Tyros Stakes, Futurity Stakes and National Stakes in Ireland, before being disqualified (he moved across the track and bumped into the second-place horse) after crossing the line in first place in the Prix Jean-Luc Lagardère at Longchamp's Prix de l'Arc de Triomphe meeting in October.

With a new jockey, Ryan Moore, aboard, *Gleneagles* picked up where he had left off in the 2000 Guineas in May 2015, when he put in a deeply impressive performance to cement the new working relationship between Coolmore and Ryan Moore, who now had first call on all Coolmore horses. It was a performance that smacked of real class and it was no surprise to see Moore and *Gleneagles* double up in the Irish Guineas at the Curragh before the pair cruised to success in the St James's Palace Stakes at Royal Ascot in June.

Gleneagles and jockey Ryan Moore prior to winning the 2015 Irish 2000 Guineas.
Courtesy of David Betts

One would have expected *Gleneagles* to dominate the 1 mile division for the summer of 2015, but when the Group 1 prizes were being handed out, *Gleneagles* remained in his box at Ballydoyle. Aidan O'Brien, who described *Gleneagles* as 'the most important horse that we have worked with', was at pains to avoid soft ground with the horse. On four separate occasions *Gleneagles* was declared to run, only for O'Brien to deem conditions too soft for his champion miler.

With *Gleneagles* now at stud, Coolmore will be hoping he can follow in the hoofprints of his own sire and leave a lasting legacy. The pressure is now on the likes of *Gleneagles* and *Australia* to emulate *Galileo*, because for all the success *Galileo* has enjoyed at stud, there doesn't seem to be a natural successor to him at Coolmore. *Rip Van Winkle* has sired a Group 1 winner in the shape of Phoenix Stakes winner *Dick Whittington*, but he hasn't really developed as a top-class sire in the way Coolmore envisioned.

The need to find a suitable replacement for *Galileo*, even though he (hopefully) has many years left in him, is important to Coolmore. *Gleneagles* offers something different to other sons of *Galileo* at stud. While the likes of *Australia* and *New Approach* excelled over longer distances, *Gleneagles* was all about speed. A dual Guineas and St James's Palace Stakes winner at three, *Gleneagles* possessed a rare turn of speed both in his juvenile and Classic seasons. His maternal side also offers the hope that he will develop into a top-class stallion. One could see during his racing career the influence of *Giant's Causeway* coming through in *Gleneagles*. Although he looked very much like his sire, he raced with the toughness and tenacity associated with *Giant's Causeway*.

While the bloodstock industry is notoriously fickle (one just has to remember the lukewarm reception *Frankel's* first yearlings received in 2015), there is every reason to believe *Gleneagles* will be a success in his new career at stud. Although he raced at shorter distances during his racing career, it is likely *Gleneagles* will sire horses capable of running over a longer distance. The fact that he was successful and mature as a two-year-old is also something upon which breeders will look favourably. Perhaps the only concern they might have is the fact that he didn't run well on soft ground and that could be something breeders will hold against him, depending on how his first couple of crops do once they hit the racecourse.

The mating between *Galileo* and *You'resothrilling* that produced *Gleneagles* is exactly what Coolmore has been aiming for in the last number of years. By producing its own home-bred champions, it is digging into the DNA that has served it so well over the last fifty years rather than shelling out millions of euro, sterling or dollars on yearlings by its own stallions. Of course there will be times that Coolmore will have to splash the cash – that is the nature of the game – but one can see a swing towards Coolmore breeding its own champion colts and fillies.

Take the 2015 batch of juveniles housed in Ballydoyle. Of the 117 two-year-olds at Ballydoyle, sixty-five of them were home-bred, with many of the dams having represented Coolmore on the track. *Imagine*, who won the 2001 Oaks for Coolmore, *Rumplestiltskin*, herself a dual Group 1 winner in 2005, and *Moonstone*, who won the Irish Oaks for Coolmore/Ballydoyle, all had two-year-olds in training at Ballydoyle in 2015. The depth of talent Coolmore has at its disposal, from both its sires and broodmares, means the chances of Coolmore finding home-grown champions have increased dramatically.

Take for instance two of Coolmore's outstanding crop of two-year-old fillies from 2015, *Ballydoyle* and *Minding*. Both horses (sired by *Galileo*) displayed abundant talent on the racecourse in their first year of racing. *Ballydoyle* landed the Prix Marcel Boussac on Arc day with a commanding performance, sprinting clear of her rivals to emulate the likes of *Rumplestiltskin* and her full sister, *Misty For Me*, who also landed the Group 1 prize. *Minding* produced the best performance from a two-year-old filly in 2015 when she ripped apart a high-class field in the Group 1 Fillies' Mile at Newmarket in the middle of October. Having been ridden at the back of the field by Ryan Moore, *Minding* powered away from the rest of her adversaries to copper-fasten her place at stud with a deeply impressive performance. *Minding* also produced three top-class displays in 2016 when she won the 1000 Guineas, the Oaks and the Pretty Polly Stakes.

When these two fillies retire they will go to Coolmore as two of the most valuable broodmares on the entire property. Not only are they by *Galileo*, but they also boast brilliant race records. One could imagine them being bred to a sire in the mould of *Fastnet Rock*, who offers that *Danehill* toughness to complement the brilliance that *Galileo*'s stock has. It is those dreams that keep the romance of horse racing alive. Although it is great to see the likes of *Ballydoyle* and *Minding* strutting their stuff on the racetrack, one can't help but look towards the future and wonder what kind of talented offspring they will produce.

It's the Coolmore way. Always dreaming and always delivering.

Minding, ridden by Seamie Heffernan. She was the world's best two-year-old filly in 2015 and won the 2016 English 1000 Guineas in breathtaking style.
Courtesy of Peter Mooney

COOLMORE ACROSS THE WORLD

On a crisp autumnal day in November 2015, a horsebox flanked by a number of police cars pulled up to Coolmore's American base in Ashford, Kentucky. The resident stallion *Thunder Gulch* was in his paddock. However, he knew that something was happening. Nothing ever happened on this tract of land without *Thunder Gulch* noticing. When one has been in residence as long as *Thunder Gulch* has at Ashford Stud, having a feel for things about the place becomes second nature.

Thunder Gulch was right to be curious, because on his way to the stud was perhaps the most famous North American horse of our generation and without doubt the most dazzling stallion prospect that has ever retired to Coolmore's American arm.

But before we look to the future, it is important to look back, because Ashford Stud wasn't always in Coolmore's hands and it took the downfall of others for the property to fall into the hands of John Magnier and company. It was July 1981 and the star turn of the fledgling Coolmore/Ballydoyle axis at the time was a *Northern Dancer* colt called *Storm Bird*. Having displayed a high level of form the previous season when he won the Dewhurst Stakes before being crowned the leading two-year-old of Europe, *Storm Bird* was expected to sweep all before him in 1981. But there was a slight problem, as up until July the colt still hadn't made his seasonal debut.

All the major Classics had passed *Storm Bird* by, but for some reason Coolmore declined to say what was wrong with the horse, or indeed if there was anything wrong. Yes, the colt had suffered an attack at the hands of an ex-Ballydoyle employee during the winter months, who chopped at his mane and tail, but he was not hurt and to be still off the track as the season approached its high point was most unusual. It later turned out that the colt had a series of illnesses, which kept him off the track.

Ashford Stud, in Kentucky, is Coolmore's American base where champion sire *Giant's Causeway* resides. *Courtesy of Coolmore Stud*

It was at the Keeneland Sales of 1981 that the story took a twist. George Harris, a well-known bloodstock agent, asked the triumvirate of John Magnier, Robert Sangster and Vincent O'Brien what their valuation of *Storm Bird* was. An initial response of $15 million was put forward by the trio, but when discussion resumed, the group asked for $28 million for the colt (with a minimum price of $24 million). It was an extraordinary sum of money, but the bidders, Dr William Lockridge, owner of Ashford Stud, and Robert Hefner II, a successful businessman with interests in oil and gas, were unperturbed.

Soon a deal worth $21 million was agreed for *Storm Bird*, with the two gentlemen paying the sum in three instalments. However, soon after the first payment was made, one of Hefner's companies ran into financial difficulty due in large part to the collapse of the natural gas market. As Hefner was a partner in Ashford Stud, the stud farm was handed over to the Coolmore Syndicate in part payment for *Storm Bird*. The racing career of *Storm Bird* came to an ignominious end when he finished down the field in the Prix du Prince d'Orange at Longchamp in the September of 1981. He was retired to stud and began his stallion career at Coolmore's new American base. Luckily for his connections, *Storm Bird* enjoyed a hugely successful time at stud. During the course of his long career, he sired the likes of *Indian Skimmer*, *Prince of Birds*, *Bluebird* and the top-class filly *Balanchine*, who won the Irish Derby at the Curragh in 1994.

Yet despite all those noteworthy successes, the horse with which *Storm Bird* is most closely associated is his top-class son *Storm Cat*. *Storm Cat* developed into one of the most important stallions of this century, siring the likes of *Giant's Causeway*, who has become one of the flagship stallions for Coolmore in North America in the last fifteen years.

Ever since he was defeated in the 2000 Breeders' Cup Classic and retired to stud, *Giant's Causeway* has led the way for Coolmore in North America. His initial covering fee of $200,000 was quickly justified when his first crop produced the likes of *Shamardal*, who was champion two-year-old in Europe in 2004 and now is himself a world-class sire. *Maids Causeway* was another star performer, along with *Footstepsinthesand*, who landed the 2005 English 2000 Guineas for the Coolmore team.

Giant's Causeway has gone on to make a deep and meaningful impact in North America, siring top-class colts and fillies who can run on dirt, grass or synthetic surfaces over short or long distances. Horses such as *Aragorn*, *First Samurai*, *Eskendereya*, *Rite of Passage*, *My Typhoon*, *Heatseeker*, *Await The Dawn* and *Eishin Apollon* have represented the sire with distinction on both sides of the Atlantic. By the end of the 2015 season, *Giant's Causeway* had sired thirty-one Group 1 winners worldwide and his progeny have made over $123 million, earning him recognition as one of the most influential sires in the history of the thoroughbred.

While one may be forgiven for thinking Coolmore America is a one-stallion show, the rest of the stallion roster at Ashford Stud consists of top-class young stallions along with phenomenal stallion prospects. *Uncle Mo* is just the latest stallion sensation to make his mark at Ashford. A beautiful-looking son of *Indian Charlie*, *Uncle Mo* arrived at Coolmore America with a superlative record to match his Hollywood looks. He was a dominant winner of the 2010 Grade 1 Breeders' Cup Juvenile, a win that saw him confirmed as the champion two-year-old for that campaign, and while he didn't quite hit those lofty heights at three, he still bagged a comfortable Grade 2 success with a win in the Kelso Handicap.

Despite his relatively underwhelming efforts at three, *Uncle Mo* has made a spectacular start to his stud career. From his first crop he sired *Nyquist*, the winner of the 2015 Breeders' Cup Juvenile and Grade 1 Frontrunner Stakes

Giant's Causeway, a champion racehorse and champion sire, at home in Coolmore America. *Courtesy of Coolmore Stud*

and the 2016 Kentucky Derby, as well as the Grade 1 Alcibiades Stakes winner *Gomo*. The likes of Grade 3 Sanford Stakes winner *Uncle Vinny* and the Sunday Silence Stakes winner *Uncle Brennie* have also played their part in establishing *Uncle Mo* as one of the hottest young sires in North America.

It isn't just *Giant's Causeway* and *Uncle Mo* flying the Coolmore flag high in North America. Every stallion that has had runners on the 2016 Coolmore America stallion list has sired a Group/Grade 1 winner, and with the likes of *Declaration of War* and 2013 Breeders' Cup Turf hero *Magician* both now at stud, the future for Coolmore in North America looks to be in safe hands.

Going back to November 2015, the scene was all very dramatic, and the police cars and flashing lights might have seemed a bit much, but in this particular case the theatrics were very much justified because in the horsebox was the *beau idéal* thoroughbred of our generation. Here was a horse that not only chased the impossible dream but also captured it and in the process thrust himself into a spotlight that is rarely shone on the world of horse racing. It was the brightest light of all and, thanks to his exploits on the track, the sport of horse racing in North America was shown off in the most positive of lights.

As the horsebox pulled up to the beautifully appointed stud in the heart of the Bluegrass State, observers craned their necks to catch a glimpse of the potential superstar stallion who was commencing his stud career there. Many people were decked out in apparel that read 'Triple Crown winner'. Three simple words but ones that perhaps carry more weight than any others in the horse-racing lexicon. In order to be a Triple Crown winner, a horse must have enough brilliance to win the Kentucky Derby at Churchill Downs in May and the Preakness Stakes in Baltimore, Maryland, and enough stamina to see out the 1 mile 4 furlong test of the Belmont Stakes in New York. Three races in six weeks, and for the winner – immortality. If a horse can win the Triple Crown, it will join the likes of *War Admiral*, *Citation*, *Secretariat*, *Seattle Slew* and *Affirmed* as a bona fide legend of the turf in North America. In 2015 another horse joined that exclusive list.

American Pharoah wasn't so much a horse as a sleek racing machine. The son of *Pioneerof the Nile* was built like a bull but could move like a Rolls Royce. Despite losing on his racecourse debut, *American Pharoah* proved to be by far the best horse of his generation, winning two Grade 1 races as a juvenile, before embarking on a three-year-old season that secured his place in history. Having won his first two starts in devastating fashion, *American Pharoah* lined up for the

American Pharoah, the first horse in thirty-seven years to win the American Triple Crown, wins the 2015 Haskell Invitational Stakes in devastating fashion. *Courtesy of Mark Wyville*

Kentucky Derby as the short-priced favourite to give his Hall of Fame trainer Bob Baffert yet another Derby success. The colt made his owner sweat, however, and it took the strongest urgings from his jockey Victor Espinoza to drive him past the second-place horse *Firing Line* and into the position of 2015 Kentucky Derby winner.

While the Kentucky Derby may have been won by sheer force of will, the Preakness was a much more relaxed affair, with Espinoza and *American Pharoah* enjoying a smooth trip throughout the Grade 1 contest, winning by seven lengths without breaking a sweat. With two of the three legs of the Triple Crown secured, all roads pointed towards Belmont Park and the final, gruelling leg over 1 mile 4 furlongs, a distance rarely tackled by the leading dirt performers in America.

As anticipation reached fever pitch, *American Pharoah* entered the stalls at Belmont Park with the weight of history against him. He proved more than equal to the challenge. Breaking from stall 5, *American Pharoah* bounded out of the starting gates and never saw another rival as he galloped headlong into the history books by becoming the first horse in thirty-seven years to land the Triple Crown. It was a scintillating performance from a horse who was plucked from the heavens. His five and a half-length winning margin was the fourth largest ever for a Triple Crown winner in the Belmont and reflected the gulf in class between *American Pharoah* and his contemporaries.

A dominant win in the Grade 1 Haskell on his next start was a prelude to a shock defeat in the Travers Stakes at Saratoga, a track known as the graveyard of champions. That defeat led many people to believe that it was going to be the last time that *American Pharoah* would be seen on a racetrack. However, his connections were determined to send him to stud as a winner, with the Breeders' Cup Classic selected as the final race of his career. Ranged against him were a number of top-class horses, including the likes of *Frosted*, *Keen Ice* and the Coolmore-owned *Gleneagles*, who was looking to give both his owners and his trainer Aidan O'Brien their first taste of Breeders' Cup Classic success.

As soon as the stalls in Keeneland cracked open, the rest of the field were playing second fiddle to *American Pharoah* and Victor Espinoza as the pair produced a cold, efficient and remorseless performance to win by a comfortable six and a half lengths. It was a performance of sheer class and the perfect send-off for a colt who did more to restore the reputation of American racing than any other in recent memory. It was also the crowning glory for *American Pharoah*'s trainer, Bob Baffert, who bounced back from a life-threatening heart attack four years previously to reclaim his spot at the top of the American racing tree.

Following his win at the Breeders' Cup, *American Pharoah* was promptly retired to Coolmore's American base to stand alongside the likes of *Giant's Causeway, Uncle Mo, Scat Daddy* and another Kentucky Derby winner, *Fusaichi Pegasus*.

The Coolmore website explains how *American Pharoah* was settled into his new role at the stud:

> It is a quiet time in the stallion division at the moment, so *American Pharoah* will be given time to slowly settle into the routine of the other stallions at Ashford. Over the next few days, he will be taken for an early morning walk and grazed in hand. Before long he will be turned out to relax in his own paddock each morning. Our resident equine 'father figure' *Thunder Gulch* will play an important part in this process. Now 23 years old and pensioned from active stallion duty, the 1995 Kentucky Derby winner will act as a babysitter of sorts for *American Pharoah* and will keep him company in an adjacent paddock.
>
> Our stallion manager Richard Barry explains how *Thunder Gulch* will provide a good example for *American Pharoah* in his formative stages at Coolmore America: 'Young horses, when they get out, tend to run around a lot, and if they have company it just encourages them to run around. But if you put a 23-year-old boy beside them, he'll kind of look at him and go, "Son, you can run on your own." *American Pharoah* will probably spend an hour looking at *Thunder Gulch* eating grass, and try to get him to run, and he won't run anywhere, and then he'll figure out that he should eat some grass himself.'
>
> So far *American Pharoah* has shown a very sensible temperament and a keen interest in everything happening around him, so we expect him to settle

into his new routine very quickly. He will be turned out in his paddock first thing in the morning and brought back into his stable before lunch to be groomed. Afternoons will be spent relaxing in his stall and also parading for any breeders who come by the farm to inspect him. Once the day is done, he will be given his evening feed and bedded down for the night.[1]

A fee of $200,000 was set for *American Pharoah*'s first season at stud in 2016, and a stellar book of mares was assembled to give him the best possible start as a stallion. He may be the horse to lead Coolmore America into the future, but the future is equally bright at Coolmore's other international base in the Hunter Valley in Australia.

Having developed both the main office in County Tipperary and the Ashford base as centres of equine excellence, Coolmore has quietly grown its influence in Australia over the last two decades to become one of the major players in Australian bloodstock, with the legendary *Danehill* at the heart of its success. While many people see *Sadler's Wells* as the bedrock of Coolmore's

Coolmore Australia, in the Hunter Valley, is the place the likes of *Fastnet Rock* and *So You Think* call home. *Courtesy of Coolmore Stud*

---

1   http://coolmore.com/american-pharoah-settling-in-at-coolmore-america/

domination in Europe, *Danehill* flew the flag for the organisation in the southern hemisphere, where he is still regarded as something of an equine god. The son of *Danzig* proved a revelation at stud in Australia with his extraordinary ability to sire top-class horses over a range of distances and ground, something which marked him out as a stallion of the highest class.

Danehill was very much Coolmore Australia's founding father. Having begun his stud career at Arrowfield Stud, *Danehill* was the subject of a bidding war between John Magnier and John Messara of Arrowfield. Messara wanted *Danehill* to spend more time at his stud farm, while Magnier wanted the horse at Coolmore. Magnier won out and *Danehill* became a fully fledged Coolmore stallion.

With *Danehill*'s success in Australia, a gem of an idea was placed in Magnier's head, one that revolutionised the bloodstock industry worldwide. Traditionally stallions only covered mares for one breeding season. In the northern hemisphere stallions worked for the first half of the year, and in the southern hemisphere they serviced mares in the final half of the year. So for six to eight months stallions would simply relax in their paddocks and munch away at grass to their heart's content. Magnier saw the possibility of having stallions do a double shift and cover mares in both the northern and southern hemisphere, and with that the shuttle-stallion concept was born.

It turned out to be a stroke of genius. Not only were the stallions earning more income, but the chances of Coolmore breeding a potential champion to follow in the hoofprints of *Danehill* were dramatically increased. With *Danehill* leading the way, Coolmore began to shuttle a number of their high-class stallions to their Hunter Valley base after the northern-hemisphere breeding season had come to an end. The stallions then returned to County Tipperary in the January of the following year, having serviced another book of high-class mares and enjoyed having the sun on their backs.

Along with *Danehill*, the other stallion to do the most to promote Coolmore Australia in those formative years was *Encosta De Lago*. A son of Coolmore sire *Fairy King*, *Encosta De Lago* didn't set the racetrack alight but his deeds in the covering shed ensured that his name would rank alongside *Danehill*'s in terms of impact on Australian racehorses. The winner of three of his eight lifetime starts, *Encosta De Lago* proved a much better sire than he was a racehorse. Having started off his stud career at a modest $8,500, he developed into a high-class stallion, winning two Australian sires' championships and siring such household names as Hong Kong superstar *Sacred Kingdom*, brilliant mares *Alinghi* and *Princess Coup*, as well as *Sirmione*, *Racing to Win* and *Ultra Fantasy*.

Upon his retirement at the beginning of 2015, Coolmore's general manager in Australia, Michael Kirwan, said of *Encosta De Lago*:

> His stud career has been nothing short of phenomenal. His progeny have earned just short of $140 million in prize money around the world and to that end he is entitled to be regarded as the most successful Australian-bred sire of all time. He has been an incredibly versatile stallion, capable of siring top-class performers in all age groups, over any distance, in any jurisdiction, with the hallmarks of his progeny being their soundness and a great appetite for racing. While he was a classy racehorse in his own right, the manner in which he rose from relative obscurity as a sire has been something of a fairy-tale. His figures to date are astonishing and the success of *Northern Meteor* has served to demonstrate his prowess as a sire of sires, while his daughters have firmly established him as a wonderful broodmare sire.[2]

The shuttle-stallion concept proved to be a tremendous success, with the quality of racing horses in Australia rising immeasurably thanks, in large part, to the quality of stallions Coolmore was sending to its Hunter Valley base. One such stallion that has carried on *Danehill*'s legacy is *Fastnet Rock*. He became the hottest Coolmore sire in Australia thanks to the likes of *Atlantic Jewel*, who raced to Group 1 glory in Australia wearing the navy-blue silks of Mrs John Magnier.

---

2   http://coolmore.com/champion-sire-encosta-de-lago-retired/

Fastnet Rock, Coolmore's premier stallion in Australia, ridden by Glenn Boss,
winning the L'Oréal Plate. *Courtesy of Martin King*

Fastnet Rock is just one horse to have graduated from Coolmore Australia's successful 'raise and graze' programme, which has seen the farm develop over 370 stakes winners on their Hunter Valley property. Along with him, one of the best horses to have been 'raised and grazed' at Coolmore Australia is the hugely talented *Vancouver*, who set the world of Australian racing alight with his achievements in 2015, including a dominant performance in their championship two-year-old contest, the Group 1 Golden Slipper. Such was the manner of *Vancouver*'s victories that Coolmore and the China Horse Club stepped in to secure a controlling stake in the Sheikh Mohammed Bin Khalifa Al Maktoum-owned colt, valuing him at AU$40 million.

Speaking at the announcement of the purchase, Tom Magnier said to reporters:

> There was obviously a massive amount of interest in the horse, so we are de-lighted to have secured him. He's a brilliant colt and we and our partners, who include the China Horse Club, Ramsey Pastoral and Peters Investments, couldn't be more excited about his future.
>
> *Vancouver*, along with another of our recent investments, *Pride of Dubai*, serve to illustrate the long-term commitment of Coolmore to the Australian breeding industry. Both of these wonderful racehorses were foaled and raised at our Jerrys Plains property in the Hunter Valley and are a ringing endorsement that there is no finer source of quality bloodstock.[3]

Trained by the legendary Gai Waterhouse throughout his racing career, *Vancouver* retired to Coolmore Australia in the middle of 2016 and left a legacy of distinguished excellence on the racetrack.

Aside from *Danehill* and *Fastnet Rock, High Chaparral* also proved to be a high-class shuttler, siring the likes of *So You Think*, who is now resident at Coolmore Australia. The story of *So You Think* is one of the most interesting developments at Coolmore in the last ten to fifteen years and shows the global appetite that John Magnier and his associates have for horse racing. Having raced successfully in Australia for the legendary trainer Bart Cummings (sadly now deceased), *So You Think* was the subject of a staggering offer from Coolmore Stud, which was looking to purchase a controlling interest in the colt from his owner Dato' Tan Chin Nam.

As the winner of the two Cox Plates, Australian's premier weight-for-age race, *So You Think* was considered one of the finest equine talents in the region

---

3   http://www.racingpost.com/news/horse-racing/pride-of-dubai-australia-coolmore-buys-stake-in-20-million-vancouver/1848453/#newsArchiveTabs=last7DaysNews

for quite some time, and Cummings was understandably keen to hold on to his stable star. However, Tan Chin Nam saw the great opportunity that was available to *So You Think* and sold the majority stake in the horse to Coolmore.

The ten-time Group 1 winner *So You Think* at home in Coolmore Australia.
Courtesy of Coolmore Stud

Having raced the likes of *Haradasun* and *Starspangledbanner* (both Group 1 winners in Australia and Europe), Coolmore was keen to test *So You Think* in Europe, and the horse was transferred to Ballydoyle in the spring of 2011, where his racing career was entrusted to Aidan O'Brien. *So You Think* began his career in Europe in comfortable style, winning his first two races with tremendous ease and authority. His star faded a little, however, when he was outgunned in his first major European test, as he lined up for the Group 1 Prince of Wales's Stakes at Royal Ascot. Despite being sent off the red-hot favourite, *So You Think*, ridden by Ryan Moore, was outgunned by the Godolphin-owned *Rewilding*, who got up in the shadows of the winning post under an inspired ride from Frankie Dettori.

It was a tough loss to take, but Coolmore and *So You Think* continued to face all comers. The Coral Eclipse made its way back to Tipperary when *So You Think* got the better of the 2010 Epsom Derby and subsequent Prix de l'Arc de Triomphe winner *Workforce* in a cracking duel, with champion race mare *Snow Fairy* a distance back in third place. *So You Think* inflicted another defeat on *Snow Fairy* next time out in the Irish Champion Stakes at Leopardstown that September, before closing out his first European season with a surprise defeat to crack French horse *Cirrus Des Aigles* in the Champion Stakes at Ascot at the inaugural QIPCO British Champions Day.

Having won his second Tattersalls Gold Cup on his seasonal debut in 2012, *So You Think* made amends for his Royal Ascot failure twelve months previously when he took the Prince of Wales's Stakes in decisive fashion from *Carlton House* to win his tenth Group 1 success of a remarkable career. It was the first time *So You Think* had really shown the ability that made Coolmore fork out the amount of money they did to acquire him. The manner of the victory led many people to believe that Aidan O'Brien had finally worked out how to train the horse correctly. Indeed, O'Brien intimated as much in the post-race debrief with journalists, as he apologised to everyone for having trained *So You Think* so poorly up to his Ascot victory.

Unfortunately for the team at Coolmore/Ballydoyle and supporters of *So You Think*, Royal Ascot was the last time the horse was seen on a racecourse. The son of *High Chaparral* was withdrawn on the eve of his final start in the Coral Eclipse, having pulled muscles in training, and retired to Coolmore's Australian base as the winner of ten Group 1 races and with a prize money total of $8.9 million. The success of *So You Think* confirmed Coolmore's belief that it was possible to bring horses from the southern hemisphere and race them successfully in Europe. Not only did it enhance the reputation of *So You Think* as a horse of global calibre, but it also showcased the excellence of the Australian breeding industry, something that has continued in recent years with the likes of superstar mare *Black Caviar* travelling from Australia to win the 2012 Diamond Jubilee Stakes at Royal Ascot.

So You Think's exploits made him one of the most exciting stallions in recent years. From Coolmore's standpoint, the stud stood to gain handsomely from his deeds as a racehorse. Not only was there tremendous interest in the horse in Australia, but having seen his talent up close and personal, a huge number of northern-hemisphere breeders were keen to send their mares to *So You Think*. That interest meant the new sire had full books in both hemispheres and *So You Think* made a tremendous impact in Australia, with some of his first crop yearlings selling for AU$500,000, AU$430,000, AU$350,000, AU$325,000, AU$310,000 and AU$300,000. With his progeny in the hands of the very best Australian trainers, it looks a safe bet that *So You Think* will go on to have a successful career at stud.

The success that Coolmore enjoyed with *So You Think* encouraged the team to send a number of their horses to the southern hemisphere for a crack at their top prizes. Their boldness paid off in 2014, when the aptly named *Adelaide* won the Cox Plate in sensational style under a magnificent ride from Ryan Moore. Having drawn a wide stalls position, Moore was forced to chart a wide passage throughout the Group 1 contest. When the field swung into the short straight at Moonee Valley, it looked for all the world that Moore and *Adelaide* wouldn't get to the front in time. But Moore delivered his challenge with a sniper's precision to drop *Adelaide's* head right on the line, giving the Coolmore/Ballydoyle team their biggest success in Australia to date.

Winning any type of Grade 1 is hugely important to the Coolmore team, but for a European-based horse to fly to Australia and win one of their most prestigious races fresh off the plane was a huge feather in the Coolmore/Ballydoyle hat. It made *Adelaide*, who was a solid horse in Europe, into a terrific stallion prospect in Australia, and he retired to Coolmore's Hunter Valley base to stand alongside the likes of *Fastnet Rock* and *So You Think*.

The Coolmore team returned to Australia in 2015 with the American Grade 1 winner *Highland Reel*, who ran an excellent second in the Cox Plate, as well as *Bondi Beach* and *Kingfisher*, both of whom finished down the field in the Melbourne Cup, which is one of the few races in the world to have eluded Coolmore.

The Australian arm of the Coolmore operation is the pride and joy of Tom Magnier, and one can see the stud farm continuing to grow and develop over the next decade and beyond. Certainly Tom has made a tremendous impression in Australia and has built the Coolmore brand, stallions and broodmares, very successfully over the last ten to fifteen years.

Their purchases of *American Pharoah* and *Vancouver* show that Coolmore is continually looking towards the future. Perhaps the stallion, along with *Fastnet Rock*, that will lead Coolmore Australia into the future will be the outstanding *Pierro*. A gorgeous-looking son of *Lonhro*, *Pierro* had the talent to match his looks and, under the watchful eye of his trainer Gai Waterhouse, he developed into a brilliant two-year-old and one of the best Australian sprinters in recent memory. His performances in his juvenile career are what set *Pierro* apart. In a glorious five-race campaign, he went undefeated and unchallenged, and he became only the sixth colt in history to win the Australian Triple Crown of two-year-old races (the Champagne Stakes, the Sires Produce Stakes and the Golden Slipper Stakes). Those performances caught the attention of Coolmore, and a move was swiftly made to ensure that *Pierro*'s stud career would take place in the Hunter Valley. Michael Kirwan said:

> We've followed *Pierro*'s career very closely ever since he made his debut and we're thrilled that he is joining what is already an exceptional line-up of stallions here at Coolmore Australia. He was a truly brilliant two-year-old,

equally effective at all distances from 1000 to 1600 metres. No other horse since 1970 has managed to secure the two-year-old Triple Crown while remaining undefeated through his first season, and I understand that he's the only Triple Crown winner to go on to win two G[roup] 1 races at weight-for-age as a three-year-old.

A horse like *Pierro* is fundamental to the continued development of our operation in Australia and in both he and *So You Think*, Coolmore is now home to the two most desirable young stallions in the Southern Hemisphere that are free of *Danehill* blood.[4]

It is that final line that is the most arresting – 'Coolmore is now home to the two most desirable young stallions in the Southern Hemisphere.' If one line can sum up Coolmore's modus operandi, that would be it. The desire to be at the very top of the bloodstock industry is what drives Coolmore, and as the sun sets at Ashford Stud in Kentucky, in the Hunter Valley in Australia or in their head office in County Tipperary, that is the place they occupy – No. 1 – now and for the foreseeable future.

4   http://coolmore.com/champion-pierro-to-stand-at-coolmore-australia/

THE JOCKEYS OF COOLMORE

After all the careful years of planning and selection, all the hours of training and preparation, it's amazing to think that all the responsibility comes down to one person. For those fleeting few minutes on the racetrack, it is the decisions a jockey makes that can be the difference between first and second, between a lifetime at stud and a lifetime as an also-ran. Not much pressure, really.

As first jockey for the Magnier, Tabor and Smith syndicate, Ryan Moore is following in the footsteps of some of the biggest names in world racing. Men like Kieren Fallon, Johnny Murtagh, Joseph O'Brien, Michael Kinane, Jamie Spencer, Christy Roche, Pat Eddery and the legendary Lester Piggott were all first jockey to the Coolmore operation, and all had their own highs and lows during their time in County Tipperary.

Before 1975, the year the original syndicate of Robert Sangster, John Magnier and Vincent O'Brien came together, the jockey most associated with Ballydoyle's horses was Lester Piggott. Lester, or the 'Long Fellow' as he was known to all and sundry, was the greatest jockey of his generation. Born on 5 November 1935, Piggott enjoyed an immensely successful career, partnering with some of the most famous horses in history to achieve victory. *Sir Ivor* and *Nijinsky* were just two of those who benefited from Lester's expert handling.

What separated Piggott from his contemporaries was his will to win. There would be times in a closely fought finish that Piggott would get his mount up through his own force of will. Cast your mind back to finishes like *The Minstrel*'s Derby of 1977 or *Roberto*'s finishing effort in the same race in 1972. Would either horse have won that day without Piggott driving them home? I think not.

Piggott was the perfect fit for Coolmore when it began its quest to turn the finest racehorses in the world into the finest stallions on the planet. For the plan to succeed, it needed to win races, and in Lester Piggott it had a jockey with an assassin's eye for hitting the target and ice water running through his veins. Coolmore's first top-class horse came in the shape of *The Minstrel*, who was among the team's first purchases from the Keeneland Sales in America in 1975. Although closely related to *Nijinsky*, *The Minstrel* was the polar opposite to the Triple Crown winner, save for the fact that they both had outstanding ability. While *Nijinsky* was tall, imposing and would 'fill your eye' whenever he walked into a parade ring, *The Minstrel* was short, stocky and, with four white socks and a big white blaze running down his face, was the definition of a 'flashy chestnut'.

Vincent makes a point to Lester. One doubts if the jockey was listening intently.
Courtesy of Jacqueline O'Brien

His looks didn't prevent him from running and, with Piggott in the saddle, *The Minstrel* was a standout performer of the two-year-old crop in 1976. A win in the Dewhurst Stakes bookended a successful juvenile campaign. This meant much was expected of *The Minstrel* at the beginning of his three-year-old season, but defeats in both the English and Irish 2000 Guineas somewhat tarnished his aura. It was thanks to Lester Piggott that the colt was afforded the chance to re-establish his reputation when he was pointed towards the Epsom Derby of 1977.

Both his trainer, Vincent O'Brien, and his owner, Robert Sangster, were unconvinced that *The Minstrel* would stay the gruelling 1 mile 4 furlongs of the Derby. They also harboured concerns that the colt would become unbalanced on the famously tricky course. The one person who wasn't worried, however, was Piggott. In a pre-race discussion with the colt's trainer, Piggott said to O'Brien, 'If you run *The Minstrel* in the Derby, I'll ride him and he'll win.'

What happened next is the stuff of legend. Piggott was exceptional. Having positioned the colt off a searching early gallop, Piggott and *The Minstrel* hit the front two furlongs from home and fought off a grimly determined Willie Carson and his mount *Hot Grove*. It was a desperately close-run finish, but Piggott refused to be denied and pushed *The Minstrel* forward with everything he had. His famous rat-a-tat finishing drive would have earned him a long ban today but not back then, and the duo won the Derby to give Piggott and Vincent O'Brien their fifth win in the race. *The Minstrel* backed up this performance with wins at the Curragh (Irish Derby) and Ascot (King George) before retiring to stud where he was syndicated for $9 million.

Piggott was also in the saddle when another of The Syndicate's horses began to carve out his own spot in the annals of horse-racing history. A contemporary of *The Minstrel*, *Alleged* took his time to find his hoofs at Ballydoyle. Having been bought at a two-year-old breeze-up sale (where horses are galloped before being offered at auction), *Alleged* was brought along quietly by Vincent O'Brien while his more glamorous stablemates grabbed the headlines. It wasn't until the August of his three-year-old season that *Alleged* began to show his ability.

With Lester riding, *Alleged* destroyed a high-class field in the Great Voltigeur Stakes at York's Ebor Festival. The colt displayed a jaw-dropping turn of pace to win by eight lengths. It was a performance of such merit that Timeform said the victory 'changed the face of European racing for the year'. While Piggott had no need to extend himself on *Alleged* that day, their next race, the St Leger at Doncaster, saw Piggott make a tactical error. He pressed on far too early and failed to hold off the challenge of the Queen's runner, *Dunfermline*.

Piggott made amends next time out, in the Prix de l'Arc de Triomphe, with a dazzling ride, lying close to the pace before sending *Alleged* on to win by one and a half lengths from a top-class field including the likes of *Balmerino*, a New Zealand horse that was raced in England that season. *Alleged* stayed in training as a four-year-old and, despite a truncated campaign, became the first horse since *Ribot* to win back-to-back runnings of the Prix de l'Arc de Triomphe, a feat unmatched until the brilliant race mare *Treve* won two consecutive Arcs in 2013 and 2014.

Piggott's excellence in the saddle was crucial in the formative years of Coolmore Stud. Without his brilliance, there would have been no Derby victory for *The Minstrel*, the horse that gave The Syndicate their all-important first wins as a group and provided the solid financial footing that allowed them to expand their operation. However, for all his talent in the saddle, Piggott was a handful away from the racetrack. His frequent clashes with racing authorities, along with his desire to 'test drive' the horses at Ballydoyle, led to a parting of the ways with Coolmore/Ballydoyle in 1981.

With the hot seat left vacant, the powers that be sought out Pat Eddery as the man to take over from Piggott. Unlike Piggott, who could be of fiery disposition one minute and calm and collected the next, Eddery remained the same throughout his career. Always reliable, always dependable, he had a will to win, just like his predecessor. The confirmation of Pat Eddery as the No. 1 jockey at Coolmore/Ballydoyle coincided with the career of *Storm Bird*, one of the most talented and talked-about horses in the operation's history.

Bought for $1 million at the Keeneland Yearling Sales, *Storm Bird* was a brilliant two-year-old. He rounded off his first season with a deeply impressive win in the Dewhurst Stakes, where he put away the highly touted *To-Agori-Mou*. His second season was expected to bring even richer harvests. However, quite bizarrely, *Storm Bird* suffered an assault early in his three-year-old year when an ex-Ballydoyle employee snuck into his stable and hacked away at his mane, tail and forelock. Although the colt wasn't physically hurt, he missed his early season engagements, including the 2000 Guineas and the Derby. As the season progressed, *Storm Bird* remained noticeably absent from the high-summer races. Royal Ascot, the Irish Derby and the King George all passed him by. It wasn't until September that he made his seasonal bow in the Prix du Prince d'Orange. *Storm Bird* flopped and was syndicated to stand at Ashford Stud in America for an incredible $21 million.

While Eddery didn't get the chance to partner with *Storm Bird* as often as he would have liked, his tenure as Coolmore's retained rider proved to be wholly successful. One of the best horses that Eddery rode during his time in Tipperary was *Golden Fleece*. A big, imposing son of *Nijinsky*, *Golden Fleece* cost The Syndicate the tidy sum of $775,000 at the Keeneland Yearling Sales of 1980. It proved to be money very well spent.

Golden Fleece debuted at Leopardstown in September 1981 and won with such ease that his name was being spoken of in the same breath as Vincent O'Brien's previous champions. It wasn't known at the time but the horse that finished second to *Golden Fleece* that day would go on to land the following season's French and Irish Derbies. *Assert*, who was trained by David O'Brien (Vincent's son), was one of his trainer's first runners and provided O'Brien with Classic glory before he retired to France to pursue his interest in the wine industry.

With *Golden Fleece* in his corner, Eddery grew into the Coolmore job with each passing day. The pair brought another Epsom Derby back to Ballydoyle in 1982, with a performance of sheer excellence from both horse and rider. Having only the fourth run of his career, *Golden Fleece* displayed a scintillating change of pace to speed away from the future St Leger winner *Touching Wood*, with *Silver Hawk* third. His winning time of 2:34.27 was the fastest for almost fifty years. After the race Eddery called *Golden Fleece* 'the best horse I have ever sat on'.

Sadly for Eddery, he didn't get the chance to sit on *Golden Fleece* again. The colt picked up a virus after Epsom and also suffered swelling on his off hind leg. He was retired to Coolmore where he stood at £100,000 a covering. The story took one final, very sad, turn. In December 1983 *Golden Fleece* was struck down with cancer and, despite the best efforts of the world's leading surgeons, the colt was humanely destroyed in February 1984.

When one thinks of Pat Eddery's time at Coolmore, one can't help but drift back to the Epsom Derby of 1984 and his ride on *El Gran Senor*. That ride is one of the most talked about in the history of the sport. Did Eddery play his hand too late or did the horse simply run out of petrol? Cast your mind back. Two furlongs from home, Eddery is sitting motionless on the 2000 Guineas winner. His nearest rival, *Secreto*, is hard at work but seemingly not making any inroads into the favourite's lead. Then past the furlong pole and still Eddery waits, with a tight grip of *El Gran Senor*'s head. Surely it was only a matter of time before the pair sprinted clear and claimed Derby glory.

A hundred yards from the line, Eddery gave his horse a shake-up and asked *El Gran Senor* to go and win the race. However, there was very little response, and despite Eddery's urgings *Secreto* and Christy Roche mugged *El Gran Senor* and Eddery right on the line to win one of the most controversial Derbies in living memory. Debate rages to this day over whether or not it was jockey error, or if *El Gran Senor* ran out of stamina in the last 100 yards. Either way *El Gran Senor* and Eddery were defeated.

That Derby disappointment proved to be one of the few blots on that 1984 campaign. Eddery and *El Gran Senor* gained a measure of compensation for their defeat at Epsom when they landed the Irish Derby at the Curragh, while Eddery guided fellow three-year-old *Sadler's Wells* to success in the Coral Eclipse and Irish Champion Stakes. However, Eddery deserted *Sadler's Wells* to ride a better fancied stablemate, *Capture Him*, and lost out to the colt when George McGrath rode him to victory in the Irish 2000 Guineas at the Curragh. Eddery sadly passed away in 2015 and will be remembered fondly by all those who saw him compete.

After Pat Eddery left the Coolmore operation for the No. 1 jockey position with Prince Khalid Abdullah, Northern Irish jockey John Reid became No. 1 jockey to O'Brien's stable. Unlike Piggott and Eddery, who joined the operation at high points of its history, Reid joined at a point in time when Coolmore/Ballydoyle was in one of its rare troughs.

During the late 1980s Vincent O'Brien and John Magnier set up Classic Thoroughbreds PLC, with John Reid in charge of riding the horses to victory. However, Classic Thoroughbreds didn't turn out to be the huge success story everyone had hoped for. With Vincent O'Brien's powers on the wane and the bloodstock industry slipping into a deep recession, the class of horse Reid needed to win just wasn't there, although one horse did stand out. In 1990 *Royal Academy*, a striking-looking son of *Nijinsky*, won the July Cup with Reid on board. However, an injury meant the jockey missed out on the colt's greatest moment, when he won the Breeders' Cup Mile. Lester Piggott was in the saddle that day.

While the jockey position at Coolmore during Vincent O'Brien's time was one of quiet certainty, the same cannot be said since Aidan O'Brien took over the reins at Ballydoyle and became Coolmore's No. 1 trainer. In the twenty years that Aidan O'Brien has been at the helm, seven jockeys have taken up the most coveted seat in horse racing. Christy Roche was the first to work with O'Brien, and the pair enjoyed a good deal of success, winning the Irish 2000 Guineas and Derby with *Desert King*. It was, however, when Michael Kinane came on board that Coolmore had a jockey in the Lester Piggott mould, someone who stayed in Tipperary for a prolonged period and ensured that the good times came back to Coolmore/Ballydoyle.

Kinane signed on for the 1999 flat season and his association with Coolmore looked like a match made in heaven. He was regarded as one of the top jockeys in the world. Success both at home and internationally earned Kinane the reputation as the go-to jockey for big-race rides. His association with Dermot Weld had brought Kinane to the top of Coolmore's wish list, and they would get their man.

Kinane's innate ability to stay cool under pressure and make the correct tactical call in a race situation proved to be invaluable. He guided *Montjeu* to Arc glory in 1999, as well as steering the likes of *Giant's Causeway* to juvenile Group 1 success in the same year. 'The Iron Horse' and Kinane continued their wonderfully successful partnership in 2000. With Kinane doing the steering, *Giant's Causeway* landed five Group 1 races in succession. However, their final race together saw Kinane suffer one of his worst days as a jockey. The stage was the 2000 Breeders' Cup Classic at Churchill Downs.

Giant's Causeway was running on dirt for the first time, in the final race, the Breeders' Cup Classic. Having taken to the surface better than anyone could have expected, he swung off the final bend very much in contention. Kinane and his mount locked up with the American favourite *Tiznow* in the home straight and they settled down to fight it out all the way to the line. With each stride *Giant's Causeway* was inching past *Tiznow*, until 50 yards from the line when Kinane went to pull his whip through from his left hand into his right. The rein disappeared, and *Giant's Causeway*, who always needed to be kept up to his work, began to slow down. The mistake would prove fatal and the pair were beaten by a nose. The defeat gnawed away at both O'Brien and Kinane.

In the excellent documentary *Written in the Stars*, Kinane said of that defeat: 'It was disappointing. When it really mattered, things just went wrong. It was the first day, the following morning, that it was very hard to get out of bed. I felt that I had let myself down a bit on the highest stage. It was one of the most disappointing days in the saddle, for sure.'

That defeat in the Breeders' Cup proved to be one of the rare blemishes on Kinane's tenure at Coolmore. During his time there, the likes of *Galileo*, *Rock Of Gibraltar*, *Hawk Wing* and *High Chaparral* all benefited from Kinane's expert handling before they retired to stud to Coolmore.

Despite Kinane enjoying huge success during his four years as Coolmore's retained rider, by 2003 cracks were beginning to form in the jockey–trainer relationship. A row at Ballydoyle with Aidan O'Brien in the weeks leading up to the Breeders' Cup was the beginning of the end for one of the most successful partnerships in the modern era. Kinane's ride aboard *High Chaparral* in that year's Breeders' Cup Turf was the perfect way to cap a period in his career during which he rode fifty-seven Group 1 winners for Coolmore.

Following the departure of Kinane, Coolmore decided to opt for a fresh face as its retained rider for the 2004 season, in the shape of Jamie Spencer. It proved to be a disastrous move for both sides. Spencer is a jockey who rides on instinct and with fearlessness. In 2004 he was seen as the ideal replacement for Kinane. He was a jockey who had enough talent to soar as high as he wanted to, but as Coolmore's No. 1 jockey the pressure was too much and Spencer crumbled.

There were mitigating circumstances, however, in the quality of the horses he was riding, which weren't up to Coolmore's usual high standards. The main Classic hope for that season, *One Cool Cat*, bombed out spectacularly when hot favourite for the English 2000 Guineas, while *Antonius Pius*, a wonderfully gifted but quirky horse, threw away the Poule d'Essai des Poulains (French 2000 Guineas) when he collided with a running rail 75 metres from the finishing line. It was the story of Spencer's season. The tipping point for the young jockey came at that year's Breeders' Cup in Lone Star Park, when he had a meeting to forget. *Antonius Pius* once again snatched defeat from the jaws of victory in the Mile, while Spencer made a monumental tactical error in the Turf when he rushed up his mount *Powerscourt* to the lead fully half a mile from home. The colt couldn't sustain his effort and was passed by the eventual winner *Better Talk Now*.

Following his own winter of discontent, Spencer informed Coolmore that he would be resigning his position in early 2005. Speaking at the time about his decision, he said:

> When it came down to it, I had been thinking about it for a while and in the end it was personal and professional things. Peace of mind is a lot in life, no matter how much money you have. I rode well last season, but every jockey will say they can ride better, even if they won every race in a season. Any jockey who said they did not feel any pressure would be lying, but once the stalls open, it is just down to instinct and any pressure or nervousness ends there.[1]

---

1   http://www.rte.ie/sport/racing/irish/2005/0209/189888-spencerj/

Spencer's decision to walk away from his role meant that Coolmore would once again have to recruit a retained rider. It looked across the Irish Sea to perhaps the most controversial jockey of his generation, Kieren Fallon. The jockey, who had struck up a successful relationship with Sir Michael Stoute in England, was never far away from the headlines. He lost his job with Sir Henry Cecil a number of years previously when his name was linked to an extra-marital affair with Cecil's wife, allegations that were never proven. Yet for all his reputation as the bad boy of horse racing, Fallon had talent that overshadowed any problems he had off the track. He certainly hit the ground running for Coolmore, guiding *Footstepsinthesand* and *Virginia Waters* to Classic glory in the English 2000 and 1000 Guineas respectively.

Kieren Fallon enjoyed tremendous success with Coolmore/Ballydoyle before they went their separate ways in 2008.
Courtesy of Racing Post

It was just the start that Coolmore was looking for. Fallon continued to show his talent in the saddle throughout that summer. He teamed up with *Oratorio*, a boot-tough son of *Danehill* to win two Group 1s, defeating that year's Derby winner *Motivator* in the Coral Eclipse and the Irish Champion Stakes. He capped a fine season by winning three Group 1s on Arc day that October, when he guided *Horatio Nelson* to win the Prix Jean-Luc Lagardère and *Rumplestiltskin* to land the Prix Marcel Boussac, before giving *Hurricane Run* a nerveless ride to win the Prix de l'Arc de Triomphe. It was a day of days for Fallon in Paris.

The jockey continued to deliver success to Coolmore the following season.

George Washington, the previous season's champion two-year-old, won the English 2000 Guineas in the style of a true champion, while *Dylan Thomas* gave Fallon his second straight win in the Irish Derby with a performance of such dominance that Aidan O'Brien said he was right up there with the best horses he had trained.

However, for all the successes, dark clouds continued to follow Fallon. On 3 July 2006 he, along with seven other people, was charged with conspiring to defraud the Internet betting exchange Betfair. Fallon was immediately banned from race-riding in England but was allowed to ride in other racing jurisdictions, including Ireland and France. Coolmore stood by Fallon during his ban, and its faith was rewarded when Fallon guided *Dylan Thomas* to a famous win in the 2007 Arc. Two months later, in December 2007, the case involving Fallon collapsed.

It looked like he and Coolmore were set for a bright future together. But just twenty-four hours after clearing his name, Fallon was handed an eighteen-month, worldwide ban for a positive drugs test, his second in just two years. His link with Coolmore came to a swift end shortly afterwards.

Coolmore then appointed a jockey who had battled his own personal demons and was now riding at the top of his profession. A Derby win in 2000 on *Sinndar* had copper-fastened Johnny Murtagh's arrival onto the stage of top-class jockeys. However, Murtagh endured a number of fallow years, with his biggest challenge coming off the track in the shape of the dreaded drink. Having recovered from his addiction, Murtagh was primed to take full advantage when Coolmore came calling in 2008.

Just like his predecessor, Murtagh hit the ground running. In 2008 he rode twenty-one Group 1 winners for his employers, nineteen of which were supplied by Aidan O'Brien. Murtagh guided the likes of *Mastercraftsman*, *Rip Van Winkle*, *Duke Of Marmalade*, *Henrythenavigator*, *Fame And Glory* and the mighty *Yeats* to the biggest victories of their respective racing careers.

For two and a half years, the sky was crystal clear for Murtagh and Coolmore.

Then the storm clouds began to gather in the shape of Joseph O'Brien, who was beginning his own riding career. The oldest child of Aidan and Annemarie, Joseph began to pick up more and more rides as he chased the apprentice jockey's championship in Ireland, while Murtagh was riding the supposedly 'second string' Coolmore horses or not riding in some races at all.

Aidan O'Brien and Johnny Murtagh were immensely successful together before their partnership dissolved. *Courtesy of Caroline Norris*

While Murtagh did have first call on horses in Group 1 races, as the 2010 season rolled on it was clear that, from a day-to-day perspective, Murtagh was being edged out of the picture by the young O'Brien, who was making a very big impression in the early stages of his career. In the end, racecourse speculation regarding Murtagh's future with the Coolmore team proved to be accurate when Murtagh gave notice in November 2010. Speaking to the *Racing Post* in the immediate aftermath of his decision, Murtagh outlined his reasons:

It was just a stage of my life. It was three years and I had a hugely successful time. I was on a yearly contract and I was finished in November. I wasn't just enjoying it as much as I was. It was my decision, there was no pressure put on me. I just said it's time to move on. I had a good relationship with all the owners and Aidan and his family, but I thought it was time to move on before I did or said something I might regret.

With Murtagh exiting stage left, Joseph O'Brien was handed the role of lead jockey to Ballydoyle, but, crucially, not to Coolmore's other horses, as had been the tradition beforehand.[2] While many people questioned the wisdom of giving such an inexperienced jockey such responsibility, O'Brien proved more than up to the job. His dazzling performance on *St Nicholas Abbey* in the 2011 Breeders' Cup Turf was proof positive of his natural ability and coolness on the big stage.

O'Brien teamed up with his father to win his first Derby when *Camelot* bolted home in 2012. However, some might say he was at fault as he chose to guide *Camelot* through horses rather than steering an easier passage away from his rivals, when the colt was denied the Triple Crown that same season, finishing second to the Godolphin-trained *Encke*. While he added to his Derby haul in 2014, guiding *Australia* to victory, doubts remained about whether or not O'Brien was the right man for the job.

The ride he gave *Australia* in the 2014 QIPCO Irish Champion Stakes was one that must have left his employers seething. O'Brien positioned *Australia*, who was the raging-hot favourite, on the outside of the field during the 10 furlong contest, before swinging so wide off the final home turn that he was in danger of ending up in the car park. The young jockey got his mount balanced and headed for home but was mowed down in the shadows of the post by *The Grey Gatsby* and Ryan Moore, who was at his brilliant best on that occasion. It

---

2   The majority of horses owned by Coolmore are trained at Ballydoyle. However a number are trained by David Wachman, who is married to Kate Magnier, and a handful in England, France, America and Australia.

was a bitter defeat for the rider who knew the best horse in the race had finished second by the narrowest of margins.

Joseph O'Brien explains how the race panned out to his father, Aidan.
Courtesy of David Betts

O'Brien's tall frame meant that he was paring himself down to the bare bones for a lot of the season. While nobody could say it had an effect on his riding ability, it was of little surprise when Coolmore announced that Ryan Moore, by then established as the world's best jockey, would be the retained rider for the organisation for the 2015 season. Joseph O'Brien has now made the transition from top-class flat jockey to National Hunt trainer, and is fully expected to thrive in his new role. Indeed, he trained his first Cheltenham winner in 2016.

Coolmore's decision to employ Moore was fully vindicated when he guided *Gleneagles*, trained by Aidan O'Brien, and *Legatissimo*, trained by David Wachman, to glory in the QIPCO 2000 and 1000 Guineas respectively at the start of the 2015 season. Moore's no-nonsense attitude in the saddle reaped a rich harvest for Coolmore at Royal Ascot 2015, when he broke a post-war record of eight wins by riding nine winners, including seven for his main employers.

It looked to the entire world that Coolmore and Ryan Moore were set to dominate the big races of 2015, but a stalls accident involving Moore at Newmarket in July saw the jockey being forced onto the sidelines for the remainder of the summer. Moore's bad luck meant that Joseph O'Brien came back in for the rides on his father's string at Ballydoyle, while other jockeys were used for Coolmore's horses stabled outside Ballydoyle.

Ryan Moore, now established as the best jockey in the world, takes the plaudits after Derby glory aboard *Ruler Of The World* in 2013.
Courtesy of Sporting.life.com

O'Brien Jnr showed that he had retained all his ability in the saddle, by riding the likes of *Air Force Blue* to Group 1 glory in the Phoenix Stakes at the

Curragh in the summer of 2015. Yet doubts remained over whether he retained the full confidence of the Coolmore owners. Seamus Heffernan, a Ballydoyle stalwart, came in for a number of high-profile rides, with weight issues cited as the reason O'Brien Jnr wasn't in the saddle.

Moore made a tremendous comeback in the autumn of 2015 and showed why Coolmore was so keen to retain his services. Victories on *Air Force Blue* (Dewhurst Stakes) and *Minding* (Fillies' Mile) showed that the rider had lost none of his X-factor, and he capped off a fine end to the season when he guided the highly talented and boot-tough *Found* to success in the Breeders' Cup Turf, where she claimed the notable scalp of Epsom Derby hero *Golden Horn*. Moore

also steered *Highland Reel* to a memorable success in the Hong Kong Vase. In 2016 he guided *Minding* to Classic success in the 1000 Guineas at Newmarket and the Oaks at Epsom. And while he endured a tough Royal Ascot in 2016 (albeit he was still leading rider over the five days), there is no doubt that Moore will carry on the legacy started by Lester Piggott and shouldered by the likes of Pat Eddery, Michael Kinane, Kieren Fallon *et al*. The position as Coolmore's retained jockey is a high-pressure, but very rewarding one – now and into the future.

Joseph O'Brien on *Air Force Blue* at the Curragh 2015.
Courtesy of David Betts

THE PEOPLE OF COOLMORE

As with any global organisation, it is people who make the difference at Coolmore. On three continents Coolmore has assembled the finest of staff within the bloodstock business to give their clients the very best service in the world. It is a principle that Coolmore Stud works by. In the same way that *Galileo* followed his sire, *Sadler's Wells*, to Coolmore Stud, generations of families have also worked on the farm in County Tipperary, passing on their knowledge to the next generation and keeping that tradition of 'horse knowledge' in the stud.

Some of John Magnier's naysayers have described the Coolmore operation as the Coolmore Mafia, with Magnier the Don of an organisation where it is his way or the highway. They speak of this rich and powerful group that does what it likes when it likes. Unfortunately for the detractors, that couldn't be further from the truth. Yes, Magnier does keep a tight circle of trusted advisers around him, but his word is not the only one that carries weight. The likes of Demi O'Byrne and Paul Shanahan are often sighted at Magnier's side at yearling sales and their advice is taken extremely seriously.

Demi O'Byrne is one of the longest-serving members of the Coolmore operation and one of the few remaining links between the Vincent O'Brien era and the dominance of Aidan O'Brien that we see today. O'Byrne hails from a County Waterford family steeped in equine know-how. His father produced horses for the British Army at his Lodge Stud, together with an array of hunters, some of which he rode in the field. O'Byrne's older brother, John, still runs the family farm, while his younger brother, Roddy, runs McCarthy's, the popular bar frequented by horsemen in Lexington, Kentucky.

When he qualified as a vet in 1968, O'Byrne was already in the inner circle at Ballydoyle. The respect he had was such that Vincent O'Brien entrusted the young vet to take his champion two-year-old *Sir Ivor* to Pisa, Italy, for the winter ahead of that colt's triumph at Epsom the following year. He also travelled with the Triple Crown winner *Nijinsky* during that colt's overseas trips.

O'Byrne became the chief vet at Ballydoyle in 1972, looking after the likes of *Golden Fleece*, *El Gran Senor*, *The Minstrel* and *Roberto* in a distinguished career that ended in 1994, when Vincent O'Brien retired from training. Not one for resting on his laurels, O'Byrne switched from Ballydoyle to Coolmore and became an instant success in his new role purchasing bloodstock for the organisation. One of his earliest purchases turned out to be one of the most important. O'Byrne paid a little over $400,000 for *Thunder Gulch*, who later won the 1995 Kentucky Derby for Michael Tabor. O'Byrne was also responsible for spotting a lightly raced French two-year-old from the stable of Richard Hammond, which he recommended to Coolmore. The horse was *Montjeu*, who went on to be one of the most dazzling horses to grace the racetrack this century. *Montjeu* was also a phenomenal success at stud, siring four Epsom Derby winners, including two for the Coolmore team in the shape of *Pour Moi* and *Camelot*.

For years O'Byrne would be the bidder for Coolmore at the various yearling sales that take place in Europe and North America every year. It has been said that when he first laid eyes on *Camelot*, O'Byrne's breath was taken away. Not all of his hunches have been on the money, however. Under his bidding, Coolmore paid an eye-watering $16 million for a two-year-old colt in Florida. The horse, *The Green Monkey*, ran three times and only finished in the money on one occasion. He has subsequently gone on to be a disappointment at stud.

Along with Demi O'Byrne, Paul Shanahan is another person who has a high rank among John Magnier's trusted lieutenants. Shanahan is Magnier's eyes and ears at Coolmore and nothing happens without Shanahan noticing it. Although he was an extraordinarily well-known figure in the bloodstock world, the first time he came to the notice of the wider public was in 2007 when he informed Aidan O'Brien that Coolmore's star three-year-old *Holy Roman Emperor* would be retired instantly to replace the sub-fertile *George Washington* at stud. Shanahan was dispatched by Magnier to Ballydoyle to deliver the bad news. 'The lads and the boss [Magnier] had to try and replace him,' said Aidan O'Brien at the time. 'We were shell-shocked about it here because *Holy Roman Emperor* was our best horse. He was the horse we were looking forward to for the Guineas and the St James's Palace. Paul Shanahan was here at 11.30 a.m. and the box came and picked him up at 11.50 a.m.'

Paul Shanahan, one of John Magnier's most trusted advisers. *Courtesy of Tattersalls*

Shanahan worked his way up from the bottom rung of the ladder to the position he holds today – John Magnier's right-hand man. His strong work ethic, combined with his knowledge and a thirst for the business, saw him rise through the ranks to become one of the most valued minds in the Coolmore operation. Not only is Shanahan one of Magnier's most valued collaborators, he has also become a very successful breeder in his own right. He breeds horses under the appellation of Lynch Bages, after the noted vineyard in Pauillac, and Shanahan's efforts do justice to the name. Lynch Bages has bred the likes of Derby winner *Pour Moi* and his three-parts sister *Kissed*, whose promising racing career came to a sorry conclusion when she fractured sesamoids in the Prix de Diane (French Oaks) of 2012.

Shanahan is far from the only Coolmore employee to breed top-class horses. With Magnier's encouragement, Richard Henry, who fronts Coolmore's advertising and public relations, has bred the Group 1 winners *Quarter Moon*, *Yesterday* and 2015 Group 1 winner *Diamondsandrubies*, who ran in the Epsom Oaks before winning the Group 1 Pretty Polly Stakes at the Curragh. Director of Sales David O'Loughlin, in a partnership that included former Ballydoyle stable jockey Mick Kinane, bred 2007 Derby winner *Authorized*. All these horses were by Coolmore sires.

Along with the likes of Demi O'Byrne and Paul Shanahan, another crucial member of the Coolmore team is Christy Grassick, who is the general manager of the stud farm. Like the majority of Coolmore employees, Grassick started at the bottom and worked his way to the top through hard work. He too comes from a family steeped in horses. His father, also named Christy, was a successful jockey before turning his hand to training, at which he was also hugely successful. He trained the speedy *Godswalk*, winner of the 1976 Norfolk Stakes at Royal Ascot. At Coolmore Grassick Jnr moved from on-the-farm duties to front-of-house responsibilities, taking over from Bob Lanigan as manager of the stud farm. Whenever a horse retires to Coolmore, the event is traditionally marked with warm words from Grassick.

Family matters at Coolmore Stud, and while John Magnier may be the main man in this part of the world, his sons and daughters have taken on their own share of responsibility for the running of the operation and have done so with tremendous success. His eldest son, Tom, is the head of the Coolmore brand in Australia. A keen farmer as well as a noted judge on horseflesh, Tom Magnier has built up the Coolmore brand in Australia to such a degree that is it now widely considered the premier stallion complex in the Hunter Valley. Not surprisingly, horses were in Magnier's blood from a young age: 'Every spare moment we had, we were out schooling our horses. My mother is very keen on eventing. We talked horses at breakfast, lunch and dinner. I would not have been any good at anything else.'

During an interview for the Summerhill Stud website, Magnier was asked if he had a favourite race when he was growing up. Not surprisingly it is *Royal Academy*'s emotional win in the 1990 Breeders' Cup Mile that gets his blood flowing and his hair standing up on end:

Diamondsandrubies, ridden by Seamie Heffernan, winning the 2015 Pretty Polly Stakes at the Curragh. *Courtesy of Patrick McCann (Racing Post)*

My grandfather persuaded Lester [Piggott] to come out of retirement to ride the horse. Vincent sent Lester to The Curragh and said, 'See how you get on today,' and The Curragh got a record crowd. Vincent offered him four rides and he rode four winners, and I think that proved to Vincent he could do it, so off they went to the Breeders' Cup.

From a young age, it is the one race that sticks out [in] my head. If anybody ever asks me, 'What is a great race?' that's the first video I would put on to show them – I think Lester gave him the most unbelievable ride, while *Royal Academy* showed what a great racehorse he was and he beat a hell of a field.

The atmosphere at that time was unbelievable – there was a lot of excitement, the stallions [*Lomond, Caerleon, Sadler's Wells, Last Tycoon, Storm Bird, El Gran Senor* among them] were getting a lot of very good mares and the horses they were throwing were very good-looking, and then they went on and did the job on the racetrack.[1]

While Tom heads up the business in Australia, his brother MV is beginning to take a more influential role at the business' headquarters in County Tipperary. MV, named after his grandfather Michael Vincent O'Brien, is traditionally spotted at the major bloodstock sales throughout the world, selecting and purchasing the next generation of horses to run under the Coolmore banner. It is a high-pressure job, but one that MV handles with aplomb. Over the last number of years Coolmore has purchased dual Derby winners *Camelot* and *Australia*, Epsom Oaks winner *Was* and Irish 2000 Guineas winner *Power* from auction sales. That run of success doesn't happen by accident. MV is one of the leading faces for Coolmore at bloodstock sales. He acquired the first foal of the mighty *Frankel* to be offered at public auction and can be found criss-crossing the globe throughout the year, searching for Coolmore's next champion.

Another one of Magnier's sons, JP, carved out his own reputation as an amateur jockey. Despite being taller than the majority of his rivals, JP enjoyed

---

1   http://www.summerhill.co.za/blog/2013/6/12/tom-magnier-a-horseman-at-heart.html

Tom and MV Magnier, the future of Coolmore Stud. *Courtesy of Tattersalls*

notable success in the saddle, partnering *Rhinestone Cowboy*, who ran in the navy colours of Coolmore, to two Grade 1 victories at Aintree and Punchestown in 2004. JP is now fully involved in the financial side of the family business.

Kate, one of John Magnier's two daughters – the other being Sammy Jo – is also involved with the family business. Her husband is David Wachman, second only to Aidan O'Brien in terms of Coolmore trainers. Wachman has enjoyed huge success in his career to date, and if the time comes when Aidan O'Brien does decide to leave Ballydoyle, it is speculated that Wachman will fill that sizeable gap. From their base at Longfield Stables, David and Kate Wachman have built one of the finest training establishments in Ireland and have been rewarded for their efforts with a number of top-class horses, including *Again*, a champion at two and a Classic winner at three, the champion French and English two-year-old *Bushranger*, the cracking two-year-old *Damson* and the American Grade 1 winner *Luas Line*. Perhaps the best horse to pass through Longfield is the 2015 English 1000 Guineas, Nassau Stakes and Matron Stakes winner *Legatissimo*, who proved a wonderful advertisement for her trainer's ability.

The future is everything to Coolmore and in 2014 a new face was welcomed into the fold as a new partnership began to bloom. Teo Ah Khing may not be a familiar name to many, but if his early successes are any indication, we will be hearing a lot more about him. Fifty-four-year-old Teo is a Malaysian-Chinese billionaire entrepreneur and Harvard-trained architect whose exposure to the horse-racing game came when he met the ruler of Dubai and owner of the powerful Godolphin operation, Sheikh Mohammed. Ah Khing was commissioned to build the futuristic Meydan Racecourse, which was opened in 2010, for His Highness.

That meeting lit a fire deep within Ah Khing and he increased his interest in horse racing when he established the China Horse Club (CHC). In August 2014 he told the website Thoroughbred Racing Commentary:

> I have come into racing as a passion late in life. In Dubai, I had the opportunity to be adviser to His Highness Sheikh Mohammed for seven years. To build Meydan properly, to make sure it was going to be everything Sheikh Mohammed wanted, and what I wanted, I needed to know about the horse and all it requires. So Dubai was the first time I really started to pay attention to thoroughbreds. It was in Dubai as an adviser to HRH Sheikh Mohammed that I was exposed to elite racing for the first time …
>
> Watching *Australia* win the Derby at Epsom and then the Irish Derby at The Curragh was very special to me. To be able to share such experiences with my family and friends was very satisfying. All owners aspire to win races like this, but it is quite another thing to see it all unfold. *Australia* has been tremendously exciting from the start. Hopefully, the ride can go on a little while longer.

Legatissimo, ridden by Ryan Moore, wins the 2015 English 1000 Guineas for David Wachman. *Courtesy of Martin Lynch*

The CHC also has a special International Advisory Council (IAC) which brings together a who's who of international racing experts and business figureheads from other industries. The IAC includes, in no particular order: John Magnier; the Honourable John Warren (racing manager and bloodstock adviser to Queen Elizabeth II); Dr Andreas Jacobs (chairman of Jacobs Holdings AG and of Barry Callebaut, and vice-chairman of Adecco SA as well as former owner of Nestlé); New Zealander Sir Owen Glenn (founder of OTS Logistics Group and the Glenn Family Foundation); Dato' Tan Chin Nam (founder of IGB and co-founder of Goldis Corporation); and Dr Joseph Deiss (former president of Switzerland and of the United Nations General Assembly), who is chairman of the IAC.

Teo explained:

> What is significant about our partnership with Coolmore is the vision and foresight of John Magnier. John has again moved faster than his counterparts. He has seen the opportunity and promise that China offers and has invested in the region for the long run. We have created opportunities in China. Others have tried without success, but Coolmore has seen what we are doing and believed in us and in the steps we are taking. The CHC is a gateway for business into and out of China; and, as a business leader, Coolmore sees the value in this.
>
> Coolmore's involvement in a breeding venture with the CHC in China is a long-term one, and a breeding industry in this region could have global implications. The only commercial racing industries that exist without breeding industries are Hong Kong, Dubai and Singapore. Every other region is supported by a breeding industry – and China will be no different.
>
> The impact on the region in terms of economic benefits, job creation in new industries, the education of a new generation to make them skilled participants, the involvement of international organisations in the importing and exporting of thoroughbreds are [sic] immense. It won't happen overnight – but it is very real.[2]

---

2   https://www.thoroughbredracing.com/articles/meet-mystery-part-owner-coolmores-dual-derby-winner-australia

While *Australia*'s successes on the track put Ah Khing's name in lights, it is only the beginning for this hugely ambitious man. The CHC is the launch pad he will use to conquer the flat-racing world:

> I've had people within the international horse-racing circuit question the possibility of training a winning Chinese jockey. Those words reverberate in my mind. One is reminded of China when a jockey wearing CHC's silks wins a race, even though the rider may not be Chinese yet. Now, people respect CHC. But that's not enough. I want them to respect the Chinese.[3]

In its short history, the CHC boasts among its Group/Grade winners *Australia*, *Tropaios*, *Zululand*, *Jazz Song*, *Ming Zhi Cosmos* and the now-retired *Casquets*. It also shares a breeding partnership with Coolmore that includes winning Australian mare *Melito*, now in Ireland and in foal for the second time to *Galileo*, and *Muravka*, dam of the 2014 Coventry Stakes winner at Royal Ascot, *The Wow Signal*. Its ambitions are global, albeit radiating from its Beijing base, and not confined simply to the matter of ownership. Teo says:

> We already race thoroughbreds in China, Australia, Singapore, France, Ireland and the United States, and we have breeding interests in Australia as well as in Ireland. But we also have scholarship programmes that see Chinese students spend time in France and Ireland to learn world's best practice in training and breeding. Hopefully this can expand into Britain in the next 12 months, where several trainers have expressed interest in taking on Chinese students.

Significantly, his plans for China are not contingent on the highly problematic question of whether or not that huge country ever decides to legalise betting. They are oriented towards the thoroughbred – and the sport – and unlike some,

---

3   http://thepeakmagazine.com.sg/2015/04/teo-ah-khing-plans-to-run-the-world-on-horseback-2/

Teo does not see betting as a precondition for the resurgence of racing in the world's most populous country.

Besides the CHC's plans for increasing the exposure of China's masses to the joys of racing, Teo offers an intriguing possibility:

> Why couldn't a world-class thoroughbred race be held in China and include participants from around the globe? China has an audience, the world's largest audience ... Motor racing, tennis, golf and football have all brought stars to China to help to grow their sports, and racing should be open to all possibilities, too. China can provide an opportunity for clubs, companies, and industries that want to spread their brand and create awareness.[4]

Teo's impact on the racing and breeding world has already been felt, and in 2015 his Desert Star Phoenix breeding operation bred the Group 1 winner *Johannes Vermeer*, who won the Critérium International at Saint-Cloud.

Another breeder who has achieved many victories with the Coolmore operation is Joseph Allen. Born in the Bronx in 1941, Allen has enjoyed more than twenty-five years of success in horse racing, and over the last number of years he has developed a close relationship with Coolmore Stud thanks, in large part, to the exploits of his stallion *War Front*, who has become one of the leading sires in the world. Coolmore has sought to have a close relationship with *War Front*, who stands at Claiborne Farm, Kentucky. Two of his progeny have raced successfully for Coolmore and now both are at stud for Messrs Magnier, Tabor and Smith. *Declaration of War* won the 2013 Queen Anne Stakes at Royal Ascot and the Juddmonte International Stakes at York before narrowly failing to win the Breeders' Cup Classic on his first start on dirt, going down by a length to *Mucho Macho Man* and *Will Take Charge*.

While he didn't have the longevity of *Declaration of War*, *War Command*

---

4   https://www.thoroughbredracing.com/articles/meet-mystery-part-owner-coolmores-dual-derby-winner-australia

flew the flag for Joseph Allen quite successfully. A much scopier horse than *Declaration of War, War Command* burst onto the scene with a devastating six-length win in the 2013 Coventry Stakes at Royal Ascot. It was a dominant performance, and *War Command* sprinted clear of his rivals to win from *Parbold*, with *War Command*'s stablemate *Sir John Hawkins* finishing three-quarters of a length behind *Parbold* in third place. Despite bombing out in the Group 1 Phoenix Stakes at the Curragh on his next start, *War Command* rounded off his juvenile career with two wins, in the Group 2 Galileo Futurity Stakes at the Curragh and the Group 1 Dewhurst Stakes at Newmarket.

Unfortunately for Joseph Allen and Coolmore, *War Command* wouldn't build on his exploits at two when his three-year-old career resumed. He finished down the field in the QIPCO 2000 Guineas won by *Night Of Thunder*, before finishing out of the money in the St James's Palace Stakes at Royal Ascot and the Coral Eclipse Stakes at Sandown Park. After this he was retired to Coolmore Stud.

Coolmore's belief in the *War Front* sire line was further enhanced when *Air Force Blue* landed the 2015 Phoenix Stakes at the Curragh to give Aidan O'Brien a remarkable fourteenth win in the 6 furlong Group 1 contest, before going on to prove himself the outstanding juvenile of his generation, with dominant victories in the National Stakes at the Curragh and the Dewhurst Stakes (both Group 1 races) at Newmarket. The success that Coolmore have enjoyed with the *War Front* bloodline adds a new dimension to their operation, one that will no doubt provide many more exciting horses to race in the Coolmore livery.

MOMENTS IN TIME

There are some moments that can never be forgotten. When those special events take place, you know life rarely gets better. Throughout the course of the last fifty years Coolmore Stud and, in turn, the wider racing public have enjoyed some of those moments that cause adrenaline to pump through your body, lifting you to places of which you dared not dream through their horses.

Sport is wonderful because there is such a depth of history. With the technology available nowadays, reliving a moment is merely a click away. One can watch the brilliant Brazilian soccer team of the 1970s or one of the classic 1980s tennis matches between Björn Borg and John McEnroe and see why they have stood the test of time. Equally, although I wasn't born when the likes of *Nijinsky*, *The Minstrel* and *Golden Fleece* were strutting their stuff, over the years I have watched their races so many times that they are imprinted in my mind.

Over the last twenty years, after John Magnier took the decision to appoint Aidan O'Brien as his trainer at Ballydoyle and get Coolmore Stud back on the road, there have been many wonderful moments that will be looked back upon by future generations as the standard-setting races of our time. Perhaps the one that tugs most on the heartstrings is a 2 mile 4 furlong Group 1 race that took place at Royal Ascot in June 2009. The race was the Gold Cup, the highlight of the five-day extravaganza which brings horses from across the globe to compete in some of the most prestigious Group 1 races anywhere in the world. The horse in question was *Yeats*, a huge, strapping son of *Sadler's Wells*, who was attempting to achieve the impossible by becoming the first horse to win the Ascot Gold Cup four times in succession.

Yet if things had worked out differently, *Yeats* would not have been at Ascot on that beautiful summer's day. Instead he would have been enjoying his summer break at Coolmore Stud having had his third season as a stallion. For when the mating plans were made for *Yeats*, nobody predicted that he would win one Ascot Gold Cup, let alone four on the spin.

Derbies were the order of the day when *Sadler's Wells* was mated with the Top Ville mare *Lyndonville*. The colt, who was foaled in 2001, was named after the Irish artist Jack B. Yeats, brother of the famed writer W. B. Yeats, and was co-owned by John Magnier and his long-time friend David Nagle. *Yeats* was sent to Ballydoyle with the dream that he would stand in the hallowed winner's enclosure at Epsom in 2004 having secured yet another Derby for his sire and his Coolmore owners.

Things began brightly for *Yeats*, when he won his only start as a two-year-old, landing a 1 mile maiden race at the Curragh by four lengths. He was then sent into winter quarters with the aim of bringing him back in a Derby trial the following season. Having emerged from his winter break bigger and stronger, *Yeats* was pointed towards the two major (from an Irish perspective) Epsom Derby trials – the Ballysax Stakes and the Derrinstown Stud Derby Trial Stakes, both of which take place at Leopardstown. Under new jockey Jamie Spencer, who had taken over from Mick Kinane as Coolmore's retained rider, *Yeats* won both his trials in impressive style and everything looked set for the horse to follow in the hoofprints of *Galileo* and *High Chaparral*, who won the Derby for Coolmore/Ballydoyle in 2001 and 2002 respectively.

However, as with the best-laid plans of mice and men, disaster struck on the eve of the Epsom Derby when *Yeats* was declared a non-runner owing to a training setback he had suffered on the gallops at Ballydoyle. It was a hammer blow for everyone connected with the horse, and the racing public wouldn't see *Yeats* again until he returned a year later, when he was beaten into second place by *Cairdeas* in a Group 3 at the Curragh.

Despite his winning the Group 1 Coronation Cup at Epsom on his next start as a four-year-old (imagine if he had run in the previous year's Derby!), *Yeats'* career was one of a stop-start nature and it appeared for a time that he may not fulfil the immense potential the Coolmore team knew he had. The pivotal

Yeats, ridden by Johnny Murtagh, on his way to winning a record-setting fourth Ascot Gold Cup. *Courtesy of Bill Selwyn*

231

moment came at the beginning of his five-year-old season when it was decided to race the horse over a longer trip.

Because he didn't have the 'sexy' race record to stand as a stallion at Coolmore, *Yeats* was given the chance to develop into a long-distance horse, something with which Coolmore didn't really associate themselves, as their ideal horse was one that was effective over a range of distances from 5 furlongs up to 1 mile 4 furlongs. The 2 mile 4 furlong distance of the Ascot Gold Cup wasn't something that appealed very much to Mr Magnier and his associates at that time.

Yet it proved to be a revelation as *Yeats* thrived on the step up in distance, and in the intervening years proved himself one of the most talented staying racehorses of his or any other generation. He had won three Ascot Gold Cups, two Goodwood Cups, one Irish St Leger and the Prix Royal-Oak, before lining up for his historic attempt at a fourth Ascot Gold Cup.

You could have cut the atmosphere with a knife as Aidan O'Brien saddled up *Yeats* in the pre-parade ring at Ascot on 18 June 2009. He knew he had his horse as well as could be, but he was attempting to make history and everyone knows how difficult that can be to achieve. As Johnny Murtagh pulled his dark goggles over his eyes and *Yeats* walked forward into the starting stalls, the racing community held its breath, before the nine-strong field was sent on their way for one of the most punishing races they could face.

When the field turned away from the packed stands for the first time, *Yeats* and Johnny Murtagh were travelling well, with the colt tugging ever so slightly for his head. It was a sign of his well-being, and as the race began to hot up approaching the final turn for home, Murtagh kicked *Yeats* in the belly and asked his willing partner for one final effort up the demanding Ascot home straight. The horse responded and quickly took four lengths out of the field. It looked for all the money that he would be able to cruise into the history books.

However, there was one final challenger in the shape of the Sir Michael Stoute-trained *Patkai*, who had been guided into the race under Ryan Moore. When *Yeats* passed the furlong pole one could see that his long, flowing stride was beginning to shorten and he was digging as deep as he possibly could to fend off *Patkai*. In the end the young pretender could not inch his way past the defending champion. *Yeats* would not allow himself to be defeated, and if you look back at the tape you can almost visualise *Yeats* turning to *Patkai* and saying 'Not today, son.' *Yeats* and Murtagh pulled away from *Patkai* and passed the line as history makers.

The post-race celebrations were some of the most jubilant ever witnessed on a racecourse, with people from Coolmore/Ballydoyle flooding into the winner's enclosure to greet their warrior. Speaking to the press corps in the aftermath of the race, and with tears in his eyes, Murtagh said of *Yeats*:

> Muhammad Ali said he was the greatest, and he was, and today *Yeats* has shown everybody that he is the ultimate heavyweight champion. He loves fast ground and he loves Royal Ascot. He comes alive here. It's one of the greatest days of my life in racing. *Yeats* is everything positive about racing.[1]

Yeats' trainer, Aidan O'Brien, who admitted to being a bag of nerves in the run-up to the fourth Ascot Gold Cup, told the media afterwards that the most comparable race, pressure-wise, was when his legendary hurdler *Istabraq* was attempting to win the Champion Hurdle at the Cheltenham Festival for a third time in 2001:

> That's the only time I've felt this much pressure, and when we got over him, I never thought it would happen again. I was afraid of the disappointment for everybody if it didn't happen. It's not for no reason that it's never been done before. This is just a unique horse.

Victory for *Yeats* secured his place in horse-racing folklore. However, he could

---

1   http://www.theguardian.com/sport/2009/jun/19/yeats-four-wins-gold-cup-royal-ascot

not round off his career on the high note it deserved, with defeats in his final two races at the Curragh and Longchamp before he was retired to stud, first to Coolmore's main base and then transferring to their National Hunt wing.

Yeats' deeds at Ascot were marked in the finest way possible when in 2011 HRH Queen Elizabeth II unveiled a bronze statue of the horse, designed by Charlie Langton, which now sits proudly in the Ascot parade ring. Three of these sculptures were made, with one residing at the home of David and Diana

Queen Elizabeth II unveils a statue of *Yeats* that sits in the Ascot parade ring.
© *2011 Horsephotos.com*

Nagle, and the final one standing at Coolmore Stud. The positioning of the statue at Coolmore shows the regard in which *Yeats* is held there.

As you cross the road from Coolmore's main office and pass the statue of *Be My Guest* (his is the first statue one sees because he was Coolmore's first champion sire), the next two statues you will see are of *Montjeu* on your left and *Galileo* on your right. They are positioned there because of their outstanding achievements in the stallion barn. Then, as you make your way to the main stallion yard, you will see the statue of *Yeats*, standing alone and proud. The statue is in this position because John Magnier considered *Yeats* one of the family during his racing career, and with family being so important to the Magniers, the decision was taken to place *Yeats* adjacent to the main yard, which the likes of *Galileo*, *Australia* and *Pour Moi* now call home.

Yeats' fourth Gold Cup was perhaps the most emotional moment that the Coolmore operation has enjoyed over the last twenty years, but another tear-jerking moment came at the Breeders' Cup meeting of 2011. The story of *St Nicholas Abbey* is similar to that of *Yeats*, albeit not with the same happy ending.

In the same way that *Yeats* was bred to be something special, *St Nicholas Abbey* was conceived with the Epsom Derby in mind. His dam, *Leaping Water*, was sent to *Montjeu* and the resulting offspring became one of the toughest and most brilliantly talented horses to step into Aidan O'Brien's Ballydoyle stable. Purchased by the Coolmore team for 200,000 gns at the 2008 Tattersalls yearling sales, the colt raced in the purple and white colours of Derrick Smith, a set of silks that he carried with distinction throughout his racing career.

When he arrived at Ballydoyle in the autumn of 2008, *St Nicholas Abbey* was just another well-bred wannabe, who had the breeding to become a superstar but would need to prove his ability on the demanding Tipperary gallops. Certainly there would have been a degree of expectation – not only was his female side full of talented horses (*Leaping Water* was a daughter of the Moyglare Stud Stakes winner *Flamenco Wave* and a half-sister of the Group 1 winners *Ballingarry* (Canadian International Stakes), *Aristotle* (Racing Post Trophy) and *Starborough*

(St James's Palace Stakes)), but he was also by the leading middle-distance sire in the world, *Montjeu.*

St Nicholas Abbey's pedigree screamed middle-distance three-year-old colt and that is exactly how he was raced during his first season under the tutelage of Aidan O'Brien. He was not rushed and only made his debut in a 1 mile maiden race at the Curragh on 16 August 2009. The colt travelled with consummate ease to win by four lengths from the Kevin Prendergast-trained *Saajidah.* It was a performance of great promise, and soon *St Nicholas Abbey* stepped up in grade when he was pointed towards the Group 2 Beresford Stakes, which was won the previous year by *Sea The Stars.* Sent off the 2/5 favourite, *St Nicholas Abbey* once again travelled supremely well and won snugly from the English raider *Layali Al Andalus* by three-quarters of a length.

The win confirmed the promise that *St Nicholas Abbey* was showing on the gallops at Ballydoyle, and he copper-fastened that promise with a silky-smooth display on his next start, the Group 1 Racing Post Trophy at Doncaster. Ridden by Johnny Murtagh, *St Nicholas Abbey* was not pushed to secure his first top-level success, winning without fuss by three and three-quarter lengths from *Elusive Pimpernel.* It was a performance to warm the heart and gave hope that if the colt wintered well, he could target the Triple Crown in his Classic season.

As he had pleased his trainer over the winter, the 2000 Guineas at New-market in 2010 was chosen as the starting point for *St Nicholas Abbey's* three-year-old campaign. An enormous weight of expectation was on the colt when he lined up for the Group 1 contest, with punters sending him off the even-money favourite. But for *St Nicholas Abbey* and his many supporters, it would be a race to forget. Despite travelling well for much of the race, the colt was tapped for speed when the field swung into the famous Dip at Newmarket and he couldn't find the acceleration required, fading into sixth place behind the eventual win-ner *Makfi.*

Despite his Triple Crown dream dying, Aidan O'Brien pronounced himself happy with *St Nicholas Abbey's* run and indicated that the colt would be seen in the Epsom Derby next time out. Unfortunately for Coolmore, he returned sore from his effort in the English 2000 Guineas and did not line up for the Derby.

It was eleven months before the racing public would see *St Nicholas Abbey* again, when he lined up as the odds-on favourite for the listed Alleged Stakes at the Curragh. Apparently ring-rusty, he could only finish third behind the Dermot Weld-trained mare *Unaccompanied*. Victory in the Ormond Stakes at Chester next time out hinted that the talent *St Nicholas Abbey* had shown at two years remained intact. He went on to emulate *Yeats*, taking the Coronation Cup at Epsom a year after he was due to line up in the Epsom Derby.

Having secured the second Group 1 victory of his career, *St Nicholas Abbey* began to make up for lost time, competing in the likes of the King George at Ascot (he came third) and the Prix de l'Arc de Triomphe at Longchamp, where he was ridden for the first time by Joseph O'Brien (he came fifth). Joseph was making a great start as a jockey when he got the leg up on *St Nicholas Abbey* in the 2011 Arc. He had ridden his first winner just two years previously when he guided *Johann Zoffany* to victory at Leopardstown, and his meteoric rise to the top continued in May 2011, when he rode his first Classic winner, steering *Roderic O'Connor* to victory in the Irish 2000 Guineas.

By the time *St Nicholas Abbey* and his young jockey landed at Churchill Downs for the 2011 Breeders' Cup Turf, both horse and rider had achieved a lot of success in a relatively short period. Kentucky proved to be their greatest moment.

Traditionally the Breeders' Cup Turf is considered a 'banker' for the European horses travelling to the event. Run over 1 mile 4 furlongs and on grass, neither of which suit the majority of American horses, the Turf usually heads back across the water, and in 2011 many people expected that to happen, with the likes of *Sea Moon* and *Midday* lining up for Juddmonte, along with crack French mare *Sarafina* and *St Nicholas Abbey*'s stablemate *Await The Dawn*.

Despite his tender years, Joseph O'Brien settled *St Nicholas Abbey* in mid-division in the early stages of the $3 million Grade 1, with *Await The Dawn* happy to cut out the early fractions. As the nine-strong field swung for home, it was *Sea Moon* and Ryan Moore who kicked on and looked to have pinched a race-winning lead. Sitting behind them was the ice-cool O'Brien, who guided *St Nicholas Abbey* off the rail and gave the colt every chance to use his explosive turn of foot to defeat *Sea Moon* and give the Coolmore/Ballydoyle team one of their most emotional victories ever. Crossing the line, O'Brien entered the history books as the youngest rider to win a race at the Breeders' Cup meeting.

St Nicholas Abbey ridden by Joseph O'Brien in the 2011 Breeders' Cup Turf.
Courtesy of galleryofchampions.com

The ride on *St Nicholas Abbey* would have been considered one of the rides of the meeting if an experienced jockey had ridden the colt, but the fact that the rider was just eighteen years of age and at the beginning of his career made it that much more remarkable.

As the horse and rider made their way back into the winner's enclosure, scenes of unbridled emotion greeted them. Aidan O'Brien, who is normally reserved in his post-race dealings with the media, was moved to tears when interviewed by ESPN. Annemarie, who rarely appears in front of the cameras, was equally moved, as any mother would be.

As had happened for *Yeats* and his fourth Gold Cup win, the winner's circle was teeming with members of the Coolmore/Ballydoyle outfit, all sharing in this most wonderful of triumphs. The young pilot, however, was as cool off the racetrack as he was on it. Speaking to the media post-race, O'Brien gave an assessment of his trip:

> Obviously, there was a certain degree of nerves. But I was looking forward to it more than anything else. He jumped good at the start, had a nice position and travelled very well. I got the gaps when I needed them and he picked up really well. It's a dream come true. I've been coming to the Breeders' Cup since I was very small and obviously looking at all the big names and big horses winning the best races. It's just something you dream about.[2]

Derrick Smith, who, along with MV Magnier, conducted the post-race interview on behalf of the Coolmore owners, was unstinting in his praise for O'Brien. 'Joseph is a world-class rider,' Smith said. 'We have unwavering confidence in him and he just gets better and better.'

For the Coolmore/Ballydoyle team, it was one of those great days that one wishes would never end. *St Nicholas Abbey* returned to Ireland a hero and

---

2   http://www.theguardian.com/sport/2011/nov/06/obriens-triumph-breeders-cup-2011

continued to race with distinction over the next two seasons. He created another slice of history when in 2013 he became the first horse to win three Coronation Cups in a row, when he swatted aside the challenge of the globetrotting *Dunaden*.

Sadly it was the last time *St Nicholas Abbey* would be seen on a racecourse. While training for another crack at the King George VI and Queen Elizabeth Stakes at Ascot, *St Nicholas Abbey* sustained a fracture of his right front pastern,

St Nicholas Abbey, ridden by Joseph O'Brien, wins a record-setting third Coronation Cup at Epsom in 2013. *Courtesy of Trevor Jones, Thoroughbred Photography Ltd*

an injury that brought an end to his racing career. Through the work of surgeons at the Fethard Equine Hospital, *St Nicholas Abbey* was saved. Twenty screws were placed in the injured leg and it was hoped that with time and patience the horse would make a full recovery, but it was only the start of the challenges he was about to face. For seven long months the horse bravely fought for his life, with the Coolmore team determined to do everything possible to keep him alive. In October 2013 'St Nick', as he was known at Coolmore/Ballydoyle, suffered a severe bout of laminitis, a difficult condition to manage, but he showed the same kind of resolution he had on the racetrack and pulled through. Thanks to video updates provided by Coolmore Stud, the ordinary person who followed the career of *St Nicholas Abbey* was kept informed of the horse's progress. However, he lost the battle for his life in January 2014, when he suffered a bout of colic so bad that he was euthanised on humanitarian grounds. It was a tragic end for such a tough and brilliant horse.

At the time of his death, Coolmore released a short statement:

> Regretfully *St Nicholas Abbey* has lost his brave battle after suffering a colic this morning. Surgery revealed a severe strangulating colon torsion that was unviable and he had to be euthanised on humane grounds. This is extremely unfortunate as *St Nicholas Abbey* had been in terrific form, the laminitis was resolving very well and the fracture had healed better than expected.
>
> Coolmore would like to thank the surgeons, the international experts and all the staff at Fethard Equine Hospital who gave him such excellent care 24/7. We would also like to thank the multitude of well-wishers for all the cards and messages of support for *St Nicholas Abbey*. He will be buried in the graveyard here at Coolmore.

Joseph O'Brien paid an emotional tribute to the horse that gave him his first taste of big-race glory on the international stage. Speaking to the *Racing Post* the jockey said:

He was a horse I'll never forget. He gave us at Ballydoyle some great days and over a mile and a half, on good ground, he would have given any horse in the world a run for their money. His win in Dubai last year was possibly his best performance and he was probably better than ever last year. But from my point of view, winning on him at the Breeders' Cup was very special. It was my first big win on the world stage and my first big win outside Ireland. What happened to him was very sad.

When the news broke that *St Nicholas Abbey* had passed away, this author was floored and I am not ashamed to admit that I shed a few tears. No doubt there was many a tear shed both at Ballydoyle and Coolmore. The passing of *St Nicholas Abbey* proves just how fickle sport and, indeed, life can be. One moment he is thrilling us on the Epsom Downs, running himself into the history books, the next he is gone, too early, and all we are left with are the memories.

While the story of *St Nicholas Abbey* didn't have a happy ending, Coolmore has enjoyed more highs than lows over the last two decades. Who could forget the 2002 Epsom Derby, when two Coolmore-owned horses, *High Chaparral* and *Hawk Wing*, streaked clear of a high-class field to lead home an Irish 1–2 in one of the toughest tests in the world. Two and a half furlongs from the finish, *High Chaparral* and Johnny Murtagh kicked for home and quickly opened up a sizeable gap on the rest of the field. Only one horse could live with *High Chaparral*'s change of pace, and that was his stablemate, the mercurial *Hawk Wing*, a horse that was seen as a potential Triple Crown winner at the start of his Classic season. As the race entered the final furlong all the spectators could see were the two Coolmore horses battling it out. There wasn't another horse in sight of the Irish pair. Crossing the line, *High Chaparral* got the better of *Hawk Wing* as Mick Kinane's mount ran out of stamina in the closing stages.

The winning margin was two lengths, but it was the distance back to the third-place horse that was truly remarkable. Twelve, yes twelve, lengths was the official distance back to the third-place horse, *Moon Ballad*, who had made the running at the start of the race, and while one could be forgiven for bashing the form given the fact that *Moon Ballad* was a 20/1 outsider, the Godolphin-owned colt later won the world's richest horse race, the Dubai World Cup, showing that the two Coolmore horses that defeated him in the Derby were of the highest class.

It was another brilliant day for the Coolmore team and one that cemented their place, once again, at the top table of flat racing. Remarkably for an organisation of its size and scope, it was ten years before Coolmore again stood in the winner's enclosure at the Epsom Derby. Despite throwing a huge number of darts at the Derby – thirty-nine horses in total – it wasn't until *Camelot* and Joseph O'Brien won the 2012 Derby that Coolmore took its place in that most hallowed of winner's circles.

Camelot's victory was a long time coming and it gave John Magnier's outfit another slice of history. With Joseph O'Brien in the saddle, the young rider and his father became the first father–son, trainer–jockey combination to win the Derby. A relieved and visibly emotional Aidan O'Brien said to the media afterwards: 'You can't even dream of days like this. I was always happy, I know [Joseph's] body language by now and he looked confident. No one can describe the feeling. Things like this don't happen.'

Yet things like *Camelot's* Derby victory do happen, at least for the Coolmore operation, and while people will point to the vast resources it has at its disposal, the fact remains that no other entity has been able to deliver success, both on the racetrack and in the breeding shed, as Coolmore has.

It is refreshing to see that, even at the very top end of flat racing, where millions of euro are staked on a horse finishing first and not second, sentiment and emotion still play a big role. It was sentiment that kept *Yeats* in training for so long and allowed the horse to rewrite the record books and win four Ascot Gold Cups. While *Camelot's* Triple Crown bid was done with commercial intentions, there was surely a degree of sentiment that saw the colt line up at Doncaster in 2012, when it would have been easier (and more sensible commercially) to run in a race like the Juddmonte International or the Irish Champion Stakes.

Yes, Coolmore is in the business of making stallions and generating huge sums of money, but at the end of the day, from the top of the organisation to the bottom, Coolmore is choc-full of horse people who live and breathe this wonderful sport. It's not work to them, but a way of life. And what a way of life it is.

Camelot and Joseph O'Brien after winning the 2012 English 2000 Guineas at Newmarket.
© *Cranhamphoto.com*

THE FUTURE FOR COOLMORE

It is September, and while Coolmore is enjoying yet another wonderfully productive season, it is nevertheless tempting to look towards the future and wonder if the good times will ever come to an end for this most wonderful of Irish sporting success stories. With *Gleneagles* at stud and with *Australia's* first-crop foals earning rave reviews, the future does indeed look bright for John Magnier and his colleagues.

The future well-being of the operation will, of course, rest largely on *Galileo's* shoulders. Having enjoyed another championship-winning season in 2015, *Galileo* continues to churn out high-class horses at an impressive rate, with the majority spending their racing careers at Ballydoyle under the care of Aidan O'Brien, before the best of them graduate to Coolmore. One can't help but wonder if Coolmore employs extra security around *Galileo's* box, but it wouldn't be the strangest sight to see someone manning the box of the legendary stallion just in case anyone ever got any funny ideas. One can never be too careful, especially with such a vitally important stallion.

With *Sadler's Wells*, *High Chaparral* and *Montjeu* all sadly departed, it has fallen on *Galileo* to keep the Coolmore show on the road. With the possible exception of *Fastnet Rock*, Coolmore do not have an 'established' Group 1-producing sire that could be mentioned in the same breath as *Galileo*. Yes, they have the likes of *Mastercraftsman*, *Zoffany*, *Canford Cliffs* and others, but if something were ever to happen to *Galileo* there would be a gaping hole for Coolmore to fill, and it is hard to see what horse could take up that mantle.

It may well be that the likes of *So You Think*, *Australia*, *Gleneagles* and, further down the line, *Air Force Blue* will come along and keep Coolmore at the top of the bloodstock world. With *Galileo* now eighteen years of age and reaching what would be considered his best years as a stallion, the hope and expectation is that he will continue to sire top-class colts and fillies for the next six to seven years, and by that time the likes of *Australia*, *Ruler Of The World*, *Gleneagles* and *So You Think* will have shown their capability of becoming Group 1 sires. Coolmore was lucky to have *Sadler's Wells*, *Danehill*, *Montjeu* and *Galileo* all stand there over the last twenty years. All four were phenomenal stallions and provided Coolmore with unbroken success. Without a ready-made replacement for *Galileo*, it would be interesting to see how the stud would manage if the worst were to happen. As we are all horse-racing fans, let's hope *Galileo* enjoys many more years at the top.

Coolmore itself must be hoping that sooner rather than later it will own a horse that can capture the English Triple Crown of the 2000 Guineas (Newmarket), the Derby (Epsom) and the St Leger (Doncaster). Having come so close with *Camelot* in 2012, winning the Triple Crown is one of the few ambitions that remains unfulfilled for the operation. I can still remember the agonising distance by which *Camelot* was beaten in the St Leger and the sheer disbelief among the Coolmore team when Joseph O'Brien came back to the unsaddling area.

That Doncaster defeat remains a sore spot and I can't help but feel that if Coolmore has a potential Triple Crown-winning horse in the coming years, nothing will stand in the way as the team attempts to emulate *Nijinsky*, who won the accolade in 1970. Perhaps *Camelot* himself will sire a horse good enough to tackle those three races, which demand lightning speed along with extreme stamina and superior class. It is for those reasons that the loss of *Montjeu* remains so lamentable. Unlike *Galileo*, who can sire top-class mile and middle-distance horses, *Montjeu* was able to sire horses that excelled at middle distances and also enjoyed a more searching test of stamina. *Camelot* was the only horse sired by *Montjeu* who was quick enough to win a Group 1 at 1 mile, and while *Galileo* has sired the winners of both the English and Irish St Legers, I have always felt that if Coolmore was to own a Triple Crown winner, it would be a son of *Montjeu* rather than *Galileo* that would end the long wait for this title.

While the English Triple Crown remains a huge domestic focus for the Coolmore team, there are goals and challenges for them to overcome both in the northern and southern hemisphere. Despite having enjoyed a tremendous amount of success at the Breeders' Cup, the one race that has eluded them is the Breeders' Cup Classic, run over 1 mile 2 furlongs on dirt in October. Since 2000, when *Giant's Causeway* failed by the narrowest of margins, Coolmore has traditionally fired its best horse at the Classic in the hope of ending their luckless run in the race. The likes of *Galileo*, *Duke Of Marmalade*, *Henrythenavigator*, *Rip Van Winkle*, *So You Think* and the ill-fated *George Washington* have all lined up in the Classic, hoping to give Coolmore its first win in what has become a stallion-shaping race in North America.

One just has to take a look at the impact both *Giant's Causeway* and *Henrythenavigator* have had at Coolmore's American base to see why Coolmore is so keen to bag its first Classic win. Both colts finished second in the race and have gone on to have highly successful careers as stallions in North America. *Giant's Causeway* is a three-time champion sire, while *Henrythenavigator* was the champion first-season sire in America in 2012. Both horses had top-class European form, but it is their ability to change surfaces and still maintain their form that attracted American breeders to them.

Declaration of War is another Coolmore horse that earned his place at Ashford Stud when he narrowly failed to bring the Breeders' Cup Classic back to Ballydoyle, losing out by two heads to *Mucho Macho Man*. The son of *War Front*, like all of Coolmore's Classic challengers, was having his first run on dirt but performed exceptionally and on another day could have been the one to end the Coolmore hoodoo. When Coolmore wins the Breeders' Cup Classic, it will rank alongside any of the big races it has won in Europe for the simple fact that to take a horse from Europe, fly it over to America, compete with the best American horses on a surface totally alien to European horses and win is something quite extraordinary. That's why there have only been two European winners of the Grade 1 since its inception in 1984. *Arcangues* caused a 133/1 shock in 1993 and *Raven's Pass* led home *Henrythenavigator* in the 2008 race.

Because the majority of Coolmore horses have traditional grass pedigrees, they are unsuited to the demands of dirt racing, with the kick-back they receive one of the main stumbling blocks, along with an inability to handle the surface. *Giant's Causeway* excelled on his first attempt on dirt probably because his pedigree was laced with dirt performers. Having acquired the breeding rights for the 2015 American Triple Crown winner, *American Pharoah*, Coolmore will be hoping to breed a number of Breeders' Cup Classic winners from its Ashford Stud base over the next number of years. Indeed, if there is one horse that could help Coolmore achieve their dream, it could be *American Pharoah*.

The Breeders' Cup Classic has become one of the must-win races for Coolmore and there is a sense of inevitability that it will win the race eventually. Speaking a number of years ago ahead of the race, Aidan O'Brien explained how seriously Coolmore takes the race:

> I've stopped just dreaming about winning it. We've brought all types of horses and we haven't been able to win it, so we'll just keep trying to find the right horse.
>
> You just continue to do your best every day. We've had some near misses, but that's the way it goes. Sometimes you make good decisions and sometimes you make bad decisions. All you can do is try to learn from the bad ones. Some people have just done a better job than we have, but that's the reality of it.
>
> Each year, you hope you have a horse good enough to run in it. You need a very good horse and he can't have any flaws. It's frustrating never to have won it, and we've had some bad luck, but there are loads of things in life that can frustrate you. All you can do is give it your best and hope someday it will happen. In the meanwhile, you make whatever changes you feel you have to make, and if it doesn't go right you learn from it and try again. I think it's great that the lads (Coolmore's John Magnier, Michael Tabor and Derrick Smith) are happy to keep doing it. And it's just great to have a horse good enough to run in it almost every year. It's very special.[1]

---

1   http://cs.bloodhorse.com/blogs/horse-racing-steve-haskin/archive/2015/10/24/never-say-die-o-brien-tries-again-with-gleneagles.aspx

Apart from the Breeders' Cup Classic, one can't help but feel that both Aidan O'Brien and Coolmore would love to win the Melbourne Cup and in the process put to bed the ill feeling that was generated when Coolmore attempted to win the 'race that stops a nation' in 2008. When *Septimus* and his two stablemates lined up for the race, it was widely expected that they would put up a bold show for the Coolmore team. However, when the stalls opened, the three Coolmore horses set a scorching early gallop not in keeping with the Australian way of racing, where the tempo gradually increases before the field sprints for home. On this occasion the Coolmore trio refused to drop the tempo and instead of finishing full of running, the three horses finished at the back of the field, with *Septimus* and one of his stablemates, *Honolulu*, both finishing lame.

It was a disastrous race for the Coolmore team and one in which the local media took great pleasure. The style of racing that Coolmore's jockeys employed also caught the attention of the race-day stewards, and Aidan O'Brien was asked to appear in front of the stewards despite the fact that he had already left the track. What followed was a tense stand-off between the local stewards and O'Brien, which was, thankfully, defused. The scars from that Melbourne Cup experience still remain and one can only imagine the delight when *Adelaide* landed the 2014 Group 1 Cox Plate in sensational style under Ryan Moore to give Aidan O'Brien his biggest win in the southern hemisphere.

There is no doubt that winning the Melbourne Cup would mean a tremendous amount to everyone involved in Coolmore. It has built a fantastic operation in the Hunter Valley, standing the likes of *Fastnet Rock* and, before him, *Danehill*, who was the breed-shaping stallion of his era in Australia. Winning the most prestigious race in Australia would allow Coolmore to tick another goal off its list.

If it is to win the Breeders' Cup Classics and Melbourne Cups of this world, Coolmore must ensure that its relationship with Aidan O'Brien continues to run smoothly. The relationship between O'Brien and his paymasters looked to be on shaky ground in the middle part of 2015, with rumours circulating that

O'Brien would leave his position at Ballydoyle and return to his old yard in Piltown. While these rumours eventually died down, as O'Brien saddled the likes of *Air Force Blue*, *Ballydoyle* and *Minding* to Group 1 glory at the end of the European turf season, one can't help but feel that if Coolmore is to retain its place at the top of the bloodstock world, Aidan O'Brien will need to remain as its principal trainer.

There are of course some people who will suggest that any trainer could do Aidan O'Brien's job given the raw material at his disposal, but that opinion doesn't hold true at all. Yes, there are a number of highly talented trainers throughout the world, but there isn't a trainer alive today who can match up to O'Brien's ability to develop and train Group 1 winners season after season. His ability to find his next superstar at the beginning of each season and bring that horse through its racing career before sending it off to Coolmore is second to none, and the way he has dealt with the 24/7 pressure that comes with training at Ballydoyle only adds to the esteem in which O'Brien is held. Despite looking forward to his fiftieth birthday in a few short years, O'Brien will surely only grow and develop as a trainer, which can only be good news for Coolmore, as its business model depends on producing the next generation of champion sires along with standing the most in-demand sires at the moment.

With O'Brien at the helm, Coolmore is best positioned to ward off the threat from trainers, both domestic and international, who are looking to knock it off its lofty perch. While the likes of Godolphin have tried to mount a renaissance over the last number of years, their racing team lacks the depth of high-class horses once associated with the operation. Since the group was hit with the news that a number of horses in the care of their former trainer Mahmood Al Zarooni had tested positive for anabolic steroids, the Godolphin team have struggled to regain their place among the elite of the flat-racing world.

When one thinks of Godolphin, one automatically thinks of *Dubai Millennium*, *Fantastic Light*, *Daylami* and *Dubawi*, but sadly for Sheikh Mohammed and indeed the world of flat racing, Godolphin has slipped further and further behind Coolmore on the racetrack. The one area in which it is making ground, and where one could see it challenging Coolmore in the years ahead, is in the breeding shed. *Dubawi*, a son of Godolphin's *Dubai Millennium*, can count only *Galileo* ahead of him when it comes to the best sires in the world. As good a racehorse as *Dubawi* was, he has developed into an even better stallion, siring the likes of *Makfi*, *Postponed*, *Poet's Voice*, *Al Kazeem* and *Arabian Queen*, the only horse to defeat the 2015 Epsom Derby and Prix de l'Arc de Triomphe winner *Golden Horn* in Europe, when she stunned the odds-on favourite in the Juddmonte International in August 2015.

Sheikh Mohammed, the ruler of Dubai and owner of Godolphin, Coolmore's fiercest rivals. *Courtesy of Tattersalls*

Dubawi has had such an impact that even Coolmore is beginning to sit up and take notice. During the Tattersalls October yearling sales, John Magnier made a winning bid of 2.1 million gns for a daughter of the Darley Stud stallion. The filly came from a beautifully bred family and one with which the Coolmore operation has enjoyed plenty of success down the years. The filly's dam, *Loveisallyouneed*, was a Group 1 winner herself. She is also a sister to a mare who is related to both *Quarter Moon* and *Yesterday*, two Group 1-winning fillies for the Coolmore team, along with *Diamondsandrubies*, who won the 2015 Group 1 Pretty Polly Stakes for the Coolmore/Ballydoyle axis.

What made the purchase so interesting is the fact that Coolmore successfully bid for a daughter of *Dubawi*, a stallion that raced in Godolphin blue and now stands in the Darley Stud farm in Newmarket. Although tensions have eased between Darley and Coolmore, it was still surprising to see John Magnier and his team purchasing a horse sired by a horse from the rival stud. It is a nod to Darley and *Dubawi* that Coolmore would pay so much for one of his offspring and perhaps a sign that Coolmore will have strong competition for the champion sires' crown in the coming years.

Coolmore does have the likes of *Australia*, *Gleneagles*, *Pour Moi*, *Camelot*, *So You Think* and others to call upon. However, Darley is cultivating its own stallion roster in Europe, which is impressive in terms of both the numbers and the quality of horses they are now standing. *Dubawi* may be their standout stallion at the moment, but Darley also has top sires *Shamardal*, *Raven's Pass*, *Teofilo*, *New Approach* and his son *Dawn Approach* within its stallion ranks, and with this fire power it is a force to be reckoned with.

Perhaps its most interesting stallion recruit is the outstanding three-year-old colt in 2015, *Golden Horn*, who lit up racetracks in England, Ireland and France, with stunning performances in the Epsom Derby, Coral Eclipse, Irish Champion Stakes and the Prix de l'Arc de Triomphe, before signing off his racing career with a surprise defeat to the Coolmore-owned *Found* in the Breeders' Cup Turf at Keeneland in October 2015. Given that he was such an outstanding racehorse, it will be fascinating to see how *Golden Horn* takes to his new career as a stallion. Certainly his racecourse performances would lead one to believe that he could develop into a top-class sire of horses over a range of distances and surfaces. Although they never met on the racetrack, it will be extremely interesting to map the respective stud careers of both *Golden Horn* and *Gleneagles*, given the fact they both retired after the 2015 Breeders' Cup meeting and will be representing Darley and Coolmore over the coming years.

The breeding world is constantly changing, and Coolmore has adapted to these changes. By having a daughter of *Dubawi* in its ranks, Coolmore has access to a bloodline that it hasn't had before. In much the same way that Sheikh Mohammed bought into the *Galileo* line via his purchase of *Teofilo* and *New Approach*, Coolmore is looking to cultivate some of the *Dubai Millennium* blood, which has been so successful in recent seasons.

While Darley may be providing Coolmore with competition in the breeding sheds and sales ring, it is the powerful string of horses owned by Sheikh Joaan Al Thani that may provide Ballydoyle with its strongest test on the racetracks across Europe. Sheikh Joaan, who has had a huge impact in the world of racing with the likes of Group 1 winners *Olympic Glory* and *Toronado*, French 2000 Guineas hero *Style Vendome*, the top-class juvenile of 2015 *Shalaa*, and the dual Prix de l'Arc de Triomphe winner in 2013/14 *Treve*, has become one of the biggest players in the world of flat racing and one can only see his string growing in numbers and quality in the next few seasons.

The sheikh's association with John Gosden, who had such a wonderful 2015 with the likes of Derby winner *Golden Horn* and Irish Derby winner *Jack Hobbs*, is one that is sure to strengthen, and with Gosden training as well as ever, don't be surprised if both Sheikh Joaan and John Gosden challenge Coolmore in the not-too-distant future as these superpowers of racing battle it out on and off the track.

In Ireland the battle for supremacy on the racetrack is still as competitive as ever. Along with the Coolmore/Ballydoyle team, the likes of Dermot Weld, Jim Bolger, David Wachman, John Oxx, Mick Halford, Ger Lyons and others keep the standard of Irish flat racing very high, and if anyone is going to win a race on the flat in Ireland, they'd better bring their A game to the track.

While some may feel that flat racing in Ireland could do with a shake-up in terms of competition, it is hardly the fault of Coolmore that it has one of the best trainers in the world at its disposal and the means to buy and breed potential champions year after year.

There are a number of challenges facing Coolmore on and off the track, but I feel confident it will be able to maintain its place at the top of the breeding and bloodstock world for the foreseeable future. What will be fascinating, from my viewpoint, is when the trio of John Magnier, Derrick Smith and Michael Tabor exit stage left, and no longer have a hands-on roll at Coolmore. One could liken it to when Sir Alex Ferguson retired from Manchester United in 2013 and the vacuum that his departure left on an organisation that was used to continual success. When Ferguson left, there was an instant drop off in the level of performance, and it now looks like it will take a sizeable investment and a number of years before Manchester United is back among the elite of world soccer.

How Coolmore manages that transition from the established order to the new generation will be fascinating to watch. Unlike at Manchester United, there appears to be a succession plan in place so that the business will continue to run smoothly, regardless of who is in overall control. As we have seen, John Magnier's sons are all actively involved in the running of Coolmore both in Ireland and Australia.

The journey Coolmore has taken over the last fifty years is nothing short of extraordinary. When one considers where Irish racing was in the 1950s and 1960s and where the industry is at the moment, it is like comparing night with day, and a lot of the credit has to go to John Magnier and the Coolmore operation. The future belongs to those who plan for it, and for Coolmore Stud the future looks to be in very safe hands.

Epilogue:
What Coolmore Means to Me

It was the conversations that fuelled my passion. Hearing about *Nijinsky, Sir Ivor, The Minstrel, Be My Guest, Golden Fleece, El Gran Senor, Sadler's Wells* and *Royal Academy*. These were the names I grew up with. Names that were the bedrock for my love of horse racing and for Coolmore Stud. It is an enduring love that continues to burn as brightly as the sun. I can still hear the conversations with my father, Michael, who provided the inspiration for this book. As a sports-obsessed young child (people say I am now a sports-obsessed big child, but that is a topic for another book), I grew up hungry for information, and sport was the only tool in my wheelhouse. People grow up to have a wide variety of interests; my all-consuming passion is sport, with horse racing at the top of the pile. I can make for a very boring dinner guest if there are no like-minded people around, as you can imagine.

Initially, when I was told of the likes of *Sadler's Wells* and others, they were just names to me, like Roy Keane and Paul Scholes from Manchester United (my other great passion), and naively I didn't place too much stock in them. Then I began to listen to the stories behind the names, about the superb feats these wonderfully bred horses achieved on the racetrack. Then they became more. They were my idols, and while teenage boys my age were beginning to explore life's different options, I had my head buried in the latest copy of the *Racing Post* or *Pacemaker*, reading about the exploits of *Montjeu* and how his win in the 2000 King George at Ascot was one of the most stunning that had ever been witnessed since the great *Nijinsky* did something similar thirty years earlier. *Thirty years*, I thought. *I've a lot to catch up on.*

So books were collected, the Internet was scanned, and soon I was immersed in the wonderful world of horse racing. For me it wasn't just similarly coloured horses running around a field, described by the immortal Sir Peter O'Sullevan, trying to be the first horse to pass the lollipop stick of a winning post before being showered with superlatives by pressmen and trainer alike. For me, it was the process. Why is a particular horse (*Galileo*, for example) so much better than all the rest? Yes, trainers play a huge role, along with the jockey on their back, but there has to be more. Latent ability is in a horse from the moment it is born. A trainer can't make a horse run faster than it is able to, although both trainers and punters alike wish that this wasn't the case. I became fascinated and constantly asked myself the question *why*. That one question has taken me on a lifelong journey that continues to this day.

A lot of people ask if there was one moment, or one horse, that kick-started this journey. My light-bulb moment was in 2001, when *Galileo* winged his way into the hearts and minds of many racing fans with his devastating displays in winning the Epsom and Irish Derbies. It was his win at the Curragh, rather than his power-packed display at Epsom, that had me hooked. When Mick Kinane, who looked like a statue on *Galileo*'s back, pushed the colt to go and win his race, *Galileo* answered his jockey's urgings and strode away from his rivals in majestic fashion.

There is a moment a furlong out that I can remember as if it were yesterday. Kinane took a look over his shoulder (he would have needed a pair of binoculars to see his adversaries) and when he turned around he allowed himself a wry smile. It was the smallest break across his lips, but it said it all. It's as if he was thinking, *Wow! This horse is just different*, which is exactly what he was. To watch Kinane and *Galileo* stride up to the winning post as one, Kinane feeding off *Galileo* and vice versa, was a moment of sporting perfection. Like when Lionel Messi runs past defender after defender as if they were all statues before scoring yet another goal for FC Barcelona, it was a moment when you knew things rarely get better than this. Whenever your passion was beginning to wane, you could just press the play button and watch it again, and your faith in the game would be restored.

256

With *Galileo* lighting the fire within me, my journey began. Soon the phrase 'by *Sadler's Wells*' was part of my lexicon. I learned that *Galileo* was considered one of the best offspring by *Sadler's Wells*, who lived in Coolmore Stud. For me, at that point in my education, Coolmore Stud could have been located adjacent to the moon as far as I knew. However, my father knew, and he began to explain what Coolmore was and, more importantly, what it stood for. He told stories about Vincent O'Brien, this man from County Cork who came from nothing and rose to become the world's greatest trainer, a title he will never relinquish. I sat there, jaw dropping, as he detailed how he had won Grand Nationals, Cheltenham Gold Cups and Champion Hurdles as if they were going out of fashion, before shifting his attention to flat racing and turning that industry on its head.

Two legends: Lester Piggott and Vincent O'Brien discuss tactics pre-race.
Courtesy of Jacqueline O'Brien

He told me of this wonderful, almost mystical training establishment called Ballydoyle. A Camelot for racehorses was how it was described. I was regaled with such wonderful stories about how Vincent, or MV as everyone called him, built Ballydoyle from nothing. About how he paid £17,000, which in 1960s Ireland was a prince's ransom, for a site that had only two things: grass and fencing. I learned how he soon turned a collection of fields into the greatest academy for training racehorses and how he built the first all-weather gallop in Ireland and an airstrip for his owners and jockeys to land if they were coming to watch or ride in a horse's last big workout before a race. *Imagine having the foresight to build an airstrip at your training yard*, I thought. I was hooked.

If that wasn't enough to fuel a young boy's dreams, I then discovered Coolmore Stud. One thing I quickly found when reading up on Coolmore was the almost reverential way people would speak about the stud, as if it were a place that could only be mentioned in hushed tones in case anyone overheard you. It was *the* place to be if you wanted to find a top-class champion of the past or breed the next generation of superstar racehorses. This is where the crème de la crème stood to breed the next line of champion colts and fillies. If you wanted to be somebody in the world of horse racing, Coolmore Stud was the place to be.

All this information was intoxicating. Even though I was living in Dublin city, which is far removed from the tranquillity of County Tipperary, I could see Coolmore and Ballydoyle as soon as I closed my eyes, imagining what it would be like to stand alongside *Galileo* as he whizzed up the famous Ballydoyle gallops, or to have a chance to touch the navy-blue silks of Mr and Mrs John Magnier. It's no wonder that navy is my favourite colour.

Following *Galileo*'s retirement, which I didn't take too well, I followed the Coolmore/Ballydoyle operation religiously. Picking up the *Racing Post* and scanning through the race cards to see if there were any Coolmore runners became a daily habit. There was nothing like looking at an unraced maiden, seeing their pedigree, watching them run (and usually win) before following them on to bigger and better things. One such horse was the imposing *Hawk Wing*, who finished his two-year-old campaign with a devastating win in the 2001 National Stakes at the Curragh. It was a spectacular performance from the son of *Woodman*, which saw him obliterate the all-aged track record for a 7 furlong race.

After I wished the winter months away, spring broke and all my attentions were on *Hawk Wing*. Opening the *Racing Post* and reading about the Aidan O'Brien stable tour was a joy, and to see the strapping *Hawk Wing* on the front page made the hairs on my neck stand up. When 2000 Guineas day arrived at Newmarket, I knew it was a big day but I could see no reason why *Hawk Wing* wouldn't win. He was the best horse in the race so there should be no reason that he shouldn't win, right? I was wrong. Very, very wrong.

One can imagine my reaction when *Rock Of Gibraltar* (*Hawk Wing*'s stablemate, no less) was called the winner and not *Hawk Wing*. Yes, the field split into two groups down the wide expanse of Newmarket's Rowley Mile. But this was a race, and doesn't the best athlete win regardless of circumstance? I had just been taught a painful lesson.

A further lesson was handed down to me when *Hawk Wing* was (yet again) defeated by another Coolmore inmate in the Epsom Derby, when *High Chaparral* outgunned him and broke *Hawk Wing*'s stamina on those famous Epsom Downs. *Hawk Wing* gained compensation in the Coral Eclipse at Sandown next time out, but even allowing for his eleven-length win in the Group 1 Lockinge Stakes at Newbury as a four-year-old, *Hawk Wing* never reached the heights that I dared dream for him. He stood, briefly, at Coolmore before being sold abroad.

Despite those disappointments, my passion for Coolmore Stud didn't diminish. *One Cool Cat* was another horse who grabbed my attention. As beautiful as one could wish for, *One Cool Cat* was one of those horses that walked into a parade ring and demanded your attention. He had that look-at-me swagger but could back it up with exceptional talent when he took to the racecourse. Like *Hawk Wing*, *One Cool Cat* was a brilliant two-year-old and once again I couldn't wait to see him in the English 2000 Guineas. In contrast to *Hawk Wing*'s races, when my heart almost jumped out of my chest as the field flashed up to the winning post, this time my heart was at my bootstraps long before the field for the 2004 2000 Guineas had gone by the winning post. *One Cool Cat* had bombed out in spectacular fashion, coming in at the very back of the field. That was a long Saturday afternoon, I can assure you.

If you are reading this, chances are you remember that forgettable 2004 season, which was Coolmore/Ballydoyle's worst since Aidan O'Brien took up the mantle from Vincent O'Brien. They registered just three Group 1 wins in the whole season and saw their stable jockey, Jamie Spencer, who had just taken on the role from Michael Kinane, leave before the start of the 2005 flat season. In a similar situation to that in which Manchester United finds itself today, Coolmore was suffering a rare fall from the lofty standards they had set over the previous twenty years.

Having bounced back to form in 2005 thanks to the likes of *Footstepsinthesand* (English 2000 Guineas) and *Oratorio* (Coral Eclipse and Irish Champion Stakes), it was in 2006 that Coolmore fully regained their place at the top of the racing/breeding tree, thanks, in the main, to the influence of stable jockey Kieren Fallon and an exceptional crop of horses, led by my favourite horse of all time, the charismatic 'Gorgeous' *George Washington*. He was a horse like no other. The son of *Danehill* did what he wanted when he wanted. I vividly remember when he won the Group 2 Railway Stakes at the 2005 Irish Derby meeting and refused to walk under the archway that leads from the pre-parade ring into the main parade ring. And he refused to walk into the winner's enclosure after his spectacular defeat of subsequent Derby winner *Sir Percy* in the 2000 Guineas in 2006. There was even an occasion, during Ballydoyle's press day in 2006, when *George* tried to take a bite out of Kieren Fallon's arm. It is on YouTube and well worth checking out if you haven't seen it yet. When he was defeated next time out on unsuitably soft ground at the Curragh in the Irish 2000 Guineas, it was another day when my lip got a bit longer. Call it youthful petulance, but it was difficult to see a Coolmore horse defeated in a big race. It still is, if I am honest.

Unfortunately *George Washington* was laid up with an injury for the better part of his three-year-old season and when he made his comeback in wayward style in the Celebration Stakes at Goodwood, I got the feeling that we may never again see him reach the dazzling heights of the English 2000 Guineas. Then came Ascot. Sweet, beautiful Ascot when redemption and glorious affirmation awaited *George Washington* in the Group 1 QEII. With Kieren Fallon sidelined, Mick Kinane was teamed up with *George* for his biggest test to date. A 1 mile Group 1 contest against the finest collection of milers of that season. Many thought it would be too much for *George*, that his temperament would get the better of him, that the opposition would pose too stern a test and that his enforced time on the sidelines would come back to haunt him and the team at Coolmore.

Oh how the doubters were silenced. Ridden with supreme confidence by Kinane, *George Washington* ranged alongside the Irish 2000 Guineas winner *Araafa* deep inside the final furlong, and with the minimum of encouragement *George* kicked in the turbo to sprint away from his rivals and win in the style of a true champion, the true champion that I knew deep in my soul he was. It was a breathtaking performance and one that stays with me to this day. I can still visualise the race, the way Kinane and *George* travelled through it, how Kinane held on to him until the last possible moment before *whoosh!* – he was gone into the distance having reclaimed his status as the best miler in Europe.

Then it was over and he was shuttled off to Coolmore Stud to produce the next generation of champions. Or so we thought. I was lucky enough to travel down to Coolmore in January 2007 ahead of the breeding season, in the hope that I could see my hero in the flesh. Having enjoyed a wonderful lunch at Coolmore, my father and I were taken around the stud farm and shown the various stallions at the complex. There was, however, only one horse that I wanted to see. As we entered the final part of our tour, we came into the Yard of Champions, which at the time hosted the likes of *Montjeu, Galileo, High Chaparral, Sadler's Wells* and, of course, *George Washington*.

He was smaller than I had imagined, but by God did he have presence. As we walked up to him, he was posing for pictures – *posing* being the operative word – and one could see he was loving all the attention. Then it was my turn to stand beside my hero and have my picture taken. You can imagine my trepidation as I approached this magnificent animal. I might have been just another person to *George Washington*, but to me this was heaven on earth. As I gave him a pat on the neck, he suddenly turned to me as if to say 'enough is enough'. With that he was led away, back into his box for his lunch. Meanwhile I stood in the middle of the yard, speechless at what had just happened.

I thought that would be the last time I would see *George Washington*, but that wasn't the case. Early in 2007 the news filtered through that *George* wasn't performing as expected in the breeding shed and that he would return to Ballydoyle. *Holy Roman Emperor*, a son of *Danehill* just like *George Washington*, would make the short journey to Coolmore to replace him. In the middle of the National Hunt season, it was a tremendous surprise and I couldn't wait until the start of the flat season to see *George Washington* in action again.

As the old saying goes, however, be careful what you wish for. *George* could never regain the winning thread and his life was cruelly taken away from him at the 2007 Breeders' Cup held at Monmouth Park. By the time of the Classic, which is the centrepiece of the two-day meeting, the track at Monmouth was a quagmire. Heavy rain throughout the day had rendered both the grass and dirt tracks unraceable. It's baffling even now, nearly a decade after the incident, how the race meeting was allowed to go ahead. Perhaps money is more important than the welfare of the horses …

The Classic was the final race of the evening, and when *George Washington* and the rest of the field reached the starting gates, the track was deemed to be sloppy, which means that the dirt surface is nothing more than a purée and horses are running on the much firmer underneath part. While *George* may not have won the race, regardless of conditions, it was worrying to see him staggering to a halt a furlong and a half from the winning post. 'This doesn't look good,' I said to myself. Then the sickening feeling came. The lump that one gets in the pit of one's stomach when something bad is happening. While the people associated with *Curlin*, who won the Classic, were celebrating their success, my eyes were fixed on the mud-stained *George Washington*. Then came the sight that no horse-racing fan wants to see – the screens were erected.

When one sees a screen being erected at a racetrack it can mean only one thing: the end. Unfortunately, *George* had suffered an open fracture to the cannon bone and both sesamoid bones in the right front fetlock. There would be no way back for this most beautiful of colts. He was euthanised and put out of the pain he was in. I was watching the coverage of the Breeders' Cup from my home in Dublin, and it took a while for the news to filter through, so I was left clinging on to the hope that *George* would recover. Then the moment came when it was announced that *George Washington* had been put down. It was as simple as that. He was gone and there was nothing anyone could do about it.

As the credits began to roll, I sat on my couch with tears running down my face. It was like losing a loved one who you are just not ready to let go. This horse had meant so much to me, had run his heart out because that's what he was born to do, and now his life had come to an end at a freezing-cold racetrack in New Jersey, in a race that shouldn't even have been run. It was wrong, just wrong.

On one of my last visits to Coolmore Stud, I went to the Graveyard of Champions to pay my respects to the past champions. Located at the side of the main office, it's where the likes of *Danehill*, *Montjeu*, *Be My Guest* and *Caerleon* were all laid to rest, along with *George Washington*. When I arrived at *George's* grave, I simply knelt down, placed a single rose on the grave and whispered, 'Thank you.' It was a private moment and one that shall live with me for ever.

When you passionately follow any sports team, or any team for that matter, you are going to have lows, but also tremendous highs. One of the earliest highs came when I took my partner, Eileen, to the 2006 Irish Derby meeting at the Curragh. Having met her that same summer, I thought I would impress her by taking her to the races. 'What girl wouldn't like that?' I said to myself. After a great beginning to the day (I even managed to tip her a winner), the main event was coming up. Having examined all the horses, she declared that she was putting her money on '*Thomas Dylan*'. Bemused, I scanned the race card to look for such a horse. Of course, she meant *Dylan Thomas*, but it was funnier to let the joke roll. In the end, *Dylan Thomas* bolted in under Kieren Fallon and she collected on her winning bet, although she is still teased about that incident whenever we go racing.

Australia, ridden by Joseph O'Brien, winning the 2014 Juddmonte
International from *The Grey Gatsby*. © *Cranhamphoto.com*

As the years progressed, my love for Coolmore grew and grew. It was the way they went about their business that appealed to me. They were super slick in everything they did and they always seemed to win the best races. Each January I would wait for the postman to arrive hoping that he had the latest Coolmore brochure and DVD for me. When they arrived, I would sit for hours watching the great races that the likes of *So You Think* had won, or the unbelievable career that *Yeats* carved out for himself, winning a record four Ascot Gold Cups in a row. Then I would read the brochure from cover to cover, analysing, scanning each and every stallion, trying to make sure that I knew everything that I possibly could about Coolmore. I would spot the pedigree of a certain horse and make a note to follow it, and sure enough there it would be a few months later winning at the Curragh or Leopardstown. The cycle never ends, and that is one of the fascinating things about the whole operation. It's never-ending. Just when you think that you have it all, along comes a new start, another horse that makes you believe anything is possible. The dream never dies. One day you are watching *Camelot* wing his way to Irish Derby glory, and just two short years later *Australia* is doing the very same thing in the very same colours for the very same trainer. Nothing less than continued excellence.

Australia is the horse that, for me, has come to symbolise what Coolmore has stood for over the last five decades. Pure, unadulterated excellence. By *Galileo* and out of the Oaks winner *Ouija Board*, *Australia* was destined to be trained at Ballydoyle. Having been bought for 525,000 gns at Tattersalls in Newmarket, *Australia* arrived at Ballydoyle in the winter of 2012 with a huge reputation. It only grew in the months that followed. Such was the latent talent of *Australia* that the colt breezed four furlongs in eleven seconds per furlong, something that the highest-class colts would struggle to do in their Classic year, never mind at the beginning of their two-year-old campaign. That gallop hinted at unlimited potential, and *Australia* would go on to fulfil that potential, slamming future Group 1 winner *Free Eagle* in a race at Leopardstown on the inaugural Irish

Champions Weekend in 2013, before landing a pair of Derbies with deeply impressive performances at both Epsom and the Curragh.

He then produced his most visually striking display in the Juddmonte International Stakes in August 2014, when he glided away from solid Group 1 performer *The Grey Gatsby* to stamp himself as a colt of the highest class. Defeat next time out in the Irish Champion Stakes took a little shine off his lustre, before an injury that October forced the colt into retirement to Coolmore. His first crop of foals was on the ground in 2016.

The process for writing this book was a long one, and while I have always loved Coolmore, I never dreamed for one minute that my words about the operation and its people would make their way to print. Then I thought of what Coolmore would do if they were in my shoes. Would they make their way to the cliff with the intention of jumping off, of taking a risk knowing full well that it could all blow up in their faces, or would they back away from a challenge and refuse to push themselves to be the best that they could possibly be? I know they would choose the former and so have I. My passion for Coolmore Stud runs so deep that my friends joke that if I am ever cut open I will bleed navy blue rather than crimson red.

Through *Sadler's Wells, Danehill, Montjeu, Galileo* and countless other horses and people, an empire has developed in County Tipperary over the last fifty years. In 2016 Ireland stands proudly as one of the world leaders in horse racing. Our horses, year on year, win major prizes both domestically and internationally. We have sent expert horsemen and women to the four corners of this earth and they have taken the affinity that we Irish have for the horse and developed horse racing as a global sport.

From the legendary M. V. O'Brien through Robert Sangster and now with John Magnier and his associates leading the way, Coolmore stands proudly as one Ireland's most successful entities. When I talk to people about Irish sport, I extol the virtues of Coolmore Stud until I am (navy) blue in the face. It has given me some of the greatest moments in my life, both professionally and personally, and will forever have a place in my heart.

Sport, particularly elite sport, where a decision can sway the fortunes of nations in the blink of an eye, can be a cold place at times. Winning, it seems, is all that matters. To hell with anything else; once the job gets done and an individual or a team gets to the top of their mountain, that's all that matters. With Coolmore, I know that isn't the case. Yes, there are huge amounts of money involved each time a classically bred horse lines up in a 2000 Guineas or a Derby, and it is vital that they win, but winning is not everything. What matters most is the horse, the four-legged animals that carry all the hopes and dreams that were wished for them long before they came into this world. The colts and fillies that have their futures mapped out for them even before mating plans have been decided.

It's the horses that are the lifeblood of Coolmore and of this story. It is not about money, be it how much Coolmore makes per year or how much one wagers on horses. It is simply about watching a majestic animal striding out and running through that invisible hole in the wind, a horse that opens your heart and shakes you to your very foundations. It's moments like watching *Camelot* win the Epsom Derby or walking into *Galileo's* box at Coolmore Stud and standing at his shoulder gazing into his eyes and knowing in your heart and soul that horse racing is your true calling. It was what you were put on this earth to do. Very few people find their true calling in life; I am one of the lucky ones.

With this book, I have fulfilled a lifelong ambition. It has been an honour and a privilege to detail the story of Coolmore Stud. I have read about the great horses they have owned, I have watched the likes of *Galileo* develop from top-class racehorses into epoch-making super stallions, and with each new winner comes the hope that another *Montjeu* or *Rock Of Gibraltar* will take my soul once again to the highest realms possible.

The navy-blue silks of Coolmore are the uniform of my heart. Alas I am not nearly skilled enough to ride a horse, but with this book I hope I have added some value to the organisation, that they know their life's work has meant so much to so many people; that their efforts to breed and race the best horses in the world have not been in vain, and for every big race they win there is somebody out there who goes to sleep dreaming about owning the next *Camelot* or becoming the next Aidan O'Brien or Ryan Moore. For those people, for Coolmore and Ballydoyle, for my father and for everyone who has dreamed a dream, this story is for you. Coolmore: now and forever in my heart.

APPENDIX:
BREEDING THE COOLMORE WAY

When *Gleneagles* stepped off the truck at Coolmore following his disappointing effort in the 2015 Breeders' Cup Classic at Keeneland, he took up residence alongside his sire, *Galileo*, in the Yard of Champions to begin his own stud career where his owners hope he will become their next superstar stallion.

At the end of each flat-racing season, Coolmore retires at least one (two or three if it has a really successful season) champion to its base in County Tipperary. When these stallion prospects make the short trip across the village of Rosegreen from Ballydoyle to their new home, there is a great degree of expectation placed upon their shoulders, with Aidan O'Brien traditionally commenting that a particular horse is 'the best we have ever had'.

While many people will sneer at such a statement being wheeled out year after year, it does help a horse's reputation when they retire to stud with such a glowing endorsement from their trainer. Take for example the comments O'Brien made after his star two-year-old colt from 2015, *Air Force Blue*, won the Group 1 Dewhurst Stakes at Newmarket in the manner of a top-class horse:

> He's something that we haven't had before. I'd say no doubt, the size of him and the scope, and the class and the way he travelled, and when you let him go, he delivers.
>
> In February, he was a totally unfurnished baby and he was still head and shoulders above everything else in very soft ground. When he was doing that, it looked exceptional, but they still have to do it [on the track]. His mind was very good today, he was in a different zone, he was relaxed and easy. He learned about the Dip and racing, and we couldn't be more happy with him.[1]

---

1   http://www.theguardian.com/sport/2015/oct/10/air-force-blue-dewhurst-stakes-emotionless-aidan-obrien-william-buick

It's that first line – 'He's something that we haven't had before' – that is the most emphatic, and one can be sure that when the time comes for *Air Force Blue* to retire to Coolmore that quote will be plastered across the racing and bloodstock world.

Once the decision has been made to retire the latest champion, the book of mares that the prospective stallion will cover begins to take shape. For the casual racing and breeding observer, it may appear that one horse is simply bred to another and from that mating comes (one hopes) a future star of the racetrack. While this is technically true, there is a lot more to the process than simply selecting horse A to breed to horse B.

Although *Galileo* is a grandson of *Northern Dancer*, much of his success has been with mares with *Northern Dancer* blood, with the *Danzig* branch achieving extraordinary success. Group winners out of *Danehill* mares feature the brilliant *Frankel*, the champion two-year-old *Teofilo*, the Italian Derby winner *Cima de Triomphe*, the Classic winners *Golden Lilac* and *Roderic O'Connor* and the un-beaten 2011 two-year-old *Maybe*. *Galileo's* triple winner *Lush Lashes* is out of a mare by *Anabaa*, another son of *Danzig*.

As *Galileo's* dam, *Urban Sea*, produced the exceptional *Sea The Stars* to *Cape Cross* and the Classic-placed *Born To Sea* to *Invincible Spirit*, mares by *Green Desert* and his sons have obvious appeal.

Galileo is an excellent mate for mares whose pedigrees include *Nureyev*, a three-parts-brother to *Sadler's Wells*. The Group 2 winner *Incanto Dream* and the Group 3 winner *South Easter* are among his first ten foals out of *Nureyev* mares. The brilliant miler *Rip Van Winkle* is out of a daughter of *Stravinsky*, while *Purple Moon* has a second dam by *Nureyev*. *Sadler's Wells'* brother *Fairy King* sired the second dam of the Breeders' Cup Turf winner *Red Rocks*. *Last Tycoon* sired the dam of an Australian Group 1 winner, plus the second dam of Group 1 winner *Lily of the Valley*.

Galileo has sired the high-class *Misty For Me* from a *Storm Cat* mare and a winner from a *Mountain Cat* mare. *Bluebird*, another representative of the *Storm Bird* male line, sired the second dam of the Classic-winning *Nightime*.

Frankel, perhaps *Galileo*'s greatest son ever, fends off Coolmore sire *Zoffany*
in the 2011 St James's Palace Stakes at Royal Ascot.
Courtesy of Trevor Jones Thoroughbred Photography Ltd

Galileo has sired a number of Stakes winners out of *Indian Ridge* mares, including the Irish 1000 Guineas winner *Nightime* and the Group 2 winner *David Livingston*. *Galileo's* Derby winner *New Approach* is out of a daughter of *Ahonoora*, while the accomplished *Rip Van Winkle* has a second dam by *Don't Forget Me*.

Mares by *Darshaan* with *Galileo* have produced a number of Group winners, headed by *Alandi*, a dual winner. A daughter of *Darshaan's* son *Mark of Esteem* produced Irish Derby winner *Treasure Beach*. *Galileo's* Irish St Leger winner *Sans Frontieres* is out of a *Shirley Heights* mare and his 2012 Group 1 Grand Prix de Paris winner *Imperial Monarch* is out of a mare by *Shirley Heights'* son *Slip Anchor*.

Galileo is shining with the *Roberto* line, notably siring the King George and Eclipse winner *Nathaniel* and the Irish Oaks heroine *Great Heavens* from a daughter of *Silver Hawk*. He has also sired Group winners from daughters of *Kris S*, *Lear Fan*, *Red Ransom*, *Dr Fong* and *Intikhab*.

The St Leger winner *Sixties Icon* and the Australian Group 2 winner *Gallant Tess* are from *Diesis* mares, so he suits the *Sharpen Up* line. *Roderic O'Connor* has a second dam by *Kris*. *Presidium*, a half-brother to *Diesis* and *Kris*, is the brood-mare sire of the top-class *Cape Blanco*.

Galileo's high-class daughter *Misty For Me* and *Battle Of Marengo* both have second dams by *Mr Prospector* and are therefore inbred 4×3. *Galileo* also sired the Breeders' Cup Turf winner *Red Rocks* from a daughter of *Machiavellian*. *Galileo* has a winning son and a performer out of *Alysheba* mares while *Majestic Light*, another *Raise a Native*-line stallion, sired the second dam of *Teofilo*.

Bering and his son *Pennekamp* represent another branch of the *Native Dancer* male line that demands serious consideration. *Galileo's* foals out of *Bering* mares include *At First Sight*, who came second in the Derby, while his Irish Derby winner *Treasure Beach* and the Group 3 winner *Quest For Peace* have *Bering* second dams. His first few foals out of *Pennekamp* mares feature the winners *Together* and *Lily of the Valley*.

Galileo sired the winner, *Galikova*, from a *Blushing Groom* mare. A *Rainbow*

Quest mare is the second dam of *Frankel* and *Lush Lashes'* second dam is by *Arazi. Caro's* son *Crystal Palace* sired the second dams of two of *Galileo's* winners.

The mixing of speed with stamina is something breeders cherish, the theory being that if one can take the best of the speed gene and blend it with a healthy dollop of stamina, the chances of breeding a champion horse over a range of distances increases considerably.

Montjeu has been one of the greatest Classic influences of modern times, with *Camelot* (perhaps his most naturally gifted son) one of his four winners of the Derby. He also had four winners of the Irish Derby and two winners of France's top mile-and-a-half test for three-year-olds, the Grand Prix de Paris. Now that *Montjeu* is sadly no longer with us, the baton has passed to *Camelot* to continue his sire's legacy of producing top-class middle-distance champions. With a CV that also included winners of the English, Irish and French St Legers and the Melbourne Cup, classic stamina was often the strong suit for *Montjeu's* progeny. This is what makes *Camelot* so exceptional. Not only did he cruise to victory in the Racing Post Trophy at two, but he also defeated seventeen rivals to become *Montjeu's* only Classic winner over a mile, in the 2000 Guineas at Newmarket.

With *Montjeu* as his sire and a granddaughter of *Mr Prospector* as his dam, *Camelot* is bred on a similar pattern to *Motivator*, sire of the brilliant *Treve*. As *Treve* is out of a granddaughter of *Danzig*, this line merits serious consideration of *Camelot* as a stallion. Therefore, mares by such as *Anabaa, Green Desert, Polish Precedent* and *War Front* are prime candidates.

Montjeu sired the winning two-year-old *Wading* from a mare by *Green Desert*, so *Camelot* should be ideal for daughters of *Oasis Dream, Invincible Spirit, Cape Cross, Desert Prince* and *Desert Style*. *Montjeu* also sired winners in both hemispheres from *Grand Lodge* mares, so daughters of *Sinndar* are interesting (they produced 4×5 to *Top Ville*).

There is every reason to expect excellent results when *Camelot* is combined with the *Shirley Heights* line, especially as *Montjeu's* accomplished son *Fame*

And Glory has a *Shirley Heights* dam. A mare by *Darshaan* produced the Derby winner *Pour Moi* to *Montjeu*, and two of *Montjeu's* sons also have winners out of *Darshaan* mares.

Montjeu's third dam was by *Zeddaan* and he has four winners with two lines of *Zeddaan*. The stallions involved include *Kalamoun*, his sons *Bikala* and *Kenmare*, and his grandson *Kendor*.

The *Blushing Groom* line should work well with *Camelot*, as two other sons of *Montjeu* have sired very useful winners from *Rainbow Quest* mares. *Montjeu* sired the Derby winner *Authorized* from a mare by *Saumarez*.

Mr Prospector will be back in the fourth generation of *Camelot's* foals, via *Kingmambo*. A second line is, therefore, attractive, in view of the scale of *Montjeu's* success with other *Mr Prospector*-line stallions. He sired the Derby winner *Motivator* and the St Leger winner *Leading Light* from *Gone West* mares and the Irish Derby winner *Frozen Fire* from a *Woodman* mare. *Montjeu* also sired *Geoffrey Chaucer* out of a *Machiavellian* mare, plus three Group winners from *Zafonic* mares.

Lyphard sired the second dam of *Authorized*, while his sons *Pharly* and *Bellypha* also sired the second dams of some of *Montjeu's* winners. *Linamix* is the broodmare sire of the high-class *Montmartre* and also of the winning two-year-old *Ectot*.

Authorized, another of *Montjeu's* Derby winners, has a number of black-type fillies out of *Galileo* mares, including the Classic-placed *Rehn's Nest*, which are inbred 3×3 to *Sadler's Wells*.

The similarly bred *Motivator* is showing promise with the *Storm Bird* line, siring a winner from a *Bluebird* mare and a winner from a *Cat Thief* mare. *Camelot* will suit daughters of *Giant's Causeway*.

Sharpen Up is a path to follow with *Camelot*, as he sired the second dams of *Motivator* and *Hurricane Run*. *Hurricane Run* and *Motivator* respectively have Group winners out of mares by *Diesis* and by *Diesis'* son *Elmaamui*. *Montjeu's* son *St Nicholas Abbey* is out of a mare by *Kris's* son *Sure Blade*.

While the *Sadler's Wells* line is currently thriving at Coolmore, there is another branch of the *Northern Dancer* line that continues to play a huge role in the success of Coolmore, and that is the line established by *Danehill*. Like *Montjeu*, *Danehill* was a prodigious sire of top-class racehorses, and like his former stablemate, *Danehill* is still mourned following his death in 2003. The likes of *Rock Of Gibraltar*, *Holy Roman Emperor* and *Danehill Dancer* have all performed with distinction at stud. However, it is *Danehill's* son *Fastnet Rock* who looks like he might carry the *Danehill* legacy to future generations.

Although the first runners by this champion sprinter did not reach the racecourse until the second half of 2008, *Fastnet Rock* has rapidly climbed to the top of the stallion ranks in Australia, ending the 2011/12 season as the champion sire by a substantial margin. His fee of AU$275,000 made him easily the highest-priced stallion in Australia in 2013. He has shown the versatility we have come to expect of *Danehill's* best stallion sons, siring everything from winning sprinters to Classic mile-and-a-half performers. His latest standout performer is the tough and talented *Fascinating Rock*, who matured into a top-class older horse in 2015. The undoubted highlight came on QIPCO British Champions Day, when he defeated the Irish Derby winner *Jack Hobbs* before fending off the late challenge of *Galileo's* daughter *Found* to land the Group 1 British Champions Stakes for his trainer, Dermot Weld, and his jockey, Pat Smullen.

Fastnet Rock is working very well with the *Storm Cat* sire line and already has Australian winners out of mares by *Forest Wildcat* and *Hennessy*. These winners are inbred to *Storm Cat's* grandparents *Northern Dancer* and *Crimson Saint*. Mares by *Giant's Causeway* would be obvious contenders. Inbreeding to *Danzig* has already proven successful with *Fastnet Rock*. He has a winner and a placed performer inbred 3×3 to this great stallion. He also has another winner out of a mare by *Green Desert's* son *Volksraad*. *Danehill Dancer*, *Rock Of Gibraltar*, *Dansili*, *Holy Roman Emperor* and *Danetime* are others who have sired Group winners with *Green Desert* in their pedigrees. *Fastnet Rock's* €420,000 2013 yearling out of a *Green Desert* mare is inbred 3×3 to *Danzig*.

Fastnet Rock is doing well with mares with more *Northern Dancer* blood, especially via *Nureyev*. For example, he has two winners out of *Peintre Celbre* mares and he sired the outstanding filly *Mosheen* from a *Stravinsky* mare. This mirrors the considerable success that the *Danehill* line has enjoyed with *Nureyev*-line mares in Europe. A 2013 yearling out of a *Peintre Celbre* mare sold for €350,000.

Found, a daughter of *Galileo*, winning the 2015 Breeders' Cup Turf from Epsom Derby and Arc de Triomphe hero *Golden Horn*. *Courtesy of Getty Images*

Fastnet Rock has Australian Stakes winners from mares by *Sadler's Wells* and *Galileo*, plus a winner out of a granddaughter of *Fairy King*. Yearlings out of *Sadler's Wells* mares sold for nearly €400,000 in 2013. *Fastnet Rock* should prove invaluable in injecting speed into daughters of *Galileo*, *High Chaparral* and *Montjeu*.

Fastnet Rock and *Dansili* are both by *Danehill* out of *Nijinsky*-line mares. A lot of *Dansili's* good winners have two lines of *Nijinsky* in their pedigrees. *Nijinsky*-line stallions whose daughters have Group winners with sons of *Danehill* include *Caerleon*, *Green Dancer* and *Kahyasi*. *Fastnet Rock* has had winners with *Night Shift* second dams.

The *Blushing Groom* line is also worth exploring. *Fastnet Rock* already has a winner with a *Nashwan* second dam and a winner out of a *Mt Livermore* mare. *Danehill* sired winners from mares by *Blushing Groom* and *Rainbow Quest*.

Mr Prospector-line mares have enjoyed consistent success with *Danehill* and his sons. *Fastnet Rock* has four stakes winners from twenty-seven foals out of *Woodman* mares. He also has winners out of daughters of *Kingmambo* and *Lion Cavern* and a winner out of a *Jade Robbery* mare.

Danehill sired a winner from a *Roberto* mare, and very smart performers from mares by three sons of *Roberto*. *Fastnet Rock* already has a winner with a *Roberto* second dam and a winner out of a granddaughter of *Red Ransom*.

Danehill had winners from mares with *Mill Reef*, *Shirley Heights*, *Darshaan*, *Simply Great*, *Riverman* and *Irish River* in their pedigree, so the *Never Bend* line looks like another very attractive option for *Fastnet Rock*.

No young stallion in Kentucky has built a bigger international reputation in recent years than *War Front*. This fast son of *Danzig* has rapidly established that his progeny can shine at the top level on all surfaces and are equally at home in the US and Europe. This was underlined at the 2014 yearling sales when his sons sold for up to $2.2 million and his fillies for up to 950,000 gns. These yearlings were sired at a fee of $60,000. One of the colts that has helped build this reputation is *War Command*. He made a great start to his career with two wins and he was notably impressive when he stormed home six lengths clear in the Coventry Stakes at Royal Ascot. Most recent winners of the Coventry have gone on to further success, and *War Command* followed suit, taking the Dewhurst Stakes to improve his juvenile record to four wins from five starts.

It isn't just his racing record that suggests *War Command* has a lot to offer as a stallion. He has no inbreeding in the first four generations and he is out of *Wandering Star*, a winner bred along similar lines to the highly successful stallion *Silver Hawk*. *Wandering Star's* sire, *Red Ransom*, is a son of *Silver Hawk's* sire, *Roberto*, and her dam was a daughter of *Silver Hawk's* dam, the Prix Jacques le Marois winner *Gris Vitesse*. *Silver Hawk* sired top winners throughout the northern hemisphere, including winners of the Derby, St Leger and Prix de Diane (French Oaks).

One notable aspect of *Silver Hawk's* legacy has been the exceptional results that his daughters have achieved with *Galileo*. Add to this the fact that *War Command* is by a son of *Danzig* and he becomes an obvious choice as a mate for *Galileo* mares. *Silver Hawk's* daughters also produced winners to *Sadler's Wells* and *El Prado*. *Dansili*, another grandson of *Danzig*, has a terrific record with *Sadler's Wells* mares.

Grandsons of *Danzig* have also enjoyed success with mares by *Peintre Celbre*, *Stravinsky* and *Theatrical*, all sons of *Nureyev*.

Inevitably, inbreeding to *Danzig* will have to be tried with *War Command*. Mares by sons of *Danehill* and *Green Desert* create only 3×4 to *Danzig*. The *Storm Cat* branch of the *Northern Dancer* male line has supplied several winners to grandsons of *Danzig*.

Other stallions bred on the *Danzig–Roberto* cross sired graded winners from daughters of *Rahy* and *Groom Dancer*. *Declaration of War*, another of *War Front's* top sons, is also out of a *Rahy* mare, so mares with *Blushing Groom* blood look sure to do well with *War Command*. They also sired high-class winners from daughters of four different sons of *Sharpen Up*, including *Kris*, *Trempolino* and *Selkirk*.

The *Mr Prospector* line has plenty to offer *War Command*. *War Front* has graded stakes winners out of mares by four sons of *Mr Prospector*, including *Smart Strike*, *Miswaki* and *Forty Niner*. This suggests that *War Command* could also do well with daughters of *Kingmambo*, *Machiavellian*, *Woodman Elusive Quality*, *Zamindar* and *Zafonic*.

Pivotal mares have produced winners to two other grandsons of *Danzig*. *Danzig*-line stallions have numerous Group winners with mares from the *Mill Reef* line, doing especially well with daughters of *Darshaan*.

Other grandsons of *Danzig* have numerous winners out of mares by *Indian Ridge* and *Inchinor*. Mares with some *Ahonoora* blood therefore appeal.

While a lot of the above detail may seem complicated, it is the lifeblood of the breeding industry. New sires retire to stud, new combinations are tried and new outcomes are determined. It's what makes the breeding industry so fascinating, because one never knows when or from where the next champion racehorse will come.

Once all the deliberations have been pored over and the book of mares has been confirmed for a stallion, the breeding season (in the northern hemisphere) will take place from February until May. Because every horse's 'birthday' is on 1 January, breeders are always hoping for a foal to be born early in the year as opposed to later. The theory is that a foal born early in the year will be that much more developed and will be capable of racing early on in their two-year-old campaign, while foals born later on in the year will take that bit longer to develop and mature into racehorses.

Of course, there are always exceptions to that rule, such as 2015 star two-year-old *Air Force Blue*, who made a successful racecourse debut at the end of May and ended his juvenile campaign with a win in the Dewhurst Stakes in the middle of October. This was achieved despite the fact that *Air Force Blue* was a May foal and theoretically at a disadvantage in the early part of the season. His natural talent bridged the supposed gap with the rest of his rivals.

Once the foals grow into yearlings, they are offered at public auctions (commonly known as yearling sales), which traditionally kick off at Deauville in France, in August. It is there that both vendors and buyers will be able to gauge how a first-season sire will be received. One thing that potential buyers like to see from a first-season sire is that he is capable of passing on his looks to his offspring. This is known as 'stamping' one's stock. It may seem rather illogical, but the theory is that if a sire is able to pass on his looks to his stock, he is more than likely able to pass on his talent. *Gleneagles*, for example, is very much like his sire *Galileo* in terms of looks. In fact, *Gleneagles'* head is a carbon-copy of *Galileo's* and Coolmore will be hoping that *Gleneagles* has the same prospects for siring top-class horses as *Galileo*.

Not only is it important that a new sire stamps his stock, it is also crucial that a horse moves well when parading around the sales complex. If one thinks of cats and the way they walk, that is the ideal movement of a horse. A low and free-moving horse is one that will appeal above all others to breeders and buyers. Having a 'good action' is not a prerequisite to becoming a successful racehorse, but it is a help. A good-actioned horse is able to run more effectively on faster ground, while it tends to find soft or heavy ground more difficult to run on. With the likes of the Guineas and Derby run on good ground in the majority of cases, it is crucial that a horse can handle this.

If a first-season sire creates a buzz at the yearling sales, it feeds into the feel-good factor that the horse created on the racetrack. Likewise, a lukewarm reaction can have the opposite effect. When *Frankel's* first crop came up for auction in the autumn of 2015, there was a buzz around his stock the likes of which was rarely seen before. Many industry experts predicted record prices from people desperate to own a son or daughter of *Frankel*. Yet when his progeny came up for sale, there was a decidedly mixed reaction to his offerings, with some of his better-bred progeny failing to impress and make as much money as their breeders may have expected.

Frankel has enjoyed a tremendous start to his stud career. His very first runner was a winner. But despite his success on the racetrack, at stud *Frankel* is still a boy in a man's world and it will take some time for him to stand alongside his own sire, *Galileo*, as one who has made a lasting impact.

Having a successful start to one's stud career is of vital importance and Coolmore places a lot of stock in it. Coolmore's latest star stallion, *Zoffany*, is a classic case of a sire who has hit the ground running. A son of the Juddmonte sire *Dansili*, *Zoffany* was a ball of speed as a two-year-old and showed himself to be one of *Dansili*'s most talented sons when he landed the 2010 Group 1 Phoenix Stakes at the Curragh under a daring ride from Johnny Murtagh. Murtagh threaded *Zoffany* through the narrowest of gaps to defeat Royal Ascot winner *Strong Suit* and the Jim Bolger-trained *Glor na Mara*.

While *Zoffany* didn't match this lofty achievement as a three-year-old, he has the distinction of having finished closest behind *Frankel* when he went down by three-quarters of a length to the great horse in the 2011 St James's Palace Stakes at Royal Ascot. When *Zoffany* retired to stud, there was a buzz surrounding him and he soon had a full book of mares waiting for him at Coolmore. During the yearling sales of 2014, *Zoffany* made a huge impression on buyers and a number of his progeny sold for up to 475,000 gns. For a horse that had a covering fee of €12,500, that is a pretty good return for any breeder who took advantage of his relatively cheap stud fee. In 2015 *Zoffany* proved that he was a new sire to be reckoned with. Royal Ascot was a tremendous success for the stallion as he sired three of the high-profile winners at flat racing's biggest summer extravaganza. *Illuminate* did the business in the Group 3 Albany Stakes, before finishing runner-up in the Group 1 Cheveley Park Stakes at the tail end of that season. *Washington DC* and *Waterloo Bridge* both won for the Coolmore team and Aidan O'Brien that season and showed that *Zoffany* was more than capable of producing high-class horses.

Speaking after *Washington DC*'s impressive win in the Windsor Castle Stakes, Aidan O'Brien was glowing in his praise of the horse and also his sire:

We've always held him in high esteem. He travelled very well and quickened

Zoffany by *Dansili* became champion first-season sire in 2015 and
continues to be a stallion to follow. *Courtesy of Getty Images*

very well, so I'm delighted. He's mature enough – he's a typical *Zoffany*, very quick and fast. He's a horse who finds it easy to go very fast and has a good mind. I'd think his trip would be five or six furlongs – maybe he'll get further but it's unusual for a horse with that kind of pace to get an awful lot further.[2]

Perhaps the standout horse from *Zoffany's* first crop was the John Gosden-trained *Foundation*, who made a striking impression on the flat-racing scene in 2015. Having won his first two races in impressive style, *Foundation* announced himself as one of the brightest two-year-olds of 2015 when he landed the Group 2 Royal Lodge Stakes at Newmarket in impressive style from the Aidan O'Brien-trained *Deauville*. However, it was on his next start that *Foundation* really hit the headlines. The Group 1 Racing Post Trophy has become one of the defining two-year-old races of our time, with the likes of *Motivator*, *Authorized*, *St Nicholas Abbey* and *Camelot* all winning the 1 mile Group 1 before going on to superstardom. In 2015 *Foundation* lined up as the hot favourite but had a nightmare passage under Frankie Dettori, finishing very fast in third place behind the shock winner, *Marcel*.

Despite not enjoying a Group 1 winner in 2015, there is no doubt that *Zoffany* will continue to make a big impact in the breeding shed, and Coolmore will hope that *Zoffany* can sire a colt talented enough to stand alongside him at Coolmore to keep the bloodline intact.

It is a high-pressure world but one that has been very successful for Coolmore throughout the past five decades, and it will undoubtedly continue to develop in the years ahead.

---

2   http://coolmore.com/zoffany-colt-washington-dc-lands-windsor-castle-stakes/

INDEX